Y0-BXR-696

STEEL TO STONE

OXFORD STUDIES IN
SOCIAL AND CULTURAL ANTHROPOLOGY

Oxford Studies in Social and Cultural Anthropology represents the work of authors, new and established, that will set the criteria of excellence in ethnographic description and innovation in analysis. The series serves as an essential source of information about the world and the discipline.

STEEL TO STONE

A Chronicle of Colonialism in the Southern
Highlands of Papua New Guinea

JEFFREY CLARK

EDITED BY
CHRIS BALLARD AND MICHAEL NIHILL

OXFORD
UNIVERSITY PRESS

This book has been printed digitally and produced in a standard specification
in order to ensure its continuing availability

OXFORD
UNIVERSITY PRESS

Great Clarendon Street, Oxford OX2 6DP

Oxford University Press is a department of the University of Oxford.
It furthers the University's objective of excellence in research, scholarship,
and education by publishing worldwide in

Oxford New York

Auckland   Cape Town Dar es Salaam   Hong Kong   Karachi
Kuala Lumpur Madrid Melbourne Mexico City   Nairobi
New Delhi Shanghai Taipei Toronto
With offices in
Argentina Austria Brazil Chile Czech Republic France Greece
Guatemala Hungary Italy Japan South Korea Poland Portugal
Singapore Switzerland Thailand Turkey Ukraine Vietnam

ISBN 0-19-823377-9

Cover photo: A group of young evangelists in the Southern Highlands

Yesterday, white men, you came from Ialibu.
And here at Pangia you made
A house of metal and barbed wire around it.
I'll jump inside it now.

Wiru song (Paia & Strathern 1977: 29).

CONTENTS

MAPS

FIGURES

EDITORS' PREFACE

From Steel to Stone is the most significant statement of the ethnographic research of Jeffrey Clark; it was also his last piece of writing, completed shortly before he died of cancer in Canberra, in June 1995, aged only 42.[1] The volume is testimony to his remarkable character, and to the strength of his determination to see the project through, once his condition had been diagnosed early in 1994. Jeffrey had only recently been invited by Nicholas Thomas and Margaret Jolly to join their 'Politics of Tradition' project at the Australian National University as a visiting Fellow. Despite numerous interruptions due to his condition, he returned repeatedly to work on the manuscript until it had reached the point where others might be able to see it through to publication. We are honoured that Jeffrey appointed us to this task.

There was little opportunity to discuss with Jeffrey how he might further have revised the manuscript, as he died within weeks of drafting the epilogue. However, his method throughout had been to revise individual chapters repeatedly, and we decided that the body of the book should be left much as it stood. With only minor editorial changes, the manuscript was submitted to Oxford University Press through Professor Nicholas Thomas of the Centre for Cross-Cultural Research at the Australian National University. In discussion with Nicholas Thomas and Peter Momtchiloff of Oxford University Press, it was agreed that a more expansive introduction, in the form of a prologue, should be prepared; Jeffrey had simply run out of time before returning to his original introduction or polishing his concluding remarks, and his numerous and inventive ideas which might have positioned his own insights within the context of other theoretical developments in historical anthropology and post-colonial studies were never set on paper. The other elements required for publication—a bibliography and some maps—have been prepared, to the best of our abilities, on the basis of Jeffrey's notes and sketches.

In addition to Jeffrey's own acknowledgement of his debts, we would also like to thank a number of people for their assistance in guiding this manuscript through to publication. The lapse of time since Jeffrey's death provides some indication of the difficulty of this task, but Nicholas Thomas has been instrumental at every stage of the process, particularly through his constant encouragement of all the parties involved. Also at the Centre for Cross-Cultural Research, Tsari Anderson and then Ian Bryson and Jennifer Newell have undertaken the laborious work of entering editorial changes, providing links between us and Oxford University Press, and maintaining the pace of progress. Tsari's labours in this latter regard have been exemplary and she has our unreserved thanks. Keith Mitchell, of the Cartography Unit at the Australian National University, kindly produced the maps from Jeffrey's sketches. At Oxford University Press, Peter Momtchiloff, in the

---

[1] See Michael Nihill, 'Obituary: Jeffrey Lawrence Clark', *Oceania* 66(1), 1995, 1–4.

initial stages, and then Anne Ashby have shown great faith in Jeffrey's writing, and strong powers of endurance in dealing with us as editors. The manuscript has also benefited greatly from the editing skills of Dorothy McCarthy and Diana Matias. Finally, Robert Crittenden, co-executor of Jeffrey's estate along with Michael Nihill, and Margaret Jolly were strong friends both to Jeffrey, as he wrote, and to us in bringing his work to a wider audience.

CHRIS BALLARD and MICHAEL NIHILL

PRELUDE

From Steel to Stone: A Chronicle of Colonialism in the Southern Highlands of Papua New Guinea is a history of the Wiru-speaking community of Pangia district. It deals in particular with the people of Takuru village, who were the focus of intense and enduring attention from the Australian administration. They also experienced the long-term residential presence of the Wesleyan mission staffed by American pastors and their families. Clark's book is a rich tapestry of the complex and often volatile interconnections between these newcomers and the local social and cultural forms which give these forces specific expression through time.

The title is, of course, a play on words, inverting the sequence of technological innovation in Richard Salisbury's (1962) classic early monograph on change in the Eastern Highlands. The Eastern Highlands region has been the subject of numerous accounts by anthropologists and geographers addressing change. In part this is due to the longer history of colonial contact in the East (relative to the Western and especially Southern Highlands). This involved concerted attempts by the administration to implement political change through suppressing warfare and introducing local police, court and council offices, together with economic change through migrant labour and cash-cropping. Equally significant, despite Salisbury's observation that exchange flourished, were factors such as the lesser importance of gift exchange relative to the West Highlands. As A. J. Strathern (e.g. 1971b, 1979) and Feil (1982) show, while ceremonial exchange systems such as *moka* may often be given a sense of timeless tradition, their most elaborate expressions are responses to external influence. In addition, they were the major frame through which the effects of things such as material changes to wealth items and the suppression of warfare were realized. In short, all these discussions show that local cultural orientation requires as much consideration as—and in—the telling moments of the colonial impact. While social transformation is considered in many of the monographs on Southern Highlands cultures, it has secondary status in relation to functional accounts of social structure or the political economy of exchange. Clark's book is different, adopting this focus on the complex intersections of the local with wider material and cultural forces through time.

Clark's monograph thus also differs from the historical accounts of the Eastern Highlands that largely focus on the material dimensions to change. Clark, like Salisbury, takes steel and stone and the shift between them as metonymic of the complex overall changes to Wiru social life. Like Salisbury, he also uses steel to refer to implements such as axes. However, Clark is less interested in any utilitarian impact these may have, preferring to concentrate on the source of desire in the political order. Like other Highlanders, the Wiru readily adopted steel axes as prized items for Wiru gift exchanges such as bridewealth. While this desire was strong in the early days of the direct Australian presence, the Wiru had been endeavouring to procure such items through trade well before the 1960s when colonial control was achieved. What 'colonial' means is thus problematic, given the substantial but indirect impact of the Australians in the decades leading up to direct domination.

The second term of the title, 'stone', emphasizes even more the significance of local culture in directing history. In contrast to Salisbury's concern with the technological aspects of material production, 'stone' was the term the Wiru first adopted for money. The hardness and thus, given Wiru logic, the strength of coins was identified with the power of ancestral cult stones. These stones were integral to Wiru ritual designed to ward off danger and pestilence and to increase wealth, health, people, and pigs. There is no better illustration of the complex, convoluted, and often contradictory history which was to come and which comprises the bulk of Clark's discussion than money. The prime symbol (not to mention wherewithal) of capitalism, and thus the power of the extraneous, was rendered meaningful through identification with the power of the local, cult stones. This was so despite the wholesale mission efforts which sought to obliterate all references to ancestor worship (deemed paganism if not actual proof of a league with the devil). The Wesleyan mission succeeded, of course, and now, as in many parts of Papua New Guinea, there are no non-Christian Wiru, and the spirit cults have long been abandoned (the theme of Chapter 6 especially). None the less, the legacies of this identification remain, with money (now as notes) possessing qualities that far exceed the merely economic. The potency of cash is not only its buying power, but also how it is infused with the political, mystical, and magical. More than any other single phenomenon, money stands as both the vehicle and key symbol for the engagement of Takuru villagers and the forces of capitalism, Christianity, and the state, both colonial and post-colonial.

Following Thomas (1994) amongst others, Clark adopts the position that not only are local social and cultural forms integral to local history, but colonialism too has its culture. ('Colonialism' here encompasses the composition of the state, capitalism, Christianity, and other forms of Western classification.) While in more recent times the Wiru have experienced the same political and economic instability as other Papua New Guineans, one notable aspect of earlier Wiru colonial days was the quite remarkable consistency of administration personnel and policy implementation. When combined with the permanent and largely uncontested monopoly of the Wesleyans, this formed a formidable instrument of control over much of Wiru social life. It ranged, for example, from economic development to forcing the abandonment of some types of exchange while regulating others such as bridewealth. None the less, as Clark shows, because colonialism has its culture, by definition it must also be arbitrary, inconsistent, and paradoxical. The interface of Wiru and colonial cultures—at any one point in time let alone through time—is thus rich and productive, and far from a smoothly operational field. Clark's debt to the South American works of Michael Taussig (e.g. 1984) is apparent in his decision to call this interweaving of local and (post-)colonial determinations the 'space of colonialism'.

The book has three parts. Following Wiru tales of their own precolonial past, the early chapters of the monograph consider both Wiru and Western imagined constructions of others. Part One deals with the Wiru experience of the West through artefacts the Australians distributed in distant parts, such as the Papuan coast, that the Wiru obtained through trade. Later there are stories from others, and then first-hand accounts of government and prospecting patrols in the region. Just as important, however, is the Western imagination of the savage in the heart of darkness. Clark helps orient this discussion with a phantom patrol at the start of the century—a 'ripping yarn' of the exploits of a character named Brewster in the Papuan hinterland. Based on little fact and ample imagination, Brewster's endeavours to seek his fortune were scuttled by his shipwreck in the Torres Strait. From the Papuan coast he went north into the Southern Highlands. This is the trail of, among other things, the trade of steel and of pearl shells. The latter gives rise to a near confluence as Brewster desired pearl, Highlanders the shells that housed these pearls. The desire for both was cultural in origin while economic in form: pearl represented Western riches, while its shell was vital to the gift exchange at the centre of Wiru culture. Brewster's is an epic tale, but not unlike the accounts of patrols actually undertaken by the likes of Champion or Hides in the Highlands during the 1930s which were received with great interest by readers in the West. The gold-seeking Leahy brothers were to follow. All heralded the permanent presence of the Australian administration a few decades later. Part of the space of colonialism, then, is provided by the colonizers through the civilizing quest for the largely imagined Other. Be it the discourse of pacifying the savage to allow for 'development' or that of the expunging of Satan and the saving of souls, administration and mission alike were motivated by, and legitimated their actions through, presumptions of what the native was and could or could not become. No doubt these first-hand experiences of Wiru were more accurate than those of the natives in Brewster's tale, but administration and mission accounts of their early days were no less framed in terms of what they thought they expected to find.

Clark's aim in recounting the culture of colonialism thus aims to go well beyond the scope of the myriad of so-called 'first encounters' in the anthropological and historical literature. These overwhelmingly focus on the local cultural response with far less attention given to that of the colonizers. Based on a variety of sources, mission cultures and their versions of history are well documented. Written memoirs of years among 'savage brothers', church literature, including cartoons depicting the more vivid Old Testament stories, verbal reminiscence, and so on, together form a detailed image of missionary life and work over a number of years. Old patrol officer memories also feature, as do government records, most notably patrol reports. While they remain important, patrol reports are often somewhat sanitized versions of these times, if for no other reason than the tension which frequently existed between field officers and higher officials. It is a major absence in Highlands history that few post-war patrol officers wrote volumes on their experiences. Though the epic accounts of the early pioneers often contrast with the more mundane day-to-day lives of later patrol officers, they warrant a record none the less. Despite the unavoidable limits of available source material, Clark does a remarkable job in reconstructing Wiru history from all sides. Chapters 3 and 4 are the result of this reconstruction, and together make up Part Two, which concerns the establishment and general effects of the ongoing presence of fundamentalist missions and administration in Pangia.

Since these are instances of the culture of colonialism, Clark does not seek to confirm the historical verity of the government reports or missionary memoirs. Indeed, his account does not claim to be the history of Takuru, nor even part of the history with spaces yet unfilled. It is, first and foremost, as his subtitle conveys, a chronicle. It is far less concerned with what might really have happened than with the discourses about what happened. His perspective owes a substantial debt to the orientation Foucault takes on such matters in works such as Volume I of *The History of Sexuality*. Foucault's power/knowledge equation in which power extends beyond the material dimensions of colonialism to how culturally and historically specific 'truths' are generated, sustained, or transformed, is a major dimension of Clark's approach. That is, while never denying the importance of the material dimensions of power, power goes beyond the instrumental in its capacity to render the world real. The great task Clark sets himself thus substantially concentrates on how a reality (or, better put, realities) is produced through the interweaving of two quite fundamentally different cultural systems.

Central to this is, once again in line with Foucault, the genesis of subjectivities of both self and other which must also exhibit historical variation. Chapter 2, 'Sons of the Female Spirit, Men of Steel' is a telling instance. While Clark still interprets 'first contacts' in cultural terms, his approach differs from most accounts of these scenarios. First, he argues that it is likely that the Wiru did not have a unitary sense of 'red men' (the common, and altogether more accurate, visual image of 'Whites' in the Highlands), as suggested in the plural masculinities of the title. In part, this is due to the significance of the different directions from which patrols or trade goods came. Second, he looks not only at the culture of colonialism, but also at the changing Western perceptions of Wiru. A simple example is that of the images some missionaries have bestowed upon them. Initially portrayed as pagan savages to be converted to the Light, once this had been achieved, the Wiru were often referred to as 'wishy-washy' due to what appeared to be a distinct lack of devotion and conviction in the eyes of Midwestern Americans. As opposed to the unitary sweep of Foucault's European 'histories', Clark's Highland history is potentially more complex. Not only is variation between cultural renditions important, but there are two mutually affecting but substantially independent and changing cultures in operation.

Clark's departure from Foucault recalls a number of feminist critiques of the latter's works, reaching beyond discourse to uncover one truism of any history— that much of it cannot be easily articulated in speech. The Wiru experience of colonialism was often less open to verbal expression than to bodily experience.

Thus, at different points in time, colonialism has been linked to madness: to controlling (literally 'taming') the Wiru through suspected contagion of the water supply; the often noted disenfranchization of Highlander men brought under colonial control is deemed to have made Wiru men physically 'shrink'; and the celebration of conversion to Christianity is hallmarked by the 'joy of jumping' when possessed by the Holy Spirit.

However, perhaps the most telling illustration of the centrality of the body comes from the engagement in work, a seemingly mundane issue but one integral to how the Wiru were involved in and came to comprehend the changes taking place. Given the Wesleyan presence, it may be apt to call this a particular form of the Protestant work ethic, since it was the product of a particular synthesis of local and Western meaning. Partly motivated by the need to instil discipline and thus achieve control, and partly prompted by the rationale for development, the administration (often in concert with the mission) adopted work projects, road building in particular, as the way forward. Yet it was for different reasons that the Wiru took upon themselves the need to engage in these new forms of work. This motivation came from their cultural tradition of what work meant, even if this now had elements drawn from capitalism and Christianity. Work in many tribal cultures goes well beyond the means and goals associated with Western utilitarianism. Work may encompass what Westerners define as manual toil and ritual. It was this dual meaning which motivated the Wiru, not to intentionally engender their own domination, but to bring the rewards their sense of development entailed. What it amounted to, in line with one of Foucault's key insights into 'history', is that 'truth' may be so firmly entrenched that discipline is self-administered. While this is a theme developed throughout Clark's monograph, Part Three deals most explicitly with the Wiru history of embodied experience.

The presence of both Foucault and Taussig indicates the variety of Clark's theoretical influences. Ultimately, *From Steel to Stone* is his particular assemblage of historical ethnography, coloured with certain theoretical points or influences from those working on anthropological histories across the globe. These include Jean and John Comaroff in Africa, Rosaldo in the Philippines, and a number of Melanesian scholars. He also returns to one of the first endeavours to (re-) insert history into anthropology, Sahlins's (1981) work on Cook and Hawai'i in which structure/culture and event are shown to be inseparable. 'First contact' scenarios are clearly amenable to the notion developed by Sahlins of the 'structure of the conjuncture' in the 'conjunction of the structures'. With Cook, British and Hawai'ian alike were both motivated to act in and could only interpret events through their own culture, as different as the meanings each culture gave rise to were. Schieffelin's (1991) reaction to Sahlins is important—his 'structure of misjuncture' is not merely a pun. Sahlins's discussion of Cook's actions during the staging of the Makahiki festival (prior to his forced return after leaving as 'Lono' should) highlights the smoothness of the way each side reinforced a commitment to radically different versions of what transpired. Fundamental to Clark's approach, however, is that real misunderstandings could arise from conjuncture as well as relatively harmonious, if differing, understandings. I am sure all Highlanders recall their absolute bemusement with the colonizers—not simply because of a lack of cultural apparatus with which to understand, but because of the sheer inconsistencies of the colonizers themselves. Colonial accounts too are littered with references to frustration when their instructions produced an unintended or even opposite effect. Labels like 'untrustworthy' abound in government reports and missionary diaries, but this is as likely to be the structure of misjuncture as any conscious disobedience. With temporality included, Wiru history is thus a succession of structures of (mis-)junctures, as awkward as the phrase may be.

To merely call Clark's work an assemblage is too simple. I would be tempted, in fact, to call it a bricolage if the Lévi-Straussian concept did not refer to a contextual problem solver with a goal in mind but no great premeditated method to achieve it. Clark was most definitely more of a 'craftsman' (cf. Lévi-Strauss 1962:17). There is an undoubted eclecticism about Clark's theoretical influences, born in part from expediency, but also through design. Those interested in how anthropology deals with history should be equally interested in how and perhaps why Clark chooses and uses the milestones the authors mentioned have given us. To this end, Clark is more engineer than bricoleur even if his project can never achieve the neatness to which engineers aspire. My main reason for likening this work to that of bricolage stems from the multiplicity of sources and indeed availability of the 'pieces' to be assembled. As Lévi-Strauss (1962: 22) puts it, the bricoleur, 'builds up structures by fitting together events, or the remains of events', the reference to 'remains of events' conveying the sense that the bricoleur works with 'secondary qualities, i.e. second-hand'.

However, Clark does not pretend to be either a neutral factor himself, or one in a position to decide just what this history really is. He arrived amongst Wiru well after the advent of colonial culture. Finding 'tradition' is thus a perilous exercise in that what we may see as change is not so or, more likely, we may easily take as tradition that which has substantially changed. Just like the Wiru and the colonists, at any point in time Clark had his biases, priorities, and assumptions about what was there, and, just like the colonizers and the Wiru, these were far from unchanging. While it may not be the old version of history, as a precise chronology of what took place and why it did so, Clark's account is most decidedly his. *From Steel to Stone* is, like the bricoleur's handiwork, non-alienated: the self is very much in the product.

The concept of bricolage has its affinities with this image of the structures of (mis-)junctures. It also conjures up senses of the piecemeal and irregular resulting from historical happenchance unintended by those involved in ways that often exceeded their intentions. This is not to deny that individuals (on both sides of the cultural divide) did not devise strategies and act accordingly. Rather, it is to say that the trajectory of history is not reducible to a grand scheming of the proportions

Lévi-Strauss gives to the engineer/scientist in opposition to the bricoleur. This is, I think, highly consistent with Clark's sense of Wiru history—not only in the way it is recounted but very much in the way it was and is. He argues against the continuity-in-change thesis, not so much to deny it but to question both what it is and what value it has. He details in great depth how Wiru culture informs how change has taken place, and how the novel is rendered at least potentially familiar. However, this is not to endorse the trite expression that the 'more things change the more they stay the same'. This has given some anthropologists an excuse for poor historical accounts even when they acknowledge that history and change may be important. Jumping for joy through possession, for instance, may be informed by a culturally constructed sense of the body and the power of the spirits transferred, at least partially, to Christian figures. However, it is a radical experience, which the change-as-the-same idea entirely negates. Clark wishes to emphasize that particular historical moments may not only be beyond comprehension—extant culture cannot accommodate them—but may also be radically transformative of Wiru consciousness of themselves and the world around them.

One of the easiest criticisms of anthropology is that often we neither define the concepts we use nor use them consistently. Change and continuity (and their synonyms) are obvious instance of these charges. It is true that one of the triumphs of anthropological history is the recognition that change retains consistencies with, and continues to be informed by, local culture through the way people sense the world and are motivated to act in and on it. Any number of works show how people make sense of and actively engage in the incorporation of fundamental dimensions of political economy originating in the West through assigning meanings from their own cultural background. Gregory's (1982) *Gifts and Commodities* or Strathern's (1984), *A Line of Power* are but two of the many works which describe how Highlanders embraced capitalism and electoral politics.

These types of orientations are very different from the 'more things change the more they stay the same'. Even when the novel is rendered meaningful, it does not mean that the long-term effects of the penetration of Western political economy will simply be the reproduction of the moment of their incorporation. The two previous examples of Gregory's and Strathern's works are sufficient to illustrate this point. A sense that politicians are like traditional big men, with their following conceptualized in terms of tribal alliance, may become a point of resistance against prevailing electoral politics in the climate of widespread dissatisfaction with politicians common in Papua New Guinea today. Similarly, if the capacity to render commodities as gifts is the dimension of greatest impact in Gregory's argument, he also argues that gifts can be commoditized. Money alone demonstrates the complexities of capitalism's impact when seen over a substantial time frame. The Wiru followed the pattern of other Highlanders in rendering money a valuable suitable for gift exchange and thus became active agents in their dependency on capitalism. But the initial rendering of money as gift does not preclude the possibility that money would later generate new forms of self-interest. This may then contradict gift exchange, where the giving of valuables carries with it more prestige than the receiving. Initial continuity and complementarity with the material wherewithal of two different political economies, capitalism and gift exchange, in other words, may create the possibility of subsequent conflict between older and newer values.

The initial continuity when the novel becomes familiar is not the only possibility. Thus Clark argues that colonialism may in fact be seen as a radical departure from the past—discontinuity rather than continuity. That is, the more-things-change is just that, they do not stay the same. The question remains, however: just what does Clark mean by radical, or, more particularly, radical for whom? While I cannot do justice to his compelling argument, I wish to indicate the scope for its wider application by extending a similarity between seaboard cargo cults and Highlands development suggested by Clark (1988) himself.

Borrowing from the words Burridge (1960, 1969) so influentially uses, the message of cargo cults may be a 'new heaven', 'new earth', and 'new man (and woman)'—a radical reformulation of society and thus self. While the colonizers profoundly feared the radicalism of the cults, are they radical departures from the past? It would seem the expectation that the dead would return is most profoundly radical. However, it remains an expectation which, if achieved, would not seem to radically transform conventional understandings of kinship but only permit the ideal realization of kinship and reciprocity in a world of pure happiness. New forms of sexual practice may be part of the message, but rarely is there alteration in the relationship between gender and power. Certainly there may be shifts in male power structures (black over, or in the absence of, white; younger for older men) but knowledge and individual prowess remain central concerns.

Cargo cult practice is a piecemeal synthesis of old and new. The means of achieving the new is usually simple and necessitates only that a few fundamental truths be followed. More particularly, even if the ritual form is reinforced by both precolonial forms of practice and the miraculous that lies at the heart of the mission message, it still remains ritual in a way highly compatible with what preceded it. An external perspective on cults may arrive at the conclusion that they are a perfect illustration of cultural persistence in which forms remain intact even if the content varies. The point is, of course, that this can in no way be reconciled with the fact that change may be experienced as radical, total, irreversible, and 'new' by people such as the cargo cultists or, in Clark's discussion, the Wiru. It seems to me that the central problematic which anthropology must address is human consciousness formed in a social and cultural setting where power and meaning go hand in hand. We need to consider 'what moves people without their knowing quite why or quite how, with what makes the real real and the normal normal', in the words of Michael Taussig (1987: 366). The central and most difficult challenge for historical anthropology is to approach this by insisting on a role for time, thereby manifestly increasing the number of issues that need to be addressed. Now the novel and the extraordinary must also be considered. Clark's chronicle of colonialism for one Highland people, the Takuru Wiru, accepts such a challenge, and the result is a lasting tribute to both the Wiru and the author.

MICHAEL NIHILL

ACKNOWLEDGEMENTS

I wrote this book while a Research Associate in the 'Politics of Tradition' project headed by Nick Thomas, at the Department of Archaeology and Anthropology, Australian National University. It is the culmination of a long period of incubation and as such its debts to individuals and institutions are numerous and varied. I lived and worked in Pangia district in the Southern Highlands Province of Papua New Guinea for a total of two years, during four trips over an extended period from 1980 to 1992. The University of Adelaide and its Department of Anthropology provided the initial funding for postgraduate research, and Tom Ernst supplied the encouragement and inspiration to undertake fieldwork in Papua New Guinea, a decision I have never had cause to regret. James Cook University in Townsville, and its Department of Anthropology and Archaeology, provided funding towards later research and allowed me a leave of absence during 1994 to take up the position at ANU.

The writing project was undertaken while I was experiencing a serious and ongoing illness, and my colleagues in anthropology and other disciplines at the University of Adelaide, James Cook University, Australian National University, and overseas have been especially supportive during this time. It is not necessary to produce a catalogue of names, for they know who they are and how much I appreciate their encouragement. However, there are people who, because of their proximity or special circumstances, have been supportive not only of my writing but of my return to a modicum of health. Chris Ballard, Margaret Jolly, and Nick Thomas deserve special mention in this regard, as do Laurence Goldman and Sandra Pannell from faraway Brisbane and Townsville, who were always in Canberra in spirit. Nick Peterson, the Head of Department at ANU, together with its administrative staff, have also been very helpful with assistance and in extending my stay in Canberra beyond 1994.

In Papua New Guinea the provincial and national governments gave permission for research, and at various times the National Research Institute, the Institute of Medical Research, and the University of Papua New Guinea have supported applications for visas and helped with accommodation and other matters in Port Moresby and elsewhere. The Southern Highlands Rural Development Project (SHRDP) was operational when I first entered the field in 1980, and the assistance of its personnel was immeasurable at all of the levels that extended fieldwork requires, from the personal to the logistic. Certain individuals associated with these institutions rendered assistance beyond the call of duty; in particular, Merle and Cathy Anders, Lyn Clarke, Bruce French, and Jim Robins. Lisette Josephides, Marc Schiltz, Don Burkins and Brigitte Krause were anthropologists with whom I stayed during the first fieldwork period, and were generous with advice, food, and good company. In Pangia, it would have been much more difficult to have achieved anything without the support and assistance of two of the missions; at St Felix

Mission, Yaraporoi, Fathers Albert and Dunstan Jones who, with the always friendly Sister Margaret Doherty, provided historical insights, cups of tea, and invigorating company. In Takuru, the settlement where I spent most of my time, the Reverend Daniel and Patti Connor of the Wesleyan Mission were unstinting in their hospitality and friendship, and I remember them fondly and with much appreciation, particularly for the many excellent meals I had at their house.

In 1985, I spent a very pleasant weekend reminiscing with the late Mr Daniel Leahy over his 1930s explorations in the Highlands. He was disgusted that I caught a truck rather than walk back to Mt Hagen town. Mrs Jeanette Leahy graciously allowed me permission to read the diaries of her famous husband, Mick Leahy, held in the National Library in Canberra, a valuable source of insights into the first encounters between Europeans and Highlanders—a moment in Highlands history that obsesses me yet. Dr Harland Kerr of the Summer Institute of Linguistics, together with his wife Marie, talked to me about their early experiences in Pangia and patiently answered many of my questions about the Wiru language. Peter Barber, who became Assistant District Commissioner after more than a decade spent in Pangia, was also very helpful with interviews about his experiences of colonialism. Andrew Strathern and Marilyn Strathern, through their correspondence and publications about Pangia, have also been of great assistance in the writing project.

It is with some embarrassment that I think of the number of people whom I must thank for having helped me in the fifteen years I have been travelling to the Highlands. I spent my first night in the bush with Rob Crittenden and Janice Baines, and I vividly remember my first meal in the company of Highlanders, duck soup, as we sat around the fire in Crittenden's house. Rob and Janice were very helpful to a novice fieldworker, although I nearly collapsed from exhaustion on my first experience of walking in the precipitious Highlands, following Janice on one of her 'short' nutrition patrols on the Nembi plateau. Rob, later a Project Manager of the SHRDP when I returned for a three-month trip to Pangia in 1985, greatly facilitated my access to patrol reports, photocopying, and items of archival interest, often from his own extensive collection of documents. Many a pleasant evening was spent in Mendi after dinner discussing early patrols, and Rob awakened my interest to the importance of history in accounts of the Highlands (see Schieffelin and Crittenden 1991). One of my oldest friends and colleagues who has also been steadfast and quietly supportive both before and during my year of illness and recovery is Michael Nihill, and without Mike it would have been much more difficult to write this book. I thank him wholeheartedly for his encouragement and particularly for his reliable hospital visits. Peter Naumann, Deborah Stokes, Toni Craig, Daniel Vachon, Chris Morgan, Paul Reser, Rosita Henry, Mike Wood, Maureen Fuary, Roger Wilkinson, Don Gardner, James Weiner, Deborah Lehmann, Michael Alpers, Dave Gibson, Dave Whiting, Lee and Linda Sackett, John Gray, Deane Fergie, Vicki Clark, and Lyn Burrows were all valuable friends during my time in Canberra.

Gratitude is expressed to the following journals and editors for permission to reproduce excerpts from the following published articles: Kaun and Kongono: Cargo Cults and Development in Karavar and Pangia, *Oceania*, 59(1), 1988, 40–57; The Incredible Shrinking Men: Male Ideology and Development in a Southern Highlands Society, in *Culture and Development in Papua New Guinea*, Chris Healey (ed.), *Canberra Anthropology* [Special Issue] 12(1–2), 1989, 120–43; Madness and Colonisation: The Embodiment of Power in Pangia, in *Alienating Mirrors: Christianity, Cargo Cults and Colonialism in Melanesia*, Andrew Lattas (ed.), *Oceania* [Special Issue] 63(1), 1992; 15–26.

This book would have been impossible to write without the generosity of spirit of the Wiru people of Pangia, particularly those of Takuru settlement. Some of the most rewarding and difficult times in my life were spent in Pangia, and I am truly grateful to have shared them with my Wiru friends and informants, as I am for their sharing with me of their narratives of colonialism. Kaiyape Wilson, friend and collaborator, made fieldwork a pleasure with his companionship and intelligence, and his father, Wili, provided much help in collecting the data upon which this book is based. To Pastor Wendeka, Angopa, (the late) Koiya, and to all those people mentioned or referred to here, *ke mane uku*, it being especially appropriate that this Wiru gloss of 'thank you' is adapted from an invocation to the spirits for the boon of good luck.

PREFACE

Let the reader imagine standing by the roadside in a place called Takuru in Pangia district in late 1980, surrounded by curious children and puzzled adults, many clothed in Western cast-offs, as the SHRDP Toyota Landcruiser which brought you to this destination disappears from view around a bend in the road, reappearing fifteen minutes later further down the valley on its journey back to Mendi, a slowly moving yellow dot in the beautiful Highlands landscape. As the afternoon rain threatens, and the leaves of the coffee trees rattle in response to the approaching storm, you find yourself in proximity to the Wesleyan church, the source of the onlookers who have emerged from an afternoon service, their Christian enthusiasm the product of a recent revival. At the centre of heaps of cargo, you prepare to negotiate the track to the house you have rented from the mission while your own is under construction. People offer to carry to your temporary accommodation what appears to them as an impressive amount of cargo. The anthropologist seems always to be defined by excess. Arrival! Finally, you are on your own, ready for fieldwork in the Papua New Guinea Highlands.

A parody of entry into the field, yes, but one that describes some features of my own arrival in Takuru, except that I had spent the previous night at the Wesleyan mission, a building of mid-Western farmhouse dimensions, complete with roaring fireplace, comfortable armchairs, and upstairs bedrooms. At the hospitable insistence of my generous missionary hosts, who made polite but strenuous inquiries into my religiosity, I had eaten well and slept comfortably. In this vignette of arrival, the anthropologist is presented as the centre of attention, the local people as merely curious and dishevelled non-Western onlookers, whereas in actuality many people remained within the church, caught up in the spirit of the revival. 'Being there', the basis for textual authenticity (Geertz 1988), is established early to guarantee the validity of the ethnography which follows, after which the ethnographer magically disappears from the text.[1] There are deliberate differences, of course, with the more traditional accounts of 'being there'; mention of the year 1980 introduces a discordant note of modernity, and the people are clearly not pagan savages, even if they remain the (contaminated) Other, Christians in Western clothing (cf. Barker 1992). I had been driven to Takuru in a Toyota belonging to the Southern Highlands Rural Development Project (SHRDP) funded by the World Bank. Takuru people are presented as

---

[1] As an authorial presence in the following chapters I do seem to disappear, but most of the events I discuss took place before my entry into the field and I find it difficult to place myself in ethnohistory. Yet it is obvious that I do not make myself invisible, remaining as the *deus ex machina*, or perhaps the smile of the Cheshire cat, that lurks on every page, driving the narrative by 'speaking' for a Wiru sense of historicity, editing accounts from archives and books, and so on. Despite the absence of a clearly self-referential position, it is not the case, I hope, that the 'authorial eye and I of the ethnographer, as humanly engaged, are carefully edited out' (Keesing and Jolly 1992: 229).

'changed', growing cash crops and articulated into a world economic system, not as pristine traditionalists on the verge of violence, ritual, or ceremonial exchange (Carrier 1992).

What the account does not capture is the uncertainty and apprehension I felt at being stranded amongst Christians. Where were the Highlanders I had read and been lectured about? Why come all this way to experience discomforts and loneliness, merely to study peaceful Christians? I had naïvely hoped to find myself in a relatively traditional society so that in the years to come I could document the effects of change, but here I was in a society that seemed so changed, so far from a 'traditional' ground zero, that I was extremely discomfited in my quest for the authentic (cf. Keesing and Jolly 1992: 227). For months I viewed Wiru as severely compromised by their contacts with the West, and in my darker moments privately agreed with local missionaries who pronounced Wiru as 'wishy-washy' for the alacrity and superficiality of their conversion to Christianity—and, in my case, for their readiness, even acquiescence, in giving up their traditions—unlike other inhabitants of the province such as the Huli who, after a good fight, appeared to take Christianity seriously to heart.

I am sure that anthropologists are growing tired of 'confessions' about the ahistorical context of fieldwork—as if admissions of inadequacy confer a legitimacy on the current project—but these admissions are necessary to make two related points. The first point is that the reader has to be made aware that the data initially collected is compromised by an obliviousness to the fact that 'what looks most culturally conservative and traditional may represent a reaction to colonial domination, not historical insulation from outside influences' (Keesing and Jolly 1992: 227); and the second, that my writing of history is very much influenced by what this data gradually revealed, namely that cultural abandonment can be as dynamic and creative a reaction to colonial domination as conservatism. This awareness led to a questioning of the ways in which some anthropologists write about cultural persistence over time, as if it was a clinging to tradition; history is introduced only for its significance to be denied (Jolly 1992a). The notion of history as deliberate loss suggests that it is not change itself but a particular attitude to the past, sometimes verging on nostalgia, sometimes abhorrence, that affects local historical consciousness.

My initial disappointment affected the fieldwork itself in so far as disillusionment with my Christian co-residents discouraged my intentions to become fluent in Wiru, an arduous task that somehow seemed more justifiable if the people were authentic, continuing their practice of a rich and complex cult life. The notion that Christians were not quite worth the linguistic effort was a failure on my part that I constantly regret. From the perspective of the time in which I write, these views are obviously 'politically incorrect', but part of the problem was with the way I had been taught anthropology (Carrier 1992), and with my expectations of what fieldwork would be like among traditional people. The Highlands was, after all, presented as the last bastion of the primitive and a laboratory for hypothesis testing

(Smith 1980). To some extent, I felt let down by the discipline and by my teachers; why was I not sufficiently prepared for the existence of a radically changed Christian community? Initially, I assuaged my doubts by telling myself that 'tradition' was probably lurking just beneath the surface of contemporary life, and time spent in the community would gradually reveal to me a strong continuity with the past. I was remarkably successful with this self-deception, but what took a long time to emerge was the knowledge that a major reason for my initial discomfiture was precisely that Takuru society *had* radically changed, and that it was discontinuity, the lack of the past in the present (Jolly 1992a: 59), as much as continuity which needed to be explained.

My own sense of discontinuity is conveyed by an idiosyncratic image of the landscape. I would observe the surrounding districts from a vantage point and see the romantic terrain of cult movement, trade routes of stone axes and other valuables, and first contact, tracing out in my mind's eye the pathways of cults and valuables as they were imported into Pangia, and the journeys of the first Europeans as they encountered Wiru. Closer examination revealed Pangia as Wiru perhaps envisaged it, with the station clearly visible down the Polu valley, the corrugated iron roofs of mission buildings glinting in the sun, roads carving brown gashes through the green landscape, and settlements of many houses huddled alongside the road—undisputed evidence for a discrete, known, and colonized universe that clashed with my own preconceptions.

Andrew Strathern (1984: 99) remarks that Wiru made a deliberate effort to forget the past; and Rosaldo (1980: 45, 46) writes of his experiences in Luzon that, 'Ilongot in 1974 often told me that they "no longer" were Ilongot . . . They seemed to think that many of their former practices—sometimes their very identity as Ilongots—had been thrown overboard as if they were excess cultural baggage.'

Like Rosaldo, my dilemma in understanding what was happening to myself as well as Wiru, who had become alienated from a past they had themselves jettisoned, 'was that I myself stood knee-deep in the rapid flow of change' (Rosaldo 1980: 46), although I blamed myself as a poor fieldworker for my inability to trace out the connections between the past and the present, to find the dynamic connections between tradition and contemporary practices. These connections were undoubtedly there, and I was gratified and pleased to discover instances of them, but how much more productive my research could have been if I had concentrated upon differences rather than giving priority to similarities. The latter, of course, created the illusion that despite change, the people were, after all, authentically primitive, a few degrees off tradition. I was not, perhaps, such a poor fieldworker, merely unprepared for the complexities of dealing with postcolonial Pangia and with people who were pacified less than two decades before my arrival. After all, how could they have changed so much in so short a time, a question which Wiru themselves found difficult to answer (although, unlike Ilongot, they never seemed to question their essential Wiru-ness, even while recognizing a dramatic difference with their pagan personas and an abrupt exodus from the precolonial 'time of darkness')? The problem, of course, was that Wiru culture *had* changed dramatically, and this is what I lacked the ability to explain; I needed to account for how the more things change, the less they stay the same. The following chapters deal with some of the issues and problems involved in such an account.

Introduction

Just as the road and travel provide an endless source of literary and cinematic metaphors for the transient and shape-shifting American condition, the road provides a core metaphor for the experience of many Highlanders with the 'other', especially through the projects of colonialism. A commonly heard expression is that a woman, through her marriage, creates 'roads' between groups for the exchange of wealth and assistance, and the metaphor has obvious relevance for imagining and directing change on the Melanesian Seaboard, as the title of Lawrence's classic monograph, *Road Belong Cargo*, indicates. For the Awa of the Eastern Highlands, 'the road remains a metaphor for culture change and "development" ' (Hayano 1990: 2). Wiru, the inhabitants of Pangia district, created many of their understandings of development by using the road to trace changing connections between images of power and wealth, from the time of their earliest encounters with Europeans to their present interactions with an independent and postcolonial state. Before pacification commenced in the 1950s, trade and exchange goods were believed to enter into Pangia along major watercourses, in a similar fashion to the way in which ghosts moved from their abode in the land of the dead back to that of the living (A. J. Strathern 1984: 20). The connections between Wiru and the 'outside', modelled on links to spirits and an extra-mundane world, are different to those amongst Wiru who inhabit the 'inside' of Pangia, following not immutable rivers but well-worn paths between human communities, the latter a 'graphic effect of intentional, creative movement across the earth' (J. F. Weiner 1991: 38). Watercourses and tracks provided different metaphors for the understanding of relationships with the 'other' as spirit or human; rivers 'can only be followed' (ibid.), while paths can be abandoned or created through human action in the world.

Tracks which lead to gardens or connect settlements are known as *ka*, also the word for womb and netbag, pointing to the connection and importance of carrying, movement, growth/nurturance, and wealth (birth initiates the most important and long-term exchange of valuables in Wiru society). The vehicular road, *ka*, constructed with much heavy and unremitting labour under the supervision, bequest, and sometimes insistence of ghost-like Europeans, came to replace the river as a metaphor for the experience of flow and power, as stories about trucks laden with cargo disappearing into rivers suggest. Colonial road-building activities were never mere labour but acts of cultural innovation to channel the flow of European wealth and power (these themes are elaborated upon in Chapters 1, 2 and 5). Road-building involved human activity but under the control of Europeans, who often followed watercourses in surveying and constructing roads (Wiru footpaths were more likely to go straight up and down hills). Roads connected Wiru to a new 'outside' where Europeans were located, and their construction initiated a transformation in Wiru conceptions of inside/outside, of the source of wealth and knowledge, of self and other, and ultimately of their consciousness as subjects under colonialism. Many of these chapters are attempts to map out the lineaments of this transformation, and are organized around the twin metaphors of steel, in the form of the axes which represented the first wave of European penetration, and stone, the term by which money came to be known and which was a sign of Wiru encompassment by a colonial order and world system. The movement of steel and stone along 'roads' created new worlds of meaning, in response to and reaction against the discourses and praxis of colonialism and development.

On a return trip to Pangia in 1989, the access road from Ialibu and the Highlands Highway, laboriously constructed decades before in the colonial era, was virtually impassable to all vehicles except tractors. People asked me why Australians had come to Pangia, and why they had initiated so many changes and made rosy promises of the benefits of development—'to lead a life free from all of the old fears' (Ialibu PR2/58–59)—if Wiru were only to be plunged back into the time before Europeans arrived? They had coffee to sell, but buyers could not get into the district, nor could they travel to outside areas or seek medical attention at distant hospitals. It seemed to them that they had come full circle, that the road had in fact brought them back to the beginning. People actually believed themselves to be worse off than they were before pacification because of their colonial expectations and, interestingly, the claim was made that the government treated them like 'wild pigs', which is a state Wiru themselves confer on their own behaviour in the pagan past. I could have attempted to answer their question with a facile explanation about the inadequacies of modernization, but for Wiru this would not have satisfactorily accounted for their own experience of the enigma of colonialism. The colonial period was only meaningful to Wiru through their own metaphors and praxis, and these need to be considered in any attempt at understanding not only their 'history', but also why it is that many Wiru are left wondering if heaven is indeed the only future, and the only real promise made by Europeans.

While socio-political organization in Pangia has significantly altered since pacification, in my Ph.D. thesis (Clark 1985) I argued for a persistence of ideas concerning wealth, status, and intergroup relations through exchange, all of which affected the course of development. This persistence, the notion of continuity through change and change through continuity, has its own history in Highlands ethnography (e.g. Brown 1973), and continues to exert an influence in accounts of change (O'Hanlon 1993; Merlan and Rumsey 1991). Brown's monograph on the Chimbu ends with the dictum that 'the more things change, the more they stay the same' (Brown 1973: 125)—arguably finishing where the analysis should have started. The continuity thesis is not to be dismissed but it does require modification, tending as it does to reify and fetishize 'tradition', denying Highlanders their capacity for the re-invention (or abandonment) of tradition, and for the radical reinterpretation of their worlds (Merlan and Rumsey 1991; see also Smith (1980), who chastises Highlands anthropologists for their deliberate neglect of social change in pursuit of the authentic).[1] The other side of the coin is that change leads to loss, to deterioration not discontinuity, sometimes expressed through an anthropological romanticism: 'When that day comes [of road arrival], the Awa will have to live with one less metaphor and one less dream' (Hayano 1990: 2), where the metaphor appears to refer to the values and strengths of tradition.[2] For Wiru, the completion of the road was all to do with gain not loss, entailing the successful completion of a contract with Europeans.

Sahlins's account (1981: 41) of one incident in early Hawai'ian–British relationships best illustrates the point I am making: '[The British] seamen began to pry nails from the ships' holds as gifts for their [Hawai'ian] women friends, even as Hawai'ian men were using their newly-acquired iron adzes to do the same from the outside, so that between the two they threatened to pull the ships to pieces.'

The ship has been discussed as a refracted representation of British society, in much the same way as early European patrols into the Highlands, with their white leaders, native policemen, and carriers, mirrored and modelled colonial relations of power based upon race and degrees of civilization (Schieffelin and Crittenden 1991). Yet the ship was more than an icon of a foreign order of power and wealth, which early patrols and later the road itself represented in Pangia. It was quite possibly for Hawai'ians also a potent image of their own transformed reality, of a perhaps unreflected-upon *colonial* world, and what they were pulling apart and attempting to reconstruct, in a mutual if not complicit project with Europeans, were the foundation stones of indigenous culture. Sahlins (1981, 1985) cogently demonstrates that signs take on new meanings and do not persist uncontaminated by the future or by the political context of their renegotiation. Tradition, then, cannot provide stumbling blocks to development, and is not to be equated with conservatism (nor is conservatism, where it exists, due to the 'dead weight' of tradition). It is discontinuity, perhaps more so than continuity, which maps the future, its topography affected by contingency rather than a linear causality of cultural themes or logical transformations, much as chance and not design affects the course of biological evolution (Gould 1987).[3]

My intention is not to discount the argument for 'continuity' but rather to question its centrality in explanations of change. Chaos theory reminds us that despite

[1] Melanesians engage in similar projects to anthropologists when they also fetishize 'tradition', as in the creation of 'kastom' categories to facilitate the construction of modern identities and nationalisms (see Jolly and Thomas 1992). The pursuit of the authentic by anthropologists may have been to some extent due to the difficulties they faced with explaining change, a situation not totally to be blamed on a functionalist heritage.

[2] The notion of 'tradition' was also important to the colonialists, but one they struggled against rather than choosing to use in their civilizing projects, a process discussed in following chapters.

[3] Modjeska (1991: 235) discusses a precolonial example of the argument when he hypothesizes that 'the displacement and weakness of symbolic power among the Duna . . . is a consequence of a discontinuity in the social processes of semiotic reproduction . . .' related, but not reduceable, to changes in the mode of production. Wiru experienced a similar discontinuity in semiotic reproduction with the introduction of road labour, cash-cropping, and so on, as later chapters demonstrate.

randomness there is still an underlying pattern, yet continuity is invariably assumed rather than explained. What exactly does it mean to suggest that exchange continues to be the major concern of Highlanders, and that 'bisnis' maps on to it (A. J. Strathern 1982a: 551)? It may seem, for instance, that Highlanders entertain the same sorts of ideas about money that they once held about pearl shells. Money, as a new wealth item, has had a significant impact on the nature of exchange, as well as on gender relations and notions of personhood and agency. While it is often used in ceremonial exchange (Nihill 1989), its deployment may radically alter the context and meaning of the event, such that what is seen as 'cultural'—the similarities between money and shells that men, at least, are often at pains to point out (A. J. Strathern 1979)—is in fact contingent. And peoples' perceptions of shell wealth, interpreted by the ethnographer as 'traditional', may have changed in response to their experience of money and labour migration. A named exchange event that occurred in the past and continues to be performed in the present does not imply persistence in meaning (Jolly 1992b). Highlanders frequently refer to contemporary warfare as a 'bisnis', an activity associated with civilization by Europeans (cf. Taussig 1987: 134). Valuables such as money and pearl shells become thoroughly 'entangled objects' in a web of colonial history (Thomas 1992), and it may be reasonable to argue that Highlanders in fact 'discontinue' the practice of exchange.

One recent account of social change in the Highlands suggests that, in the colonial years, Highlanders 'underwent a crash-course in modernity' (O'Hanlon 1993: 10). They had to become familiar with voting, censuses, taxes, buying and selling, motor vehicles, local government councils, police, the state, and so on. As observers have pointed out, many Highlanders saw their first aeroplane before the wheel (or, to be accurate, both when the aeroplane landed). Signs were presented to them in the total absence of a Western developmental sequence in which to locate them. Highlanders were inserted into the twentieth century with the idea of making them 'modern', perhaps, but it is hard to resist the notion that their experience of colonialism and independence was thoroughly post-modern: signs came from everywhere and it was rare that their signifieds were immediately obvious or connected. Conflict between the 'old' and the 'new' defines this experience, not a transition to a better form, even if the latter was an outcome devoutly wished for by many Highlanders. From the tribal to the modern assumes too much, a Western continuum of change and development, whereas it may be that many of the problems that face the Highlands today are traceable to the ways in which people were flung into postmodernity, living on 'the edge of chaos', to borrow a term from recent biological writings on evolution. Highlanders are still trying to make sense of their postmodern predicament, which is for many less a stage after tribalism than a time of confusion, alienation, and anxiety—which the documentary film *Black Harvest* (1992) captures so poignantly—particularly if the colonial experience resonated with local notions of the millennium and entropy (see Clark 1995 for Huli; Lattas 1992: 29 for Kaliai).

The colonial history of Pangia is not just a recounting of the activities and influence of patrol officers (kiaps) and missionaries. History is also more than a product or description of structural processes within a society, more than just a series of progressive transformations or permutations which Sahlins (1981) argues for in his monograph on the meeting and confrontations between Europeans and Hawai'ians. The meta-narrative type of history that is criticized by Foucault may be written by the colonialists, but as a type of discourse it demands analysis for what it reveals of power/knowledge relations, as Chapters 3 and 4 demonstrate. The events which constitute this history are experienced by the colonized, often in terms not recognizable to the colonialists, and it is with this experience that Chapters 5 and 6 are mainly concerned. Ethnohistory sometimes runs the risk of using the categories of the 'other' to perpetuate a Western category of 'history', and I am more concerned with examining how Wiru represent events to themselves rather than with mapping them in any temporal sense. Yet history 'from the native's point of view' can only be understood against the background of colonial discourses designed to produce the colonial subject as a particular type of 'docile body'—in this case the Christian peasant (Foucault 1979). Ethnography, like 'tradition', should not be a static concept. 'Before and after' views of society present a distorted picture of social change, value the past as more authentic, and inhibit an understanding of the processes which transform, reproduce, and reinvent society. Contemporary Wiru culture is less a version (or product) of a precolonial or future culture than it is an uncertain process taking place at 'the edge of chaos'. Its autonomy in reproducing itself has been compromised and diminished by the praxis associated with colonial discourses about self, personhood, and agency. Many Wiru talk of the present Christian society as indicating a total break with the past, and we need to pay attention to their statements rather than emphasize continuity (cf. Taussig 1980), which offers a comforting illusion when faced with the need to account for the chaos of social change. Arguments for continuity are the anthropological equivalent of the Piltdown Man, 'logical' missing links which ethnographers expect to discover and that are indeed found, despite evidence of radical change.

The following chapters are not meant to provide a standard ethnography of the Wiru, and readers looking for accounts of social structure or exchange will look in vain (see Clark 1985). My major concern remains with bringing out certain points about colonialism and the writing of history. This will be achieved by contrasting various narratives of the colonial experience, both Wiru and European. The book is divided into three parts, the first dealing with stories of origin and settlement, and told from colonial and indigenous perspectives. An imaginary account of a journey into the Highlands by shipwrecked sailors is compared with Wiru stories of migration for their different concerns with the 'other'. Part I concludes with a lengthy account of European exploration of the Pangia region from the 1920s onwards, and its gradual pacification during the 1950s. I argue that 'first contact' was basically a dialogic encounter between Wiru and Europeans, involving 'the gradual clearing out of a space of shared meaning' (Harkin 1988: 102). Chapter 2 draws together some of the themes and conclusions presented in Chapter 1 about the 'other', and suggestions are made as to why a particular colonial history was created in Pangia out of varying perceptions of Europeans as cult spirits, ancestors, or sorcerers, providing a supporting basis for explanations offered in later chapters.

Part II examines some of the reasons for the particular Wiru response to Christian missions and the Australian administration's development schemes. This examination is carried out with specific reference to the fieldwork settlement of Takuru, although analyses are invariably set in the general context of Pangia District itself. Chapters 3 and 4 examine the period from pacification to the early 1970s and consider, in terms of Pangia's relatively late encapsulation into the colonial order, how Wiru constructions of Europeans and European resources led to the creation of a colonized culture. A Western history of development and missionization, encountered in patrol reports and books written by missionaries about the necessity and benefits of progress and conversion, is considered and contrasted with a Wiru 'counter-history' that deals with their responses to and understandings of administration and mission demands. This 'history' emerges through a consideration of ritual attitudes to labour in road-building, indicating that Wiru had their own agenda in development, namely to become European.

Part III begins with a more detailed examination of Wiru historical understandings, arguing for the importance of an embodied history given the central role of the body in Wiru thought and exchange, especially as a vehicle for the imaging of change. The context of Chapter 5 is outbreaks of madness immediately prior to pacification, and later outbreaks in Christian revival activities. Madness is related to the later Wiru engagement in development in which the construction of new bodies was the desired outcome, and the chapter continues with an analysis of an idiom of male emasculation, shrinking bodies, that arose in response to feelings of disempowerment by the colonial regime, and to the gradual recognition that becoming European was impossible. The relevance of Foucault for a Western understanding of embodied history, and for the creation of a colonized culture and new subjectivities is discussed in Chapter 6. The final chapter of the book looks to the end of the colonial era and discusses Wiru attitudes towards the independent state, foregrounding the analysis by examining the influence of money on the colonization of consciousness in Pangia.

Selling and exchange with Europeans, together with the role of material culture in social change, are investigated for their processual importance in transformations of subjectivity. I seek to demonstrate that exchange and ritual informed the interaction of Takuru Wiru with new institutions and beliefs, and to argue that their discontinuous nature, together with new dependencies, had a particular effect upon historical praxis and the reproduction of culture. The epilogue, through a brief account of a cultural 'revival' in one settlement of Pangia, considers a Wiru re-examination of their own past to understand the present, shedding light on the postcolonial awareness of ethnic identity within parameters of power defined by the state. The book concludes with no predictions for the future but it does, hopefully, provide a guide as to how an anthropological history may be written and understood for people such as the Wiru.[4]

A final comment about the style of the monograph is required before Chapter 1 is introduced. Chapters 1 to 6 follow a trajectory from precolonial times to 'first contact' to independence, and I am aware that such an emphasis might betray a Western preoccupation with history as a developmental continuum. Wiru themselves make a tripartite division in their understanding of the past, beginning with the time of darkness, when they were all pagan savages, and followed by the colonial period when expectations for development were great and people felt that major transformations were possible, with Pangia being described at this time as the home of peace, place of love. The time immediately after independence is recalled by Wiru in terms reminiscent of the biblical Fall, in which the potential of the second period came to naught and a return to the anarchy of the pagan past was entirely possible (cf. Errington 1974). I have tried to follow their cyclical chronology of colonialism—from being 'wild pigs' to being treated like 'wild pigs'—which, while it refracts more than reflects the type of history that might be produced by a Western observer, accounts for the apparent linear bias of this monograph.[5]

[4] The monograph is part of a wider ethnographic project in the Southern Highlands, involving fieldwork in Pangia and Tari districts. The Wiru material is more concerned with the history of colonialism up to the granting of independence in 1975, while my articles on the Huli, based upon intermittent fieldwork since 1989, document a much more 'recent' history of change in the context of the postcolonial state, particularly in the areas of sexuality and gender, myth, illness, and ethnicity.

[5] This is not to deny the potential for a linear sense of time emerging out of, or existing prior to the colonial experience; nor is it suggested that Wiru history is subject to a mythic mode of thought, as Chapter 5 demonstrates.

PART I

1

Tangenemo *and Other Stories*

It may seem unusual to start a chronicle of colonialism with Wiru *tangenemo*, stories of origin, migration, and settlement in Pangia, but I do this deliberately to evoke a contrast with narratives of colonialism and European exploration, themselves providing other kinds of myths for dealing with time, space, and the 'other'. *Tangenemo* (*tangene* is 'begin' or 'come to be'; *-mo* is an information suffix) are not regarded by Wiru as fictional stories but as true accounts of their origins in the not too distant past, and they help to explain certain features of the Wiru response to colonialism. Wiru consider themselves to be not the autochthonous inhabitants of Pangia but rather migrants into an empty and forested land, and locate their place of origin at Lake Mbuna in the present-day Imbonggu-speaking area to the west of Mt Ialibu, a short walk from the Highlands Highway (see Map 1). Ialibu station, from where the Australian administration launched their pacification patrols into Pangia in the 1950s, is several kilometres to the south of Lake Mbuna. Close by the

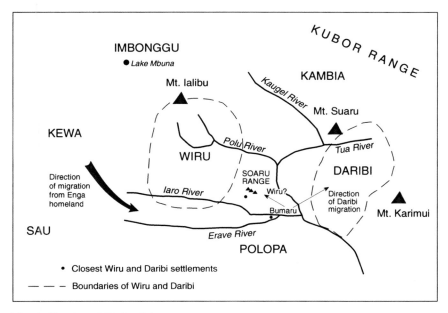

MAP 1. Pangia and Karimui Areas

lake, and visible from the station, is a hill called Polukepo from which death and generational life were introduced into the world, a revelation of particular import for Wiru; talk of the European God, of death and resurrection, was later brought from the same location.

From the perspective of Wiru their origins are to the north-west, although another oral tradition claims their ancestry with *akolali* (man on top, or above), a race of giant people who lived a long time ago to the east, and it is claimed that their huge bones can still be found on the summit of Mt Suaru in the dense rainforest close to the Tua river, far from any present-day Wiru settlement. Bone fragments of these ancestors are sometimes sought for their magical healing properties, and I was shown some by an Undiapu man who sells them all over Pangia. He told me that to collect them he had to walk many days through the bush, then climb to the top of a mountain where the bones were scattered about on the ground and in caves, possibly an ancient burial site or ossuary of Wiru. The healing properties of the bones are derived from their embodiment of ancestral power, and perhaps from an association with a benevolent sky being who shares the same name as these ancestors—Akolali, nowadays an appellation for the God that Wiru 'knew' before missionization. These two references to *akolali* suggest the possibility of Wiru descent from sky beings, a belief held in other parts of the Highlands, although I only occasionally obtained hazy allusions to this possibility. The links between 'god' and colonization are, however, demonstrated.

Early patrol reports from Ialibu refer to Wiru as Wiritaru, which is the Imbonggu or Kewa term of reference for the people of the Poru plateau. I was unable to determine the meaning of *taru*, but central plateau Wiru consider the term to identify people who are authentically Wiru, and point to the eastern settlements as the location of Wiru Taru, which is the direction in which *akolali* once resided (Huli have a word *tara*, which can be glossed as 'other', although it is unlikely that authentic Wiru would be known as 'other' Wiru).[1] This presents an apparent contradiction, as many *tangenemo* clearly point to north-west origins while 'true' Wiru are to be found in the easternmost parts of Pangia, where the giant ancestors of Wiru lived (see n. 4). There is no archaeology of Pangia, but *tangenemo*, and their equivalents from the neighbouring Daribi people across the Tua river (Wagner 1967, 1972, 1978), provide enough details to make some educated guesses about the settlement of Pangia district. Many Wiru maintain that long ago they lived much further to the south, in caves between the Iaro and Erave rivers. In the 1960s there were still some Daribi living in caves, and at a rock shelter close to the confluence of the Tua and Erave rivers (Wagner 1967: 9; 1978: 71). Andrew Strathern (1971a) first pointed to the possibility of ancestral connections between Wiru and Daribi peoples, although they are from different stock languages

---

[1] A patrol report states that the 'Taru are alleged to be pygmy-type natives living to the east of the Wiru but no-one seems to know very much about them' (Ialibu PR1/56–57).

and represent different patterns of migration into the southern edge of the
Highlands. Daribi ancestors were coastal people who were moving into the hinter-
lands, whereas it is possible that ancestral Wiru were pioneers at the frontier of a
migration out of the proto-Engan homeland in the Highlands several millennia ago
(Franklin and Franklin 1978: 72), at some stage settling the lower altitude regions
along the Erave river. It was here that contacts with Daribi were made, and it is
claimed that a group of Wiru clans once settled the west of Daribi territory, later
to be driven out, although one Daribi line claims descent from these Wiru (Wagner
1972: 12).

It is on the basis of similarities in beliefs about matrilateral exchange that
Andrew Strathern argues for a past connection between Wiru and Daribi of the
Karimui area in Simbu province (the latter are also known as *taru*). The distance
today between the closest Wiru and Daribi settlements is approximately twenty
kilometres, but it seems likely that several hundred years ago both societies were
living further south than their present habitations and in closer proximity.
Wagner makes several interesting statements about Daribi origins and migrations
to account for their present-day location, statements which in general terms
could be equally as applicable to Wiru. He suggests that the ' "centre of gravity"
of the Daribi population was at some time in the past in the valley of the Tua, to
the west of Mt Karimui' (1967: 5), and that stories and legends support their
origins on the Bore (Erave) river, into which the Tua flows, and Bumaru, a grass
plain alongside the Tua river. Some Daribi still live in this vicinity but the majority moved to the north-east, 'facilitated by the introduction of the sweet potato;
and . . . by the introduction of malaria into the low-lying lands along the river'
(Wagner 1967: 6).

The significance of this for Wiru is apparent in that 'the tribal environment of
the [Daribi] people seems . . . to have changed in the past few centuries; legends of
the time when they lived at Bumaru in the Tua Valley tell of continual warfare with
the Baria [Wiru]' (ibid.). If warfare was continual there must have been a population of ancestral Wiru living near the western edge of the Tua Valley which, in
response to the same factors precipitating the Daribi migration to the foothills of
Karimui, may have been moving to the north-west following the drainage pattern
of the Iaro and Polu river valleys.

The linguistic evidence needs to be considered before a history of migration
and settlement in Pangia is suggested. Wurm puts Wiru in the Eastern Central
Trans-New Guinea Phylum, and suggests that it is a family-level isolate of East
New Guinea Highlands Stock. He goes on to write that,

Wiru was originally classified tentatively as a sub-family level isolate in the West-Central
family, but to some extent, there have always been problems in attempts at classifying it. Its
lexical relationship to other East N. G. Highlands Stock language is comparatively low and
rather diffuse . . . However, much of its lexical resemblance with at least the languages of the
West-Central family may be due to borrowing, and . . . regular sound correspondences are
not greatly in evidence . . . [Wiru] shares some structural features . . . with languages

outside the stock such as those of the Tebera [Daribi] sub-phylum-level family. (Wurm 1975: 471–2)

Karl Franklin (pers.comm.) considers that Wiru is definitely a member of the West Central family, all members of which, except Wiru, show a lexicostatistical relationship of well over 40 per cent (Wurm 1975: 155). The percentage of cognates which Wiru shares with the West Central family varies from 35 per cent to 45 per cent; with the Central family from 20 per cent to 25 per cent; and with the Teberan family 15 per cent (Wurm 1975: 471). The original southwesterly migration into the Pangia-Erave area from the posited Enga homeland may have left behind an isolated population pocket which formed the basis for the emergence of Wiru as a family-level language isolate, with cultural features influenced by interaction with Daribi. Franklin (1975: 263) states that 'Wiru is clearly at a more extreme historical horizon than other members of proto-Engan', perhaps indicating the frontier status of the culture. According to Kerr (1975: 277), the nearest neighbours of Wiru in the West Central family are 'linguistically remote', although Wiru shares 'sufficient probable cognates [with them] . . . to justify the assumption that this reflects genetic relationship rather than convergence and borrowing.' He also writes that even if this genetic relationship can be proved, it would be a remote one (ibid.: 292).

The original Wiru pioneers, one may assume, followed the Erave river eastwards along the southern edge of the Poru plateau, and it seems likely that the plateau was gradually colonized from the south. It is possible that the limits of north-western expansion were only being reached in the last hundred years or so. At some stage in their occupation of the southern rim of the Poru plateau, ancestral Wiru came into contact with ancestral Daribi who were then living around the junction of the Erave and Tua rivers. Although Wiru and Daribi are from different stock languages, their 15 per cent of shared cognates suggests that some cultural interaction took place, regardless of any hostility. Andrew Strathern (1971a: 461) postulates that 'Wiru social structure is a transformation of the Daribi structure', although this tends to give to the Daribi a primordial and enduring polarity, it being equally likely that Wiru had as much influence over Daribi as the reverse. During periods of warfare the two enemies possibly experienced similar cultures and modes of production, and intermarried.

Possibly within the last 3–400 years, Wiru and Daribi started to move further north and away from each other to the west and east respectively, during which time Wiru came under the influence of Highlands groups and adopted pig-raising and sweet potato cultivation. That the Wiru were expanding their territory to the north and moving away from their easternmost settlements is supported by Hughes, who bases his claim on accounts of garden locations in Champion's 1936 patrol report, and on the strong possibility 'that the Wiru-Lower Kaugel contact was first made at about the time the Daribi moved north over the Tua, perhaps as recently as 100 years ago' (Hughes 1977: 179). He also records that Alia people at some stage in the past lived further to the south of their present location (ibid.:

177).[2] Additional support for Wiru living further east than they do today is the presence on Army Survey maps of large areas of abandoned gardens around the confluence of the Polu and Tua rivers. This movement to the north-west was perhaps a result of the realization that the future—in terms of trade and innovations—lay with the Highlands and not with the increasingly unhealthy Erave–Tua region.

As the Daribi and Wiru moved apart, their trading contacts became more attenuated and probably ceased altogether in the 1940s with the introduction of European goods in the central Highlands, and the changes this forced in traditional trade routes. The only remembered contacts that informants had with Daribi were with those of the Tive plateau, whom Wiru called Pumi, which is well to the north of Bumaru (Karimui Daribi were known to Wiru as Mikaru; see Map 1).[3] These Daribi traded stone axes to the more eastern Wiru settlements. Daribi refer to Wiru as Pobori, and one of Wagner's maps (1967: 13) refers to Pobori as a Daribi clan which is a member of the Noru phratry that originally lived at Bumaru. The Daribi use of the term 'Pobori' for Wiru could indicate a connection between Wiru and this Daribi group; possibly at some stage they were one and the same, intermarried, or allied, with fission or hostility eventually dividing them into separate groups. In effect, this is proposing that Wiru are the cultural and linguistic product of an interaction between two different cultures, Bumaru and Highlands, which finds some support in Wiru accounts of their origins. The likelihood of Bumaru origins is supported by the Wiru expression for returning to one's natal place, *ewa yori-ka pine okokoiya* ('sago-leaves-tree-base-shed'), referring to the way sago leaves collect at the base of the tree and do not blow away. Sago grows only in lower areas to the south and is not found in Pangia.

The Wiru land of the dead, Apera Takela, is indicated by two huge limestone escarpments occasionally visible from Pangia, marking the confluence of the Erave and Tua rivers far to the south-east where *akolali* once lived, and a boundary which has to be crossed before descending to a beach along a watercourse. These escarpments, known as Kegena Samanawe on the Karimui side, are important in Daribi myths of origin and relate to a marriage between a primal Daribi man and a Wiru woman (Wagner 1978: 120–1), indicating the importance of this area to both Wiru

---

[2] The 1978 nationwide village survey identified only 23 per cent of the Wiru population as living north of the Polu river, which roughly bisects the district, but this may reflect the poorer soils to the north. If a line is drawn through Takuru from north to south, also roughly bisecting the district, the population is evenly spread over the eastern and western halves, although the eastern half contains perhaps 2,000 Kewa speakers. This suggests that the bulk of the monolingual Wiru population is to the south and south-east of the Polu river, which supports claims made about the direction of Bumaru Wiru migrations.

[3] Hughes (1977: 177) provides some information which suggests that Wiru may have partly understood Daribi, unless this is a reference to a trade language. I am intrigued by one statement from the patrol reports: 'intrepid souls from Undiapu and Koia have irregular and rare contact with Wiru speakers on the western slopes of Mt Karimu' (Pangia PR4/70–71). One *tangenemo* tells of fighting between Wiru and Pumi over the Wiru theft of a stone axe. Wiru say that Pumi have withdrawn much further eastwards towards Mt Suaru (cf. Wagner 1967: 4).

and Daribi. Why is this region associated with the dead for Wiru if their ancestors
once lived in this direction, especially as authentic Wiru Taru are found only in
eastern communities? Partly it is because the land of the dead is usually downstream, but the situation is more complicated and reflected in the two opposed
stories of origin. In the central plateau area in which I worked there is a predomi-
nance of *tangenemo* in which ancestors came from the area to the north-west of
Pangia. Not one person with whom I discussed origins claimed that their ancestors
had always lived in Pangia; all identified an extra-district genesis. While Mbuna
origins are stressed for their contemporary relevance, the more ancient Bumaru
origins of Wiru are rarely mentioned, perhaps because these people became more
'Wiru' as they came more under the influence of the Highlands and, as suggested
above, came to identify more with the Highlands to the west and north as this
region became increasingly the direction of their principal interests. J. F. Weiner
(1988: 35) notes, for contemporary times, 'the increasing cultural hegemony of
Central Highlands societies over their southern fringe neighbors', which perhaps
masks the strong influence the latter had on Highlands cult practices and sorcery
beliefs. He does capture a certain dominance of the Highlands in fringe imagination, although perhaps 'hegemony' is not the word I would use, at least until
Europeans became identified with the Highlands.

There are many problems, however, with accepting informants' accounts of
what they regard as true movements in the past (cf. Hayano 1978). The emphasis
on north-west origins could comment on the proposed identification ancestral
Wiru made with Highlanders, and on the direction in which they were moving
(towards, not away from) in terms of trade and their view of the future. It could
also be a denial of Bumaru origins by inverting south-east for north-west, in order
to obscure the former for a closer identification with the Highlands. In many
instances, origin stories from different settlements refer to the same reason for
leaving the homeland, namely a disagreement over the distribution of cassowary
meat. The widespread sharing of elements of this story (which also occurs among
the Kewa people to the west) suggests the creation of culturally appropriate histories of migration and settlement. The two different origins of Wiru, one relatively
recent, one ancient, do tell us something. Ialibu patrol reports of the 1950s refer to
Kewa clans living in Pangia within living memory, and extensive intermarriage and
movement between Wiru and people living in the vicinity of Ialibu station.
Bumaru Wiru were moving to the north-west and intermarrying with people in
Ialibu district, but also meeting a barrier to further migration and settling back into
a relatively underpopulated Pangia. Mbuna stories point, perhaps, to intermarriage
with Highlanders in Ialibu and a movement back into Pangia and a more intensive
settlement of the district, accompanied by agricultural intensification with the
adoption of pig-raising for Highlands-influenced ceremonial and exchange occasions. This accounts for both the stress on Mbuna origins and the fact that Wiru
Taru are located to the east, well away from a Ialibu genesis. Significantly descent,
as an idiom of community, is emphasized only in respect of north-west ancestors,

providing a moral link with the Highlands (the stature of *akolali* may relate to a perception of Bumaru ancestors as different from latter-day, Highlands-influenced Wiru).

Several centuries ago Wiru were perhaps similar to so-called 'fringe Highlanders', characterized by an emphasis on swidden cultivation and hunting, and even today their culture shares similarities with that of the Daribi, as well as those of central Highlanders. In a way, Wiru were more 'successful' in their northern adaptation than were Daribi, the former having moved to a higher, healthier area and one where topography suited a more intensive cultivation of sweet potato. At the time of Wagner's fieldwork, the Wiru population was about three times greater than Daribi (16,000 compared with 5,000), although this may not accurately reflect a population expansion of the original Bumaru Wiru stock because of intermarriage with Highlanders, which never occurred with Daribi. Wiru adopted more labour-intensive gardening techniques from the Highlands, leading to a shift away from swidden agriculture towards a more intensive fallowing system of shifting cultivation.[4] Daribi claim not to have had domesticated pigs or polished stone axes until contact with Highlanders around 1900 (Wagner 1967: 6, 15). Wiru claim that sweet potato and the practice of mounding were introduced from the northwest, and the more open terrain of the Poru plateau and an earlier access to more efficient Highland stone axes for clearing may have led to an increasing concentration by Wiru on pig husbandry. The introduction of new agricultural techniques would have encouraged the domestication of pigs and a rise in pig populations (domesticated pigs would also have been introduced through the marriage payments of Highlanders in frontier areas where intermarriage occurred).

Wagner states that in their progress northwards Daribi were deluged with Highland cults and cultural practices (1967: 7). Bumaru Wiru also underwent much the same experience—implying to some degree a desire or willingness to accept 'outside' influence—and were probably more affected as their contacts with Highlanders were earlier and more direct, including marriage. The cults adopted were imports from the north-west and as such had the traditional Highlands emphasis on the mass killing and sacrifice of pigs. This provided a stimulus to pig production—although the emphasis in Wiru pig-killing was as much on ritual performances as on the politics of exchange—which transformed the agricultural scene and, as a consequence, affected aspects of social and political organization. In his comparison of Wiru and Daribi, Andrew Strathern (1971*a*: 461) writes that the

greater size and density of the Wiru population, their more extensive dependence on sweet potato agriculture and on pigs and pig-killing festivals, as well as their closer proximity to other large Highlands population, suggests that they have expanded faster than the Daribi

---

[4] Agronomists, with many years of work experience in the Highlands, invariably opined that Pangia appeared relatively 'new' in terms of gardening practices, suggesting that the Poru plateau has only recently been more intensively settled, perhaps in the last few hundred years.

possibly (but not necessarily) after the introduction of the sweet potato . . . With this expansion may have come a greater intensity of warfare and with this a greater fragmentation and dispersal of social groups.

I have suggested some reasons for this expansion, hence cultural divergence, in terms of different patterns of migration from a common area of interaction or origin, and of a more intensive contact of Bumaru Wiru with Highlanders which led to their transformation into 'Wiru'. Prior to 1900, Wiru did not develop largely independent, as did Daribi, of Highland genetic and cultural influence. It is likely that both Bumaru cultures (Wiru and Daribi) moved to higher elevations in the recent past but an explanation for their different expansion rates is not to be located solely in variant systems of production. The historical factors contributing to a more pronounced dependence on sweet potato need to be considered, as well as intermarriage with Highlanders, and the likelihood of Highlanders following affinal links to settle in Pangia.

Patterns of warfare, marriage, and exchange emerged in response to the ecological and cosmological changes which Bumaru Wiru experienced and these, too, affected the form and content of Wiru culture. This form could perhaps have owed more to the structural determinants of Bumaru Wiru culture, and its content to an appropriation of Highlands social, political and ritual practices: 'Many of the peculiarities of Karimui are explicable in terms of its situation on the edge of the Highlands; it is a region of overlapping influences from the Highlands and the low country to the south' (Wagner 1967: 11). The 'peculiarities' of Pangia may be traceable to the same influences, and the Wiru capacity and readiness for innovation under the colonial regime partly traced to their own changing 'histories' which are embodied in *tangenemo*, to which we now turn.

In the Beginning was the Cassowary

There is some difference amongst *tangenemo* in terms of content; many stories are a more or less straightforward recounting of movement and places, and of actions engaged in by people before their eventual settlement in one place, similar to the stories collected by Rosaldo (1980) for the Ilongot. Other *tangenemo* have a more fantastic dimension to them (I stress that this is my classification, and that Wiru do not make this distinction). The following is an example of the first kind of *tangenemo*, which recounts how people came to settle in the fieldwork site of Takuru (told by Koiya of Takuru).

We are Mbuna Koliri. We came here with our brothers, fathers and mothers after the father [of the first migrants] died at Mbuna. For the mourning ceremony they [his agnates and co-residents] killed a cassowary and cooked it. While it was cooking they roasted its insides in a fire and ate them, without giving any to the dead man's [immediate] family. Because of this his family [said to consist of his wife and two sons] left and walked around Mt Ialibu to Loroapa, then to Tindua and on to Korau village in Pangia, where they stayed the night. On this long journey they brought with them a tree which they planted in Korau. This tree was a *wiru* tree. The next morning they went to Poloko where they decorated themselves and danced to help one of their grandfathers recover from *kauwa* sickness. At that time in Koiyapu [a settlement close to Poloko] there was some sugar cane growing in an old garden and one brother was sent to fetch it while the older people waited. When it was becoming dark and the brother had not returned, a Koliri man told some boys who were playing nearby that they were going on and to tell the brother to follow them later. The brother came to where Koliri had waited but it was dark and the group Yumbiri took them to Koiyapu. The group Koliri living in Koiyapu today is called Kima Koliri [Kimari] because the brother started a new group as sugar cane suckers [*kima*] grow out from the main stem. The rest of Koliri continued travelling with their mother, who was the bravest and led them. When they reached Lomoi the groups Poriri and Tuando asked them why they were coming into their district, they replied that they left their Mbuna people because they were not given any cassowary meat. Poriri said they were looking for men to join them, so Koliri could settle with them in Lomoi, and showed them a house to live in. While at Lomoi they heard about a 'singsing' to be held at Melike by the Kaimari, so the men of Lomoi decorated themselves and practised dancing. Only one Koliri man [the other brother] participated but he was such a good dancer that Poriri chose him as their leader in the 'singsing'. When this man led the others in dancing around the ceremonial ground at Melike a girl called Komikiame was attracted to him. She ran away with him and they married. Komikiame gave birth to a son Bai, a second son Kawali Kango, and a third son Wanu. The last born was Toe. There were now many people at Lomoi and too much faeces accumulating around the houses, so Koliri left to find their own settlement, which they did at Pokoropini and Talowai Yapu. They moved to Takuru after buying the land from Piendi group of Wambi for two valuable pearl shells. Later other groups came to live in Takuru with the four *tapinango* ['place-base-men'] groups [Baipo, Kawali, Wanuwane, Toe].

So far as I could determine, the claims of residence by Takuru people in the settlements named in the narrative of migrations in Pangia are accurate. What is startling is the number of places where people lived before Takuru was established, suggesting that Takuru Wiru wanted their own ground and independence from other co-residents with primary land claims, and/or that endemic warfare forced a continual fission of co-residential groups and movement throughout Pangia. The four sons of Komikiame are the eponymous founders of the *tapinango yarene*, or land-owning groups, of Takuru, together known as Koliri (which is a group found in many other settlements in Pangia). The interesting features of the narrative, apart from its 'one thing after another' structure, are that Koliri as an entity existed before the migration and its fourfold division into subgroups, and was associated with an area, Mbuna, where no Wiru now live; Koliri left Mbuna after a quarrel over cassowary meat; they brought with them a *wiru* tree, the hoop pine; and a 'mother' led the group, which seems to tie in to the fact that the Wiru mother of the four sons is named, but not the Mbuna son who fathered them.

Basically, I would analyse the story as a commentary on Wiru–Highlander interaction, perhaps commenting on marriage and warfare; there is a marriage of a woman to a Mbuna man, his death and the cassowary dispute, a denial of exchange, possibly reflecting the latent hostilities between Wiru and Highlanders at the frontier (the cassowary is a symbol of aggression, dominance and warrior-hood). She enters into Pangia (it is women who move in marriage) with her sons and the icon of their ancestral identity and power, the *wiru* tree, which is replanted in Pangia, and one of the sons marries a Wiru woman and fathers four sons who came to settle in Takuru.[5]

In this scenario, the bold statement 'We are Mbuna Koliri' indicates that ances-try is claimed from a Highlands man, whereas in the narrative the emphasis shifts to women—the mother who leads, Komikiame who carries the four sons—once Koliri are in Pangia. The story starts with Mbuna and the unnamed father, progresses to unnamed male siblings who found groups, and ends in Pangia with the named mother and her four named sons. Connections to the Highlands are conceived of as 'male', whereas it is woman, particularly as 'mother', that figures importantly when the narrative shifts to Pangia: Takuru Koliri refer to themselves as the sons of an autochthonous woman, Komikiame. This importance is a reflec-tion of the importance of matrilateral exchange in Pangia, captured in procreation beliefs which stress the total physical creation of the foetus by the mother (see Clark 1985). What also seems indicated by the story is that in a sense the 'male' Highlands gave mothers rather then daughters in marriage to Wiru, reversing the structurally superior position of wife-givers. Resonances of this claim, and of the connection between marriage, death/conflict, and exchange, appear in a *tangenemo* considered below (cf. LeRoy 1985: 150).

The cassowary is an animal of immense symbolic significance in the Highlands (Bulmer 1967; Gardner 1984; Healey 1985*a*), admired by Wiru for its aggression and 'strong thoughts'. A renowned warrior is known as *ali kembi*, cassowary man. I take the cassowary as a symbol of the Highlands for Wiru, a claim I will return to below. The dispute is not over the meat of the cassowary but over the bird's insides, particularly its stomach. For pigs, at least, the insides are reserved for women, and Wiru women were prohibited from eating the flesh of the cassowary because of its strong identification with men (if women did eat cassowary, their skin—a symbol of maleness in Pangia—would peel away). The body under the skin is pre-eminently female, and the stomach stands for this in a more diacritic fashion. For the cassowary, the stomach is a place of regeneration, where seeds are processed such that new life emerges out of its faeces/death (Healey 1985a). The cassowary is a beast of cosmological import; the term for stomach, *imu*, is probably derived from *mu*, the word for testicle, cult stone, and egg, conflating 'both unitariness and open-endedness in an ongoing cycle of life and death' (Kerr 1987: 114); Mbuna, as

---

[5] Daribi also know the hoop pine as *wiru*, and one of their myths refers to its planting, to mark a new residence, by a man who became a bush-spirit after fleeing from a violent argument about the distribution of food (Wagner 1972: 116). These bush-spirits, *sezemabidi*, lived in the mountains and comprised tall and short races who fought; the tall ones were vanquished and fled to Mt Suaru (ibid.: 115). It is possible that Wiru accounts of *akolali* are a mythical trace of these tall bush-spirits, and the myth itself resonates closely with the Takuru *tangenemo*.

a lake, is also *mu*.[6] One of my informants described the stomach as 'very precious and sweet tasting', and related these claims to its coloration, consisting of red, blue, and black markings (which are the external colours of the bird, particularly around the neck, the point of ingestion). The insides of the cassowary are known as *kange tepe*, and *kange* is the name for the most prestigious and competitive, if voluntary, mortuary exchanges in Pangia. Men paint their bodies black and wear a conical black hat in *kange* gifting of pearl shells to the mother's people, the hat being modelled on the cassowary's helmet, *waire yaparoi*. The Mbuna story of death, failure to exchange, a mother leaving with her sons to Pangia, while appearing to be a more or less straightforward narrative of migration and settlement, has themes which sublimely capture the cultural emphases of Wiru.

The cassowary is emblematic of the tension between affinity and warfare, femaleness and maleness, inside and outside. Claims to true knowledge and ability are contested by the query, 'Do you know how to cook cassowary?' Wiru came to depend upon, and were married to, the Highlands, the 'outside' source of wealth and cults, and in my argument the cassowary and the failure to gift its 'female' insides represents the Highlands as a locus of creation and indebtedness, identifying the region with regeneration out of death/digestion and defecation. Paradoxically the 'male' Highlands is also a 'mother', although Wiru debt is always to a mother's brother, *opianango*, men who bear. Other stories confirm this analysis, and I now present a *tangenemo* of the second kind, which again links death, the Highlands, and creation (told by Philip Kawai of Mele).

Before, at Ialibu, there lived one woman and her young daughter, with an old woman. They left this area because there were too many men and travelled through the bush to Pangia; they came to Takuru and left behind the old woman. The mother and daughter went on to Pokale, and from this hill they looked at all the bush surrounding them and saw no men at all. They walked down from the hill through the bush, just as it was getting dark. They came across a big *walea* tree, which had been blown down by the wind, and underneath the base of this tree was a sheltered place where they could sleep. They realized that there was no fire to warm themselves so the mother got up and said, 'Let's cut this vine and pull it from side to side across a piece of wood to start a fire'. Smoke appeared and they made a fire at this place. Next morning when it was light they climbed the hill again and looked at the surrounding bush; in the afternoon they went back down, the mother going first, the daughter following. A marsupial, *kioli*, 'held' the daughter's breast while they were walking back. She told her mother who replied, 'Let's go, we don't know what this means.' They returned to the place where they slept, and next morning they arose and decided to make a small garden nearby; they had no tools, only fire to burn the base of the trees. They went to find some sweet potato runners to plant and returned to Takuru, where the old woman gave them some runners, as well as banana shoots and other things to grow. They returned to Pokale and planted them there. When the garden was producing food it was found that the

---

[6] Harland Kerr, a linguist specialist in Wiru, suggests (pers.comm.) that Mbuna means 'a long, long time', or 'everything', and posits a connection between this concept and *mu*, as a cycle of continuity, that generates a notion of infinity. This certainly fits with the Wiru interpretation of the Highlands as a *locus classicus* of the past and future, and relates to the perception of the longevity of Highlanders.

daughter was pregnant, and later she had a son, who was named Kioli. Kioli then married his mother, and she had another son called Walea. After this, she had three more sons who, with their father, went to live at Apenda; Walea remained at Pokale [where he started the group Pokale Leri]. The first son of Kioli was Angopiri, second was Epa, and third was Alamari. At a time when it was sunny and it had not rained for a while, Kioli and Angopiri were at their house in Apenda, and the other sons went to the creek Poio where they built a dam to catch fish. The creek was like a snake and they dammed it from one side to the other. Angopiri arrived and saw them doing this and became angry and asked them what they were doing. He said, 'You didn't ask me my opinion on how to do this and you've made it wrong.' This started a big fight and much blood was shed. The last two sons decided to leave Apenda to the first son; Epa decided to go to Pomba and marked the river Ipe as his boundary; Alamari decided to go to Mele and marked the creek Lua and went to the bush towards Mt Ialibu. [The story goes on to tell of making fires whose smoke attracted other people from the rainforested slopes of Mt Ialibu, who were fleeing from a disagreement over cassowary, and who wanted to learn how to make houses, eventually founding other settlements in Pangia.]

There are many interesting elements in this story and I will only address those with relevance to the aims of this chapter. Again, it is women from the Highlands who enter the bush of Pangia; one brings fire, another has sons who found groups and settlements, and the old woman supplies sweet potato runners. Unlike the previous *tangenemo*, there are parts of the story that are closer to some definitions of myth; there is the marsupial which makes the daughter pregnant (for a similar Daribi story, see Wagner 1978: 109), and the incestuous relationship between mother and son which leads to other sons who go on to found groups (the first fight is traced to a disagreement between siblings over knowledge, leading to fission and migration). The *kioli* possum is perhaps a transformation of the son from Mbuna who fathers the four groups in the first story, but in this case it is an autochthonous animal. A possum (of the folk genus *tuu*, of which *kioli* is a type) appears in the *tangenemo* of many other groups, scratching the breasts or thighs of a primal woman, or being eaten by her, to make her pregnant, and it is obviously a phallic symbol (demonstrated in the use of marsupial tails and scrota in men's decoration and headwear). The sites of original settlement in Pangia are known as *tuumu*, possum testicles, suggesting a connection between an autochthonous possum/phallus/maleness and the Mbuna cassowary/stomach/femaleness. Regeneration is still associated with the woman who comes from the 'outside', which may appear to contradict the message of the first *tangenemo* until it is remembered that it is a woman from Mbuna who brings the sons that create local groups.

Kioli is also the name for compulsory death-exchange payments made to matrilateral kin, so that the connection between sexuality and death, between the gift of life and compensation through exchange, is once more stressed. *Kange*, similar to *moka*-type competitive exchanges of the Highlands (cf. A. J. Strathern 1978), is associated with the 'outside' of Mbuna, while *kioli* is an 'inside' indigenous practice (the categories of 'inside' and 'outside' are emic and used by Wiru when these sorts of distinctions are made). The *tepe* region of a woman's body is where life is formed, and the second story could be interpreted as a male attempt to contain femaleness, to appropriate the regenerative power of the Highlands that is assimilated to the *kange tepe* of the cassowary. The women take refuge in a *malea* tree and, as Wagner (1978: 119) states, trees 'both shelter (contain) people and model their generative abundance'. There are reversals in motifs between the two *tangenemo*, particularly around the themes of life and death, which merit further consideration (and recall the Daribi and Wiru identification of Apera Takela as origin place and land of the dead respectively; paralleling the Bumaru/Mbuna origins is a more ancient Wiru story which locates the emergence of human life from the egg of an autochthonous spider; see Clark 1991).

These reversals are captured and displayed through another reference to Daribi: 'Water, like the sun, moves inexorably from east to west, coming eventually to rest in a large lake; streams are the "roads" along which souls of the dead travel to their final abode within the lake. Consequently . . . lakes . . . acquire an ominous significance: to dream of a lake is an omen of death' (Wagner 1978: 98).

Water, for Wiru, moves from the west to east, towards the land of the dead and away from a lake, Mbuna, which is associated with a death but more importantly with a 'primal' woman who travels to Pangia and creates life—Wiru people and groups. The relationship between Wiru, death, and the Highlands requires elaboration through a final look at Wiru and, this time, Kewa stories. In Pangia, I could only obtain partial and cryptic references to the origin of death. These references were said not to be *tangenemo* because no one had the complete story, but it was known that death originated at Polukepo hill, close to Mbuna lake, for which Wiru were believed to hold some responsibility. It was the time of the first people, and they climbed Polukepo, which was described as being like a 'stage', to hear an announcement. One man said '*pipere yangure*', which meant that people would be immortal, but another man said '*komai telai*', which meant that people were going to die, after which this man left for Pangia. Wiru have a notion that their ancestors in some way committed an (ab)original sin, after which they travelled to Pangia, condemned to die while people at Ialibu (the Highlands) would live a very long time, perhaps forever. These words are not Wiru, except for *pipi*, a tree known for losing its smooth bark and growing another. *Pipi* is also a Kewa term for this same tree, and it is to this language and culture that we must look for a more complete version of the story about an argument between two of the first men, recorded by LeRoy (1985: 181, the interpolations in the text are his).

The word at that time was '*pipi-e yakura-e*! It is the *pipi* tree, it is the *yakura*!' (These men were like the *pipi* trees, which shed their bark, and like the *yakura*, the caddis flies that shed their skins. Eternal renewal was possible in those early times.) This was before a Palea (Wiru) man arrived on the scene. This one came and asked the others, 'What did you say?' Someone replied, 'We said *pipi-e yakura-e*!' Then the Palea man responded, 'No! You must not say that. Say *komanu-e ralanu-e*! It is them all dying, it is them all growing up!' (And thenceforth that was the word: *koma*, 'dying', and *rala*, 'growing up', for all. In other words there would be death and then the birth of a new generation.) If the second man had said the same as the first one, we would not die but just stay on forever (shedding our old, wrinkled skin and becoming youthful in appearance), like the *pipi* and *yakura* do. But because the second man refused the first's words . . . now we die and others grow up in our place. After that, men divided and spread to different places.

As LeRoy (1985: 182) comments, the story is about 'substituting the renewal of skins for that of generations', a common enough theme in Melanesia. What is interesting for our purposes is the role of the Wiru man in bringing death into the world, and that Wiru seem to have adopted this Kewa story as an explanation for their own origins. The cryptic Pangia version has Wiru-ized the key Kewa words, which I thought at first belonged to an archaic language, but does not identify the second man as Wiru; rather he introduces death and then leaves for Pangia and becomes Wiru, as if in punishment. Another Wiru interpretative twist is that the ability of the *pipi* tree to shed its bark and expose a new, smooth 'skin' underneath (cf. LeRoy 1985: 182) is described as *toe takako*, comparing its loss to the dry skin flaking off the foreskin of the penis, particularly of babies. Trees, like the possums which inhabit them, have phallic connotations, but *toe* more properly refers to fire, the 'spirit' smoke from men's house fires causing growth. From this, *toe* is associated with ripeness and the attainment of full growth, such that *toe* can be used to describe men who hold back their prized bananas and sugar cane, instead giving only scrapings or peelings. The *pipi* tree, also described as *pipi toe*, is a complex symbol. It relates to new growth and babies, the start of another generation, as well as to the phallus and skin changing, ripeness, and failure to exchange.

The obvious missing referent is the snake, but again Wagner's account (1986: 62) of mortality in reference to Soux, the Daribi culture-hero, and his snake-like giant penis, suggests a connection:

The revelation of the snake as a penis . . . provides a retroactive motivation for [the] substitution [of] human beings as immortal beings, for it shows the penis as the snakelike implement of a continually enacted rejuvenation, shedding its (fore)skin in the erectile act by which the flow of vital fluid is passed from man to woman.

The connection between the phallus, immortality, and skin-changing captured in the bark/foreskin-shedding *pipi* tree suggests or obviates its snake-like attributes. This connection helps to explain the puzzling absence of sexuality leading to the loss of immortality that is common to Melanesian myths of this type (cf. Brumbaugh 1987: 31–2). Sexuality remains implicit in Wiru accounts of the origins of death, although its importance in the origin of life is demonstrated in the second *tangenemo*.

Northern Kewa stories introduce Yakili, a creator being, into accounts of the origins of death (Apea 1985: 219–23). Yakili, half man and half vegetation, reflecting his creation of people and the world, calls four primal men to hear his speech promising immortality, but one man from the east is late arriving, and when he asks Yakili what he said the deity replied 'death, increase', disappearing into the sky. Pangia, which is to the east, the direction of the Kewa land of the dead, seems to be implicated again in the introduction of death. Daribi have a similar myth to the Mbuna story, in which there is a failure to distribute pig viscera after a pig-feast at Bumaru, leading a mother to leave with her two sons, one of whom was Soux, who later cursed humankind with death after an episode of sexual shaming (Wagner 1972: 28–30). There are many interesting inversions taking place in these Wiru and Daribi stories of origin. The site of Mbuna, a lake, is assumed by the grassy plain of Bumaru, and instead of Soux there is Yakili, who introduces death into the world, not because of sexual shaming but because he was questioned about his pronouncements by a late-coming man. Wagner suggests that the mother's shaming through not receiving meat is later replicated in the myth by her son's sexual shaming, and it is possible that Yakili is shamed by a man interrupting his speech at Polukepo hill. Soux leaves for the Highlands, whereas Wiru come from the Highlands after Yakili sends them into Pangia.

The Wiru story refers to climbing Polukepo to hear a speech, and it is possible, although none of my informants mentioned it, that Yakili was involved. This sky being, associated with *akolali*, is nowadays assimilated to the Holy Spirit and punishes people for sin—so the connection of a deity to the origin of death, and later to Christianity, is certainly possible. The *tangenemo* discussed seem to build on these themes of death, regeneration, and migration, and indicate the complex, dynamic, and historical nature of the relationship of Wiru to the Highlands and Bumaru, foreshadowing the nature of a future relationship to Europeans and the landscape of colonialism. As Wagner (1972: 12) says of the Daribi, 'their history presents a kaleidoscopic array of blurred boundaries and transformed identities.' A new cosmology of power and knowledge begins to emerge as Europeans enter the Highlands in search of gold and souls, mystified in the name of exploration and progress. While boundaries and identities once more transformed and blurred under colonialism, is it possible that Europeans became the modern equivalent of the maleness, autonomy, regenerative power, and externality represented in the cassowary?

Colonialism as Ripping Yarn

In the early 1900s a pearling schooner, the *Southern Cross* out of Sydney, was shipwrecked in the Gulf of Papua at the mouth of the Kikori, and its intrepid party of three Europeans and an assortment of Malay and Papuan seamen saw no choice but to head inland away from the swamps rather than journey along the dangerous coast eastwards in their attempt to return to Kerema mission station. Their remarkable expedition took them northwards into the Southern Highlands, across the Papuan border into New Guinea, where they eventually turned around and headed south to follow the Purari river system back out to the eastern side of the gulf, emerging on the coast at the mouth of the Vailala river, from where they managed to make their return trip to Kerema. Their journey, recorded in Captain Henry Brewster's *Pearls of Papua*, published in 1934, brought them into contact with the strange and wondrous inhabitants of mountain Papua, including Kewa and Wiru, and preceded by decades the various expeditions of discovery into the Southern Highlands led by Leahy, Hides, and Champion. Histories of exploration into interior New Guinea are strangely silent about this momentous journey for the very good reason that, although presented as true, it never took place.[7]

LeRoy (1985) claims that the telling of Kewa tales creates a fabricated world out of dialectic between the experienced and the possible, most clearly exposed in the interaction between people and ghosts. The world in which Kewa live, garden, and reproduce is real but, in part, fictional; it is the praxis of their own ethnography (cf. Geertz 1973: 15). Colonialism also tells tales and, in so doing, creates a similarly fabricated world, an imagined landscape peopled by savages and Europeans: 'Colonial cultures are not simply ideologies that mask, mystify or rationalize forms of oppression that are external to them; they are also expressive and constitutive of colonial relationships in themselves (Thomas 1994: 2). 'Colonialism's culture', as Thomas phrases it, is created out of the tension between the imagined and the real, between notions of treacherous, cannibalistic savages and the actual savages themselves (cf. Taussig 1984). For this reason, I see no difficulty in taking as one of my texts on colonialism an account of a journey which never took place, in the genre of romantic fables concerned with the distant and exotic terrain of the wild man. Indeed, treating colonialism as narrative through this fictional account captures more precisely and with less distortion the tension referred to above. Jack Hides, in his *Papuan Wonderland*, the public account of his historic 1935 Strickland-Purari patrol, fabricates the primitive in a manner not too dissimilar to Brewster, Commander R. D. and R. N. R. (cf. Schieffelin and Crittenden 1991). The lineaments of power and knowledge are not absent in these colonial constructions, and it matters little that I take a fictional rather than a 'true' account for my own exploration of the way in which so-called savages become subject to, and sometimes desirous of, European control. A new geography, namely the colonial state, is created out of this process of subjectification.

The endpapers of Brewster's book contain a map, reproduced here as Map 2, which, as in any patrol report or narrative of discovery, authenticates the expedition (the author may have borrowed from the administration reports of Ryan's and Staniforth Smith's 1913 and 1911 patrols respectively, and probably read Hurley's similarly titled 1924 photographic journal *Pearls and Savages* (Schieffelin and Crittenden 1991: 33–40)). *Pearls of Papua* is not just a deceit, it is an example of colonialism as travelogue, of journeys which inscribe the other as a particular kind of subject (cf. Thomas 1994). The book may have been written to appeal to the young and credulous, ignorant of Papua and its inhabitants, and in this sense it may be rather 'obvious' as an exemplar for the colonial project, but it reveals the skeleton of

---

[7] Brewster's story fits into a tradition of fictional accounts of interior New Guinea, often written for polemical purposes (see Krauth (ed.) 1982), and dating back to the 1870s. Not mentioned in the chapter is a strong anti-Japanese sentiment in the book—a different but not savage 'other'.

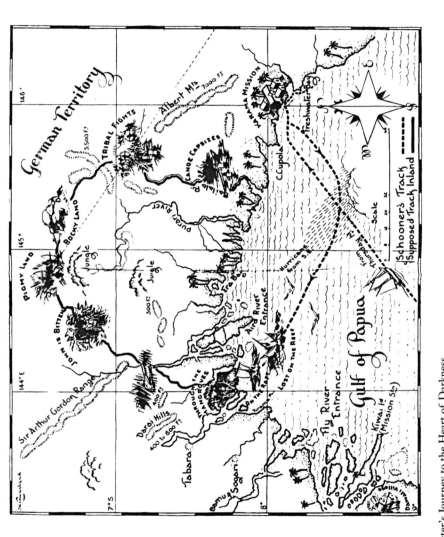

MAP 2. Brewster's Journey to the Heart of Darkness

colonialism's culture which later chapters will flesh out. The tone of the book is captured in the following quote, describing a cruise by an Australian government launch in the Gulf of Papua.

one of her boats, while skirting the coastline, saw several large white heaps near the beach. At first sight they appeared to be human skulls, so the officer in charge decided to go close in to investigate. Probably thought to himself, 'Here's a chance . . . [to teach] the bloodthirsty savage a lesson!' Visions of himself as a gory hero, and so on. Instead, imagine his astonishment—and disappointment—at finding, not skulls, but heaps of freshly opened pearl shell. (Brewster 1934: 31)

This is all the encouragement the crew need to go off in search of new pearling beds after meeting with little success in the Torres Strait. This is a story of the romance of the savage driven by the quest for pearls, displaying the connection between exotic wealth and the primitive, skulls and pearls. As we will see later a similar quest, this time for gold, opened up the Highlands to Europeans.

Anthropology also discovers things in the Highlands including, as Wagner (1967: xiii) remarks about 'the last unknown', African lineage systems (and one may add big men). What is intriguing is that many of the shells from the Torres Strait pearling industry were traded up into the Highlands, expanding the pearl-shell 'economy', so that when Europeans arrived in search of gold, they quickly realized that they would have to trade in pearlshell for food, labour, and the sexual services of women. Pearl shells, although embedded within a thoroughly indigenous symbolic logic, were in a sense forerunners of the colonial presence. In one of those arresting coincidences of history, Jack Hides, on the first administrative patrol into the Southern Highlands, failed to take shell, the local desire for which was partially generated by colonialism. Hides had many difficulties and misunderstandings, some fatal, because he could not engage Highlanders in exchange (Clark 1991; Schieffelin and Crittenden 1991).

Captain Brewster, from the deck of the *Southern Cross*, an aptly named icon of colonialism, contemplates the landscape before him:

I gazed fascinated at its great mountains, and wondered what strange inhabitants and barbarous mysteries lay locked away in their unexplored fastnesses . . . we were destined to make a much closer acquaintance of this land of mystery, and some, at least, of its secrets would be revealed to us. (1934: 66)

The combination of the mysterious exotic and destiny are the twin aspects driving colonial desire, although declarations of responsibility have to be made, such as 'It will never do for us to show the white feather to a canoeload of naked savages' (Brewster 1934: 95). Shipwrecked after a hurricane at sea, the crew make it to shore:

Miles of unexplored country, a maze of narrow water channels through mangrove swamps with but little footing anywhere, and a few scattered villages inhabited by natives far from trustworthy and reputed to be cannibals, just about summed up this part of the coast of New Guinea.

Also, if our surmise was correct, it would be somewhere in this vicinity that Bishop Chalmers, the Rev Mr Tomkins and ten mission students had been murdered and eaten quite lately! (Brewster 1934: 138)

It seems a deliberate plot device that the shipwrecked crew come ashore at the most barbarous part of the coast, although the punitive raids of the administration, exacted on the local populations after the massacre of the Chalmers party would certainly have discouraged people from harming the crew. A friendly village is encountered after winning over its chief and sorcerer by their talking parrot, another familiar device in this genre, ranking with predictions of the eclipse of the sun. It is worth quoting at length the description of their arrival, as it is a derivative and cliché-ridden classic of its kind, presenting one dimension of 'colonialism's culture' as travelogue:

they were a light coffee color, bodies well proportioned, features good but also disfigured by paint, and nose and ear ornaments, lips and chin streaked and stained with betel-juice. Their hair—artificially bleached with lime, we learnt later—stood up from their heads in huge frizzled mops. In stature, they were short, compared to a European . . . As we came in sight they commenced to stamp the ground in unison, to the accompaniment of a slow beating of tom-toms and a high monotonous chant by the women. Two men stepped forth to meet us. One, evidently the Chief of the tribe, tall, stately and grey-bearded, strode forward with graceful swinging strides. The other, whom we took to be the village sorcerer—a short, wizened old man carrying a palm branch in his hand—danced beside him with mincing steps. His hair, decked with long feathers of brilliant hues, was bound with a girdle of green leaves, and a belt of bones, which rattled as he danced. Eyes, nose and mouth were streaked and smeared with lime, and every bone of his ribs was outlined with it . . . a fearsome object! (Brewster 1934: 167)

The racial and evolutionary stereotypes in this extract are legion, complete with the beating of native drums. 'Compared to a European', the common natives are disfigured and short. This comparison is expressed at another familiar political level; the Chief is tall, stately and graceful, the nearest thing to a European, while the sorcerer (relegated to a lower case 's'), the epitome of the superstitious savage, is short, wizened and effeminate, and frightening in his strangeness. The crew pass the sorcerer's test, mainly through his chicanery because he wants to learn the secrets of the talking parrot, at which 'The villagers, thus far silent and watchful, now gave free rein to their pent-up emotions. They shouted and stamped, twirled round and round and jumped into the air; women and children broke into a shrill chant, tom-toms thudded and banged' (Brewster 1934: 168).

The depiction of the savage as a creature of the emotions, as childlike, emerges clearly, and the cavortings of the villagers clearly resemble the supposedly irrational actions of the 'head-he-go-round' people of the Vailala Madness, described by Williams in 1923 (Williams 1976). Later, the crew are fully accepted into the tribe, introducing them to such European delights as musical chairs and, in a Papuan predecessor to *A Man Called Horse* and *Dances With Wolves*, even become fully initiated! The time comes, however, when they have to leave their gracious hosts, who utter cries of grief at their departure, to return to civilization.[8] They head north into the mountainous and unknown interior, and have to continue northwards because of the nature of the terrain to the east and the jungle that they encounter. The description of their thwarted attempts to go south through the 'jungle', certainly a botanical fiction, is pure Conrad with a dash of Bosch. The party manages to lose all its food and few pieces of equipment in half an hour(!).

Horror was on our faces, nausea filled us. It was pure primeval jungle, trackless, dismal, dripping-wet, the air hot, stifling and loathsome, not a ray of sunlight piercing the gloom. My hair was on end, I had the nightmare feeling of pursuit by a nameless evil. Countless winged insects and creeping monstrosities swarmed, leeches dropped from moss-covered trees, huge bat-like creatures flopped against my face, snakes of every description lay on the mud or twined around roots and branches. (Brewster 1934: 186–7)

After leaving the friendly natives behind, passing through the necessary colonial fiction of the evil jungle, we are prepared for meeting the distinctly unfriendly savage. This time it is a tribe of pygmies, who attack the crew with poisoned arrows; when one of the Europeans is hit by an arrow and fails to die, instead joining the fray with renewed gusto out of revenge, they flee in terror, later returning unarmed.

As we waited for a move on their part, we scrutinized the pigmies [*sic*] with interest. In height not above four feet, their hair hung in a long matted mass below their shoulders; features flat and repulsive, with bone or ivory rings through nose and ears, a few even with rings through their lips. Well-proportioned and muscular, they moved with a stealthy gliding motion. In colour they were almost jet black. (Brewster 1934: 205)

The more remote and unknown the natives are, the further from civilization, the blacker, shorter, uglier, and more violent they become. According to the map of the journey, the party was in the vicinity of Pangia at this time, and Wiru are certainly neither pygmies nor cave-dwellers (as the pygmies prove to be). As remarked above, the fictional nature of Brewster's account tells us as much about colonialism and its construction of the 'other', and the landscape he inhabits, as a 'true' one. During the attack the pygmies killed the loyal Papuan servant 'boy', the Europeans proving invulnerable to poison through either luck or stronger constitutions. A request for food is made, although there is a nagging worry that their new hosts may be cannibals, somewhat offset by a belief in European superiority: 'Well, it'd be rather a disappointing shock, to say the least of it, if they brought us something suspiciously like human flesh to eat, under the impression that gods preferred it! We'd have to inform them, politely but firmly, that white gods preferred the flesh of animals and birds' (Brewster 1934: 212). The pygmies take them to their settlement of caves in a huge outcrop of basalt boulders, the women

---

[8] The depiction of natives as friendly or treacherous compares strikingly with Hides's two experiences of the savage, often met within the short trip from one settlement to the next, which puzzled him in the extreme (Schieffelin and Crittenden 1991: 244).

living almost permanently for protection in the upper rows of caves—'climbing like monkeys from cave to cave by means of ropes' (ibid.: 230)—and the sight of so much primitivity moves the Captain to exclaim:

We could scarcely credit our eyes. Here before us stood and lived primeval Man, armed with primitive weapons, his home a hole in the rock, his speech but a succession of monosyllabic grunts. Here, in this natural fortress, in the foothills of unexplored mountains, surrounded by tribes of hostile natives, cut off from civilization by virtually impassable jungle and a network of rivers and creeks, he was making a last bid for existence. (Brewster 1934: 222)

The evolutionary biases hardly need to be pointed out, and the construction of the cave-dwelling pygmies, beyond and above the horrible barrier of the jungle, as survivors of a more backward and primitive race of humans emerges clearly. The party, having acquired divinity because of their descent from the sky (actually a common enough interpretation of Europeans in the Highlands), are asked to remain behind and guard the women and children while the pygmies depart—'a wild disorganised mob of excited savages' (Brewster 1934: 226)—to kill off another hill tribe who had raided them the day before. During the absence of the pygmies the remaining people are attacked by another savage tribe, but by the clever ruse of dressing up as a monster, the Europeans manage to confuse and intimidate their enemy, who flee in terror. The pygmies are late in returning because they discover, after successfully wiping out their foes, the latter's stock of liquor(!), delaying the return trip until sober once more. The crew decide to leave soon after because of the stench of their hosts but, as usual, the latter do not want them to leave, and one more ruse is called for to trick the superstitious pygmies. One of the Malay crew is a ventriloquist, and he imitates a voice from above telling the crew to return to the sky. The pygmies are, of course, dumbfounded, and the crew reduced to silent laughter at their discomfiture, 'They wanted badly to run away and hide in the caves, but amazement and curiosity rooted them to the spot' (ibid.: 245). The crew depart from 'the mysterious heart of New Guinea' (ibid.: 247), and leave the sun-worshipping pygmies behind to find a pass through the cloud mountains. From a vantage point they are able to spy the sea and a number of large rivers winding their way down to the coast. They decide to follow one of the rivers back to the sea, avoiding native villages whose smoke they had observed from the mountains.

During the journey back the crew encounters a raiding party of headhunters about to attack a village and decide to thwart their intentions: 'The quarrel was none of ours, but each felt that it would be more than flesh and blood could endure to sit back calmly and listen to an attack on a peaceful village by such a horde of bloodthirsty-looking savages' (Brewster 1934: 277). Such is the white man's burden! As usual, the crew rely on the shock value of their size and whiteness to terrify and disperse the raiders, who have already entered the village.

Here and there among the prostrate bodies moved big powerful savages, yelling, capering, and covered with blood. They were engaged in removing the heads of their victims, dead and wounded alike! The terrible shrieks of the wounded at the approach of the awful doom made our blood boil. We saw red . . . We hit, punched and kicked, tripped them up and pushed them over, caught friend and foe by the scruff of the neck and flung them to the ground. We drove a lane clean through the mass, turned, and fought a passage back, leaving a medley of amazed savages sprawling in the dust. They fell like ninepins before us . . . savage as the very savages themselves, the light of battle in our eyes.

The shouts and yells died away, ceased, a stupefied silence reigned. They stared at us, transfixed with fear and shock. Then, with one long-drawn scream of extreme terror, both sides dropped their weapons, flung their arms above their heads, and fled pell-mell out of the village. (Brewster 1934: 285–7)

The raiders meet a gruesome end, clubbed to death by the villagers or forced into a crocodile-infested lagoon next to the village, reptiles that the villagers kept docile through sacrifice. The crew find canoes and depart for the coast, away from 'a country of mystery and barbarism' (Brewster 1934: 299).

Apart from an encounter with tree-climbing alligators, they make it safely to the coast by foraging off the countryside, at which point their canoe capsizes and they have to hide from coastal villagers. After a few days of starvation, they plan to hijack the next passing canoe, but to their surprise it is paddled not by bloodthirsty savages, but by clothed natives. 'We jumped to our feet. Was that a man in a white, white suit under a white topee, sitting amidships? Or was it our imagination, the effect of starvation? There *was* a white man in it!' (Brewster 1934: 320). A mission boat has arrived, come to check out rumours of half-naked Europeans, and with it comes the presence of the redemptive colour of whiteness. The narrative of the journey records a transition from coffee brown to utmost black to pure white, from nakedness to clothes. Complete 'whiteness' is finally achieved when the bag of pearls carried throughout their trials is brought safely to civilization and sold, realizing the personal ambitions of the crew.

'Pearls' often feature in the title of books written at this time; in addition to Hurley's volume there is the missionary Florence Young's *Pearls from the Pacific* (1926), the pearl in this case referring to the underlying humanity/whiteness of the savage, whose value and worth can be redeemed through embracing Christianity and the transformative power of plantation and domestic labour. The exotic— pearls, gold, savage labour, savage soul—is once again turned into a commodity for European appropriation. Brewster's fictional voyage through the landscape of colonialism comes to its inevitable conclusion; the white men with their loyal servants have again triumphed. It is their story, a 'boy's own' story, and the native is reduced to background colour (cf. Schieffelin and Crittenden 1991: 13). *Pearls of Papua* is an example of a colonial *tangenemo*, providing another version of the 'other' and the country he inhabits, but this story is grounded in different relations of power and knowledge, relations that had dramatic consequences for the savage. The next chapter considers 'real' events in the history of Pangia's exploration although, as we shall see, fiction is never far from colonial truth.

2

Sons of the Female Spirit, Men of Steel

Wiru tell stories of cannibalistic ogres who have vegetation growing out of their man-like bodies, and of how a human being was created out of another hybrid beast, half-man, half-reptile. This creature possessed no anus and could not defecate until it was pushed into a pit filled with sharpened stakes, one of which punctured its backside, creating an anus, the ability to excrete, and a man at the same time. In not so different a fashion, early government patrols into the Samberigi area, to the south of Pangia, based their reports of cannibalistic feasts on the most slender evidence; a house with a few human skulls and bones was sufficient to earn condemnation, with the departing patrol officers, or kiaps, indicating the government's displeasure at such barbaric acts: 'we spoke very severely to [them] about their raiding, murdering and cannibalistic ways. We impressed upon them that it must terminate at once, as they were terrorizing the whole country' (Kikori PR13/21–22).

The first European patrol officers into Takuru in 1952 made little mention of the Wiru people encountered, except for their attempts to keep the location of the ceremonial ground hidden, and for the officers' curiosity about a hermaphrodite observed once the settlement was entered:

No women were seen here, although one apparently bi-sexual native was sighted. He was dressed after the manner of a local woman but carried a tomahawk and moved with the other men. His outward characteristics were definitely male but perhaps the woman's garb was to indicate that he was abnormal. (Mendi PR5/52–53)

In this instance, the kiap was perceptive, for the man's attire did in fact mark his 'abnormal' status as an *ailaroa*, or sky/man-woman.

These narratives seem to share similar epistemological and essentialist concerns about alterity and humanity, which converge around themes of duality—animality/humanity for Wiru and primitivity/sexuality for Europeans. For the latter, however, racial myths act as a colonial charter, justifying programmes of government expansion, pacification, and development 'for their own good'. The colonial mirror reflects both the savage and the European, and looking into the mirror, no matter how perfect its surface, can only produce distortion and further narratives of difference, themselves embodying a theory of power (cf. Taussig 1993: 66). This chapter is a reflection upon the hall of mirrors in which Wiru and Europeans first encountered each other.

My analysis, here and in other chapters, of the consequences of first encounters between Europeans and Wiru has several influences: Sahlins's attempts (1981,

1985) to wed history to anthropology within a structuralist framework; an anthropological history of the first government patrol into six Papuan societies of the Southern Highlands in 1935 (Schieffelin and Crittenden 1991); and Foucault's (1979) emphasis on changing power-knowledge relationships, which I adapt to the production of 'civilized' bodies under colonial regimes.

Sahlins shifts these 'first-contact' encounters away from the simplistic view of a transitory collision of cultures, a mere historical event, to a situation in which the confrontation leads to long-term and widespread consequences, perhaps even structural transformation, for the 'contacted' culture. These initial meetings between 'others' are explored by Sahlins through the notion of a 'structure of the conjuncture', by which he means, 'the practical realization of the cultural categories in a specific historical context, as expressed in the interested action of the historic agents, including the microsociology of their interaction' (Sahlins 1985: xiv). In terms of this structure, differing perceptions of the 'other' are confronted, leading to new or revalued meanings which may, in their practice, re-order cultural schemes (ibid.: vii). Sahlins (1981) tells how Captain Cook, upon his arrival in Hawai'i, was perceived as the god Lono, so that his actions intersected in a historically meaningful way with the rituals being performed with profound consequences for Hawai'ian society.

Schieffelin and Crittenden (1991: 284–6) point to the range of interpretations of the Strickland–Purari patrol of 1935, as well as its varying historical consequences, among the six Papuan societies it encountered. There was a ritual response on the part of the Huli, which continues to influence their present-day millennial concerns (Clark n.d.), yet an almost complete lack of long-term historical effects in other societies. They account for this variation by modifying Sahlins and suggesting a 'structure of *mis*juncture' (Schieffelin and Crittenden 1991: 285, their italics). In other words, a lack of fit between the cosmological and practical concerns of Europeans and Highlanders, combined with demographic fluctuations resulting from endemic warfare or introduced disease, led to the patrol being almost 'forgotten' in some areas. Just how Wiru fit into this schema will be discussed below.

Before Europeans even imagined the existence of Highlanders, there was a discourse of colonialism which constructed savage bodies within a particular field of power relations: Highlanders were *known* before they were first encountered. This discourse changes as Highlanders move from being 'savages' in a wild landscape to workers on plantations and government stations. This transformation is mirrored by a change in the tone and content of patrol reports as people become known less as figures of romance in an unknown and fantastic landscape, and more as productive subjects in a colonial world. The 'anthropology' section in patrol reports tends to disappear, not surprisingly, after pacification and involvement in local development. Discourse alone cannot account for the divergent responses to contact cited above, but it has to be considered to explain the particularities of these meetings within the discursive space of colonialism. It is in explicating the relationship between colonial discourse and processes of subjectification that Foucault provides useful insights.

Just as Sahlins discusses the perception of Captain Cook as the god Lono in terms of Hawai'ian cosmology and the timing of Cook's arrival, I will consider Pangia's geographical location, its connection to trade routes, imported cults, and Wiru beliefs about sorcery and the dead, as factors which affected the way in which Europeans came to be incorporated within a particular system of historical relations. The isolation of Wiru from major trading networks, together with their interstitial position between so-called 'fringe' and central Highlands groups, influenced Wiru attitudes to Europeans and gave a certain direction to Pangia's colonial history, as well as to the 'history' created and experienced by Wiru. The term by which Wiru understood a newly introduced item of European provenance, steel axes, became in some settlements conflated with Europeans themselves, an identification which, because of a connection forged between steel and sorcery, was to have deleterious consequences on several occasions. In other areas, whites were associated with the recently introduced Female Spirit cult, or were believed to be spirits of the dead. Rather than any monolithic understanding of whites, perceptions of them were based on the directions in which they travelled and the period during which contacts were made. The terms by which Europeans were known became metaphors for a different understanding of power, knowledge, and wealth, upon which pacification and the structuring of a colonial reality were based.

Western Society and the 'Other'

Before considering these points in more detail, a brief digression on the nature of the relationship between Western society and the 'other' is required. This relationship is mirrored by, and sometimes stands as a metaphor for other relationships, namely those between self and other, and self and unconscious. Anthropology embodies, and turns into a science, a capacity in Western society to identify and reflect upon its 'self' in relation to the 'other' (M. Strathern 1990, 1992). This preoccupation with the 'other' is often given cultural expression by the contrivances of artefacts such as cinema or literature (*Black Robe* and *Dances With Wolves*, both novels later made into films, come to mind). Part of the enduring fascination of encounters between the West and the savage results, for the anthropologist and layperson alike, from the intensely enigmatic quality of a meeting between extremes (a statement I do not intend in an evolutionary sense). Anything is possible in this situation, the dimensions of time and space are no longer precise and become charged with the possibility that the self, and perhaps a more authentic self, may be finally discovered. There is an inherent danger in this revelation, apart from the possibility that people may be killed, as the self could be made problematic or even repudiated (a potential of Christian revivals also; see Chapter 5).

The films *First Contact* (1982), a documentary dealing with the entry of the Leahy brothers into the Highlands of Papua New Guinea in the 1930s, and *Close*

Encounters of the Third Kind (1977), which presents a possible scenario for the first meeting between humans and extraterrestrials, owe some of their success to a fascination with the enigma of knowing the self through a truly different 'other'. In the film *Close Encounters*, the problems of self which the hero experiences are resolved by an encounter with alien others. A major difference for the audience between the aliens of *First Contact* and *Close Encounters* is that the former are savages while the latter are 'civilized', in the sense of a technological and perhaps moral superiority. The black savage inhabits a 'heart of darkness', part of what Taussig (1993: 66) calls the 'colonial mirror of production', in which the European traveller is driven to madness through experiencing his own primitivity, or is at least caused to reflect upon his humanity (cf. Torgovnick 1990). The shining white extraterrestrial, by contrast, inhabits a 'heart of brightness', and journeys towards it can ennoble the self and heighten consciousness of positive human potential. In other words, new potentials for an understanding of self and of one's place in the scheme of things are possible from these dialogic encounters.

In Randolph Stow's Conradian novel *Visitants*, he depicts a visiting patrol officer's experience of the Melanesian 'heart of darkness', embodied in the malignant figure of the sorcerer. Stow, capturing nicely the duality of 'contact', writes of the consequences for a patrol officer and the inhabitants of a Melanesian island of a supposed UFO landing. The UFO serves to increase the officer's own sense of alienness derived from dealing with the natives, and he kills himself, whereas for the islanders the UFO is the stimulus for starting a cargo cult. This is the metaphysic of culture contact. The danger inherent in knowing the self through a foreign other is indicated by the patrol officer's suicide, while the cargo cult represents an attempt to know and control the colonial other through the ritual channelling of desire, attracting not the white man's aeroplane but the Visitants' (ancestors/gods?) spaceship and wealth. *First Contact* is less a revelation of self for the Melanesian than of what the 'self' can do (M. Strathern 1990). The knowledge produced or desired has profound consequences for both parties, if to varying degrees. The self–other relationships which generate 'first contact' and colonialism confirm its projects, whereas the relationship acts more as a hermeneutic for Melanesians. *Visitants* combines the themes of *First Contact* and *Close Encounters*, the UFO being a literary device for dealing with the clash between European and Melanesian cultures: one possible contact experience between people and extraterrestrials becomes a metaphor for contact with others, between whites and blacks, and between self and other.

The intention of my reference to these two films is to make the point that both perceptions of the alien are contained within the Highlander–European encounter. If the film *First Contact* is essentially a Western view of the Highlander 'other', each still recognizes the other as human, whereas in *Close Encounters* the presentation of the 'other' is in distinctly non-human terms. The initial perceptions of Europeans by Highlanders were often, if not always, of the *Close Encounters* kind; whites were not human. For the hero of *Close Encounters* and the Highlanders of

First Contact, the experience of the 'other' was of a techno–cosmological nature, encouraging a view of the alien as in some sense morally superior. The problem for Highlanders was to seek to understand what Europeans were and the motives for their sudden appearances and departures, for their establishment of permanent patrol and mission stations in nearby areas, and for their eventual setting up of these stations in the region of the Highlanders making these observations. Some aspects of this problem for Wiru will be discussed below, but first an overview of the European presence in the Highlands is presented.

First Patrols in the Highlands

There were varied interpretations of Europeans throughout the fringe and central Highlands, and they had different consequences for colonial history. Before elaborating on this claim, the use of the term 'fringe' has to be clarified; it is not meant as a residual category. It is not my intention to perpetuate a pernicious distinction between the two areas, with the fringe devalued for having comparatively low population densities, an emphasis on ritual with a corresponding 'absence' of large-scale ceremonial exchange, for being a pre-Ipomoean version of Highlands societies (see J. F. Weiner 1988). I use the term 'fringe' in a double sense: geographical, to indicate peoples such as Foi, Daribi, and Bosavi; and to refer to peoples such as the Ipili, Paiela, Fore, Mountain-Ok, and Duna, who inhabit the Highlands but who are in many ways 'closer' to the fringe than to bordering Highlands groups such as Enga. Fringe is not meant in a peripheral sense, geographically or culturally, and people described as fringe Highlanders are not to be considered as dependent on a more 'evolved' Highlands but as members of autonomous cultures within regional networks (see J. F. Weiner 1988; Biersack 1995).

In the Highlands, Europeans were often seen as ancestors or spirits returned from the land of the dead (Berndt 1965: 99; Reay 1959: 201; Salisbury 1962: 114; Finney 1973: 142; Leahy and Crain 1937) or as sky beings or their associates (Lacey 1982: 13; A. J. Strathern 1971b: 108).[1] For fringe people, whites were often thought to be related to characters in cosmogonic myths. Leahy and Dwyer, on their 1930 expedition, were thought by Daribi to be 'men who had formed the

---

[1] Consider this account of the Taylor, Leahy and Spinks patrol encountering Chimbu: 'We shall never know precisely what the Chimbus thought at the first sight of the expedition, but we know that Leahy concluded from the action of one of the women that she believed that one of the native members of the exploratory group was the reincarnation of a lost relative. The unprecedented appearance of an expedition of white and black strangers made a tremendous impression upon the people. The Chimbu have certainly never been the same since' (Brown 1973: 25).

Brown suggests that Europeans may have been thought of as ancestors or spirits from another world (ibid.: 79). The first patrol remains 'a source of story and awe' (ibid.: 78), yet despite the evidence for a metaphysical interpretation of whites, she remains unwilling to accept Chimbu accounts of first encounters (ibid.: 79). Surely a systematic collection and account of oral histories is better than stating the impossibility of 'knowing precisely'. Still, the impact of whites on Chimbu is clearly shown, indicating the need to understand events in terms of models like the 'structure of the conjuncture' (see Brown 1992).

land' (Wagner 1972: 26); even if whites could not be categorized (Schieffelin 1976: 2), they were often believed to herald some cosmic disaster on the scale of the end of the world (see Rappaport 1968: 9; Wagner 1972: 26; Schieffelin 1991). In the fringe, more so than in the central Highlands, people often 'seized upon these events as the occasions for epochal innovations of their own' (Wagner 1972: 12).

While I hesitate to set up dichotomies between such culturally different areas, some analytic mileage can be obtained by contrasting fringe and central Highlanders in terms of the presence or absence of cosmogonic myths (see also Clark 1988). For central Highlanders, particularly those of the Wahgi valley from Enga to Simbu, the universe is immanent in and constructed through practice, particularly exchange, through which people discern motivation and ascribe (a type of) humanity (cf. M. Strathern 1990). Interpretations of events for fringe people appears to be located more in a folk epistemology based around mythology and ritual; this is not to minimize the importance of exchange but rather to suggest the extent to which it is dialectically informed by mythological beliefs about such things as ground fertility and entropy. Similarly, ritual often played a large role in the exchanges of many Highlanders; the point being that the parameters of time and space which constructed 'first-contact' events were influenced more by practice than mythology, despite Highlands perceptions of Europeans as spirits. This characterization of Highlanders is in no way meant to suggest that they are more materialistic than other Melanesians.

The continual exception to these generalizations are Highlanders such as the Huli who, along with the Fore and Ipili, interpreted an actual or rumoured European presence in terms of millennial beliefs (Sorenson 1972: 362; Meggitt 1974; Frankel 1986: ch. 2). The Huli area is densely populated and covers a large territory; they are intensive sweet potato horticulturalists and pig-raisers, and in architecture, dress, and other respects appear to fit into a Highlands stereotype. Despite this, at the level of cosmology Huli are classically 'fringe', perhaps because of their strong connections to the Bosavi and Duna areas. Like the Fore (Berndt 1962: ch. 4), Huli have an extensive and elaborate mythology in which creator heroes figure prominently, and they share Fore concern with a linkage between apocalypse and the arrival of Europeans, who were initially feared because of a belief that they would destroy society by killing pigs and pregnant women (Finney 1973: 139). Both Huli and Fore areas experienced an early participation in millenarian movements. Despite these similarities, and the strong mythological tradition in terms of which the European presence was interpreted among both Fore and Huli (Frankel 1986: 16–26), the ethnography indicates that Fore viewed whites as spirits of the dead, in common with many central Highlanders, and not as non-human spirits as did the Huli (Allen and Frankel 1991).

The millennial cult entered the Huli area from the Ipili region to the north (Frankel 1986: 28). For Ipili the millennium would take place only after the end of the world, in the sky (Gibbs 1977: 15; Meggitt 1974: 29; Biersack 1990). This type of belief is common to the 'epochal innovations' made by fringe Highlanders, contrasting with the apparently more secular and less traumatic responses to whites made by their Highlands counterparts. While the focus of millennial activity was in regions far removed from white administrative stations and with infrequent exposure to patrolling, equally as important was the interpretation of Europeans in terms of a cosmological system grounded more in myth than practice. What also has to be considered is that, regardless of regional differences in beliefs about the supernatural origins of whites in the central Highlands, their presence was more permanent there than in the fringe and consequently involved significant interaction with local people, especially in the trade of shells and steel for food and labour. A permanent European presence in the fringe usually occurred decades later than it did in the central valleys, and Europeans (other than missionaries) continued to be more transitory than permanent in many fringe areas.

The quantity of goods possessed by Europeans led to their characterization, by Melpa at least, as the 'true owners' and source of these valuables (A. J. Strathern 1984: 21; see Brown 1973: 79 for the Simbu), although for Melpa their association with cannibalistic sky beings, who were connected in some stories with the origin of pearl shells, contributed to this view of whites (A. J. Strathern 1971b: 235). Whites were also seen as powerful and wealthy in the fringe, and there is evidence for their similar characterization as the owners of steel if not of pearl shells. A patrol report about the Lake Tebera region states that the local people (Daribi) 'said that when they saw a "plane" they exclaimed "Ah—there go the owners of all the axes and knives", and then ran into the bush and hid' (Kikori PR2/37–38).

This quote is interesting because it is the only evidence I could find of fringe people identifying an aeroplane (a sky being?) as one of the 'true owners' of steel. The report gives no indication of the kiap being associated with the aeroplane, although this may have been the case. Daribi further to the north associated Leahy and Dwyer with Soux, the creator being, but the ethnography makes no mention of the early perceptions of steel. Iqwaye people of Menyamya believed the first aeroplane they saw, in the early 1930s, to be the creator deity (J. Mimica, pers.comm.), and would not accept steel from McCarthy's first patrol into this area in 1933 (Simpson 1954: 41), perhaps because steel was associated with sorcery and witchcraft, as it was for the Onabasulu of the Papuan plateau who rejected offers of steel from Hides in 1935 (T. Ernst, pers.comm.; cf. Radford 1987: 17). In the Bosavi area, Europeans were fitted into origin myths which classified them as pale-skinned descendants of Guni, a primordial woman and ancestor of Bosavi people, who left the area and became witches. Steel was identified as the property of these witch beings, so that the first patrols were believed to be witches returning to the centre to reclaim their steel, presaging the end of the world, this being the reason that Hides could not exchange steel tools for food (Schieffelin 1991). Unlike the Europeans' experiences in trade with Highlanders, their attempted exchanges with Bosavi and Iqwaye people were largely unsuccessful and did not construct whites as human. In the central Highlands it was frequently trade between Europeans and local people which led to the perception that whites were, after all, human: 'When they saw [Patrol Officer] Taylor's white skin, they thought he must be one of the pale-skinned cannibals who figure in Hagen folktales, but "then he gave us shell valuables in return for pigs, and we decided he was human"' (A. J. Strathern 1971b: xii).[2]

It is interesting to compare fringe and Highlands differences in regard to attitudes to steel, Europeans, and exchange, with the mythological dimension to interpretations of patrols in the fringe, clearly demonstrated. In some regions of the fringe steel is dissociated from other trade goods such as shell, and associated with whites in a malignant or dangerous fashion. Steel and shell are both associated with whites in the Highlands, and apparently not in a malevolent manner once exchange had commenced. Perceptions of Europeans in the fringe were influenced by a cosmology in which interaction with whites was in terms of mytho-praxis, and not through a cosmology based on the practice of exchange.

This account of the fringe response to Europeans makes for an interesting comparison with the Siane perception of the 1933 Leahy brothers' patrol:

Only a few warriors and 'big men' dared to come near the 'spirits' and collect pieces of waste-paper, lids of tin cans, and portions of food. They took these objects back to the villages as 'ancestral relics' and hid them in the men's houses. Ceremonies were performed, sacred flutes blown, and pigs killed in anticipation of the relics turning into shells. But after some weeks nothing had happened. The natives now realized that the visitors were men and not spirits . . . [and] saw nothing to prevent them taking valuables by force. (Salisbury 1962: 114).[3]

The inevitable outcome of such attempts 'by force' was that they were rarely repeated, but when trade replaced violence as a means of interaction the Siane viewed this as exchange and not, as whites viewed the situation, as the purchase of pigs: 'As the natives saw it, pigs were killed in honour of the [white] visitors, who later made presentations of valuables in return' (Salisbury 1962: 115). However, the idea that Europeans were human preceded these later exchanges. It came about not by transaction but by a failure in transaction. In other words, despite the initial ritual response to the white presence, it was disappointment in the ability of the 'spirits' to make the expected returns in a ritual exchange, disappointment that the spirits were generically human after all. Reciprocity, not myth, determined the type of interaction with Europeans in this instance.

----

[2] In Hawai'i, it was the commerce in sex that helped to change the Hawai'ian perceptions of Europeans from gods to men (Sahlins 1981: 53). Certainly sexual intercourse played a role in changing Highlanders' perceptions of whites but, as in Hawai'i, this change proceeded in the context of a culture-bound empiricism and influenced the unfolding of events.

[3] This appears to have been a common pattern in the Highlands (Connolly and Anderson 1987). The return of a patrol, initially greeted with awe or hospitality, was the occasion for an attack to obtain the patrol party's valuables. I would relate this to the fact that whites were perceived in terms of a cosmology of practice, and suggest that even if whites continued to be seen as spirits they would not have been immune from attack (cf. A. J. Strathern 1971b: 108). This point is expanded upon in later chapters but for an alternative, and hopefully complementary explanation in terms of Highlanders and exchange, see Marilyn Strathern (1990).

There were, then, ritual and mythic elements to Highlands interpretations of whites but, at a general level of classification, they were the result of a cosmology based on practice. The arrival of whites did not initially herald fundamental and cataclysmic changes to society.[4] An explanation of Wiru perceptions of Europeans would not, however, fit comfortably into an either/or type of cosmology, although their perceptions were ultimately grounded more in practice than myth (Wiru, unlike Fore and Huli, do not have an elaborate mythical tradition). This chapter will consider how a 'mythic' interpretation of whites affected events which were to occur decades after the first patrols, and how it was that an interpretation based on practice eventually emerged.

The Europeans in Pangia

Unlike many Highlanders, Wiru had access to steel axes from the 1920s. These tools came up from the Papuan coast via the same trade route as pearl shells, up the Kikori river, to Samberigi, then to Ialibu and northwards to Hagen. Wiru had an earlier access to steel but the initial quality appears to have been inferior. Ivan Champion reported in 1936 many 'very old' steel axes in Pangia (Champion 1936: 98). It seems that the best steel remained in the north–south trade route and that Wiru, because of their disadvantageous trade position (Hughes 1977; Clark 1985), were fobbed off with older and blunter axes. Andrew Strathern (1968: 551) comments that 'Ialibu and Kewa men still say that they drew off the best (stone) axes from Hagen . . . and blocked the road of shell exchanges for the Wiru in the past.' There is no reason to believe that Wiru access to good-quality steel axes was not similarly restricted. What is important is that steel was known as *kapona bina*, and that *kapona* was later a term used to refer to white men (if Europeans and steel were known by one term, then obviously the former were its true owners).[5]

The first steel axes were thought by Wiru to have come from two white men who were patrolling in the Samberigi valley. The first Europeans to come into this valley were members of Staniforth Smith's disastrous patrol of 1910–11 (Sinclair

---

[4] There are broad differences between fringe and central Highlands perceptions of Europeans but some similarities exist. For the Enga and Melpa, whites had some mythical significance through their association with sky beings, especially for Enga, who are descended from them (Lacey 1982: 9, 13). This significance does not appear to be as intense or elaborate, however, as it is for societies like Daribi where mythical heroes such as Souw created the landscape and culture, rather than people (Wagner 1972).

Maring people of the northern fringe appear to be an exception to the type of cosmology I have characterized for fringe societies, particularly those that have been influenced by the 'flamboyant coastal cultures' (Wagner 1972: 19) of Papua. Maring had a reliance on the central Highlands to the south for innovation and trade, just as southern fringe societies had migrated from the Papuan coast. This may account for the lack of mythical exegesis among the Maring (Healey 1988) but there are still many similarities between their reactions to Europeans and those of the southern fringe.

[5] Kewa of the Sugu valley also knew whites as *kapona* (L. Josephides, pers.comm.), although apparently this was not a Kewa term for steel. In Pangia, individual axes, and varieties of axes, were named in a similar fashion as pearl shells. *Kapona* appears to be a generic term for steel rather than for a type of steel axe.

1969). Leahy himself recorded a Kewa term for white men, 'Binekar Boricle', just before his entry into the Wiru area in 1934, and intuitively remarked on its origins 'in stories from the Samberigi Valley, visited by Staniforth Smith years ago from the Papuan side' (Leahy 1991: 186). Leahy was no linguist, and what he recorded may have been closer to Bine Karboricle, or *bina kapona*. The Staniforth Smith patrol, however, comprised three Europeans and preceded the arrival of steel in Pangia by about a decade. The patrols of Flint and Saunders (Kikori PR13/21–22) and Faithorn and C. Champion (Kikori PR19/28–29) appear as more likely candidates for the source of *kapona bina*; there were two Europeans in each and they engaged in trade with people of the Samberigi area. The problem is that when steel arrived in Pangia, it came from the north–south trade route to the west of Pangia, and not from the very occasional patrol which, when it did trade, did so in relatively small numbers of steel tools which were not usually passed on much further (Hughes 1977: 47).

The derivation of *kapona bina* may now be impossible to discover, but there is a fascinating possibility of its origins in a myth held by people living to the south of Mt Murray, who were middlemen in the Kikori–Samberigi steel trade. The myth was recorded by Flint on his 1921–22 patrol:

> The legend of their tribe was told to me by a sexagenarian. Long ago, he said, when there were no mountains, two dogs, a male and a female, known as *Hope* and *Irua*, journeyed across the Kiko river, to a village called Ugobe, and there [each] swallowed an infant of their own sex. Returning in great haste, they became ill, and vomited up their victims alive. The infants were named *Wini* (female) and *Kebuna* (male). As a prevention against theft of these children by wandering tribes, the mountains which surround their village were made by their captors. When the children married, *Hope* went to the mountains to the south, and *Irua* to those in the north. 'They are not dead' said the old man, 'they patrol the mountains and guard the people'. (Kikori PR13/21–22)

The myth may be interpreted as a commentary on trade, especially given the important trading position of these people. The two dogs travel south, the source of shells and steel, where they eat the infants and later regurgitate them in their own country (the Kiko is undoubtedly the Kikori river, see Hope 1979: 35–6). The infants are treated as 'valuables' which the dogs guard by patrolling the mountains. The infants, Kebuna and Wini, are produced and guarded by their captors—the patrolling dogs—and it is in respect of these categories that the connection between steel and patrol officers takes on a possible significance.[6]

While patrol reports of this era do contain references to legends, it may have been no accident that the old man chose to tell the two patrolling whites, themselves trading steel, this particular story. The hypothesis, then, is that this myth

---

[6] Some support for this interpretation of the myth is that the Wiru terms for 'steel axe' and 'dog' are the same word, *tue*, except for a difference in intonation (A. J. Strathern 1984: 21). This has to be reconciled, however, with the fact that Takuru Wiru are adamant that *tue* was also the term for stone axes (which were traded in from the north not the south).

provided a commentary on steel and the presence of Europeans, which was passed on with steel in trade and ultimately resulted in the use of the term *kapona bina* (*Kebuna Wini*) for steel in Pangia, and in patrolling whites and steel becoming inextricably and terminologically linked, even though Europeans were not to enter Pangia until 1934 (the resemblance between these terms may have been even greater given the frequent errors made by patrol officers in recording native words). That is, *kapona* refers to steel and its source, Europeans, so that the latter were 'men of steel' (and people to the east of Samberigi appear to have had direct trading links to Pangia, Kikori PR13/21–22).

Although the steel/white/*kapona* linkage was commonly made, whites were not perceived as *kapona* in all settlements. The distrust and fear of Europeans as 'red cannibals', *kewa kulopia*, appears to have been more prevalent in central Wiru settlements which did not experience patrols until the 1950s, although why this was so I am not sure.[7] It may be that the cannibal aspect of whites was in any case a feature of their *kapona*-ness, in that *kapona* and cannibalism were intimately associated with the Kewa area to the south. This association implied malevolent attributes to Europeans as this was also the region where powerful sorcery was (and still is) believed to be practised. Stories of first encounters in Takuru, my fieldwork site (see Map 3), continually refer to the extreme apprehension felt towards kiaps, who Takuru people thought wanted to kill and eat them (whites and steel were both known as *kapona* in Takuru; see n. 10).

Differing but often complementary interpretations were also made of aeroplanes observed during World War II, even in the same settlement.[8] For some people aeroplanes were inexplicable, while some thought them to be *ipono*, spirits, sent by Kewa or *kapona* to kill Wiru. Others believed aeroplanes sighted during World War II to be flying axes, also called *kapona*, propelled by Kewa sorcery (cf. Brown 1992: 30). Interpretations could also be influenced by the context in which first sightings were made: Mele people were terrified by the noisy presence of 'black birds' while mounting a surprise attack on Poloko settlement, and concluded they were the spirits of Poloko dead come to protect their descendants (Paia 1977: 50). Wiru women would expose their genitals to aeroplanes to make them go away,

---

[7] *Kulopia* is a Wiru rendering of the Kewa term *kula pae aa*, 'man without foreskin' (Franklin and Franklin 1978: 162). Wiru did not offer this interpretation of whites, the term obviously being passed on from the Kewa area, although border Wiru may have been aware of its meaning. 'Man without foreskin' is a Wiru synonym for a *tomo* poisoner. Wiru associated whites with sorcery and cannibalism, so the use of *kulopia*, unbeknownst to Wiru, was quite close to the mark.

[8] During World War II, bombs were jettisoned after raids to Wewak to lighten the load for return to Port Moresby. Stories abound in Pangia of aeroplanes crashing; most likely these were bombs which were immediately used for steel tools. Lacey writes of Enga being injured trying to cut metal from unexploded bombs (1982: 15), while the Miyanmin made tools from shrapnel (Morren 1981).

People from Warababe recount how a bomb exploded there, scarring a tree. Mick Leahy carved his name on a tree in Warababe when he passed through there in 1934, and it may be that *kapona* bombs and *kapona* whites are linked in this account (if in fact a bomb did not drop, although it seems too coincidental that *kapona* scarred a tree twice in Warababe). Aeroplane *kapona* were sometimes blamed for the fatalities at Laiyo.

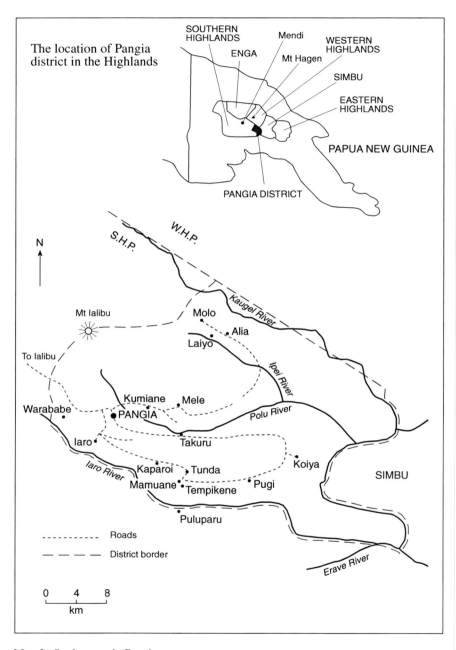

MAP 3. Settlements in Pangia

just as they would if sorcerers were suspected of being in the vicinity. The logic of this action was that the polluting power of women was stronger than sorcery. Men suffering from sorcery sickness would sleep on their wives' skirts to regain their health, an act which would appal most Highlanders (yet see Meggitt 1974: 12). There is a story of a pregnant woman being killed by a *kapona* bomb (or by an aeroplane dropping steel tools!) at Wapere for exposing herself, and speaking 'bad words', to drive away aeroplane sorcery during World War II. It is possible that this event occurred but the apocryphal overtones of the story, and the fact that variations of it occur throughout the Southern Highlands, suggests that the killing is a comment on the power and arbitrariness of *kapona*/whites/sorcery/Kewa.

Yet another interpretation was that aeroplanes were some manifestation of Akolali, a benevolent sky being, so that people were not clear if these sightings boded ill. It was partly because of this that whites were thought by some Wiru to be Akolali—now God for Christians—although this explanation was encountered only rarely. Paia (1977) records that Europeans were thought by Wiru of Mele to be sky people, although it is not clear if this was based on a connection with Akolali, aeroplanes, or the existence (which I could never verify) of an autonomous domain of sky beings as found amongst the Enga, for example. The point is that the perception of *kapona* as steel, Europeans and, later, aeroplanes, appears to have been made earlier and more forcefully in Southern Wiru settlements, or in those settlements which had contacts with the Leahys' 1934 patrol.

That the category *kapona*, including aeroplanes, was thought to be a type of Kewa sorcery is interesting, as it was at about the time that steel arrived in Pangia that beliefs in a new type of Kewa sorcery, *ulo*, were emerging. This apparent coincidence merits closer examination. Elsewhere in the Southern Highlands elements of Western society may be used in sorcery; for example, broken glass and wire. This 'new' sorcery is, though, a product of incorporation within, and long-term exposure to the Western economic system. Wiru are unusual in that the connection between whites and sorcery was made earlier (the 1920s) and probably did not involve Western elements, with the exception of steel. The 'botol' type of sorcery of the Mendi described by Lederman (1981) does not, as far as I can tell, occur in Pangia today. This may be partly because Wiru had a very different experience with development and the Australian administration, but this is speculative. It is possible that 'botol' and *ulo* are both meta-commentaries on incorporation into colonial spheres of control (cf. Taussig 1980).

Ulo was a new type of sorcery found on the southern fringes of Wiru society in the 1920s, but today spread and feared over the entire Pangia region, possibly relating to an increasing experience with inequality and Western systems of wealth generation and ownership (cf. Lederman 1981). *Ulo* sorcerers are still, it is thought, imported from the south, and are said to be recognizable by their *white* faces (suggesting that *ulo* is a transformation of the notion of *kapona* as white sorcerers). Many such sightings were reported in Takuru during a fieldwork trip in 1985. Although *ulo* is said to be of Kewa origin, it may have been based on or influenced by a Wiru concept of a malevolent and powerful spirit entity called *maua*. These entities were not sorcerers because they were not human, having the ability to turn into various animals, trees or other malevolent spirits such as *uali* (Kerr 1984: 8). *Maua* also came from the south, outside Wiru territory. Many people initially thought Europeans belonged to a spirit rather than a human or ghost category, especially in the area to the south where the *ulo* fear was created and nurtured.

Today, informants confuse *maua* with *ulo*, or spirit agency with human agency in the cause of death (this conflation had already occurred by 1967 in at least one settlement (A. J. Strathern, pers.comm.)). This is perhaps related to the fact that whites are now seen to be human. *Ulo* has become less *maua*, apparently replacing it as a feared cause of death, or becoming conflated with it. Another feature of *ulo* which supports its association with Europeans is its practice. The *ulo* sorcerer points a bamboo tube, with a stone at one end, at his intended victim, all the time uttering a phrase indicating his desire for the victim's death.[9] The tube 'fires' the power of the stone, *kue*, at the victim, killing him. The similarity with the action of a rifle, a long implement which fires a projectile at a target, is striking (McCarthy [1963: 102] reports that the Angan word for European and rifle was the same, *boong*—'presumably it was an association of ideas').

I am not suggesting that the arrival of Europeans pre-dated *ulo* or directly created it as a category of sorcery, but that the appearance and actions of patrol officers were roughly coincident with the spread of *ulo* beliefs (and with the spread of steel, also connected to sorcery fears as attitudes towards *kapona* would indicate), so that whites became associated with this form of sorcery. A massive *ulo* attack on Takuru in the late 1950s was believed to have been perpetrated with the aid of a mirror, another artefact of European origin. Certain stones have a strong, immanent power in Wiru society, and the possibility that bullets—and, later, coin money, also called *kue*— could have been interpreted in these terms is not unlikely. The timing of the arrival of *ulo*, the white faces of its practitioners, and the manner of its performance, are strong evidence for equating the spread of *ulo* with the arrival of European patrols in the Erave area in the 1920s. That Wiru do not make this equation is no evidence for its rejection. The perception of European power was given a cultural form, as a type of sorcery, to make it intelligible in terms of prevailing beliefs. The *ulo* concept arrived and was established in Pangia before the actual arrival of whites. *Ulo* is a Wiru interpretation of this arrival, part of an ethnohistory of colonialism.

[9] The Huli had a concept similar to *ulo*, a form of sorcery called *toro gamu* (Glasse 1965: 41), although it was not as 'accurate' as *ulo* (Glasse 1968: 102). *Toro* is a spirit of some kind, and it would be interesting to speculate on a link between the *maua* spirit, as the basis for a new corpus of sorcery beliefs, and *toro*, especially if the latter was somehow related to patrols in 1934 and 1935 or to patrols into Enga, with whom Huli had strong connections. Frankel records that the spells for *toro* were acquired from the Duna people to the west of Huli, and that many deaths were attributed to *toro* in epidemics after the first patrols (1986: 28). It is quite likely that *ulo* is in fact derived from the word 'Huli', as Mendi imported *uli temo* from the Huli (Longley n.d.), and this form of sorcery was then passed on southwards to the Erave area through Kagua, and then to the north into Pangia (incidentally giving some insights into the strange circularity of trade routes).

Whites as *kapona* constituted a puzzling type of entity. They were associated with spirits, steel, and sorcery, and were perhaps a new weapon in the armoury of Kewa sorcerers, while at the same time providing benefits to Wiru in the form of steel tools. Wiru desired steel in much the same way as Hawai'ians coveted British steel, which contained British *mana* (Sahlins 1981). Steel was worn by Wiru to appropriate the power of *kapona* in their first attempt to become 'like whites', as will be seen below. It is not surprising that the various characteristics of *kapona* led to an ambiguous Wiru view of whites; it was not even known if they were controlled by Kewa or acting autonomously. By the 1950s, when patrols were more frequent, it seems that a common interpretation of Europeans as *kapona* was that they were quasi-human sorcerers. *Kapona* did not fit neatly into any one of a range of extant categories but they were understood in terms of their synthesis. Some sort of perception of Europeans, however, preceded their arrival by many years, unlike in other parts of the Highlands where they suddenly burst upon the scene with little notice of their coming.[10]

A negative view of *kapona* was compounded by an incident which occurred during the Faithorn and Champion patrol of 1929 (Kikori PR19/28–29). After crossing the Erave river, the patrol eventually came to a Kewa settlement called Kaparoi (Kabire in the patrol report), south of the Iaro river.[11] Some of the inhabitants of Kaparoi stole several blankets and tomahawks from a patrol box, a theft not discovered until the patrol had moved on. Champion and some native police were sent back to recover the goods and to impress upon people that such actions against the 'government' would not be tolerated. According to men from Tempikene, a Wiru settlement to the north of the Iaro river, some Wiru men of the Kaimari group, from a settlement just south of the Iaro river (perhaps Puluparu), were visiting Kaparoi for trade at the moment when some native police returned. The men were surprised and either ran away or attempted to defend themselves, and one of the police, obviously thinking these were the culprits, fired at the men. According to the patrol report one man was killed after firing an arrow at two police; my informants thought several men had been shot 'by accident' (that is, because they were not the thieves).

This was the first fatality related to white penetration north of the Erave river (R. Crittenden pers.comm.) and, if my informants are correct, then Wiru had the dubious honour of being the first Southern Highlanders to experience death from a patrol led by Europeans. Kaparoi was a major entry point of steel into Pangia, so the association between *kapona* as steel, whites, and 'bad' things was reinforced.

[10] The fear of Europeans was partly because Wiru had heard of a white man being killed and eaten in the Samberigi or Kikori area, a transit point and source for steel respectively. This was possibly the missionary Chalmers who was killed on Goaribari island in 1901. Wiru thought that whites would kill and eat them in revenge for Chalmers's death. It is not unusual that these sorts of stories made their way so far north as a major trade route connected the Kikori area to the Highlands, and more than material goods were passed along it.

[11] That Faithorn and Champion were in Kaparoi puts them much further north than one would expect from reading the patrol report, in fact only a few hours' walk from the nearest Wiru settlement.

Some Takuru men believed it was the hostilities at Kaporoi which discouraged further European penetration into Pangia, making this district one of the last to be colonized in the Southern Highlands. Accounts of the Kaparoi death(s) and of the actions of *kapona* soon spread to Tempikene and other Wiru settlements near the Iaro river, and led directly, as far as I am aware, to the only overtly hostile encounters initiated by Wiru in a 'first contact' situation with Europeans. This hostility occurred in 1955 when a patrol, camping near Puluparu and led by a kiap from Erave (in the south), was attempting to ford the Iaro river and climb up the steep cliffs on its northern side, prior to entering Tempikene.

At first light working parties were sent to repair the bridge and assemble ladders which are necessary to scale the limestone walls . . . It was soon apparent that the previous ones had been destroyed. Upon our arrival at the river . . . we were met by a large party of natives from across the Iaro. They were fully armed with bows and spears and it was obvious at once that they were to prevent our crossing. I signalled our peaceful intentions and through feeble interpretation told them that we meant no harm. They were obviously moderately satisfied with these explanations and with much gestulation [*sic*] and shouting indicated we should return from whence we had come. This I had no intention of doing, even if it meant bloodshed. Making sure my party could look after itself, we advanced slowly towards the river. Four arrows were loosed and they fell harmlessly amongst us. I gave the order to fire over their heads . . . but the natives stood their ground. At this stage I thought that we might have more trouble than we had bargained for as more arrows fell amongst us and I again gave the order to fire into the air. At the same time I fired my .38 into the river lapping their feet and they retired with a sound like the whirring of wings. (Erave PR3/55–56)

After an uncomfortable time scaling the Iaro cliffs, against the background of continual yodelling and calling from the warriors, the patrol reached the top and followed a garden path, coming 'across the body of a man, tied to a pole, lying across our path. The assumption I drew was that here was a very palpable warning to us all to advance no further. The body seemed quite fresh and I observed no marks of violence' (ibid.).

Having avoided a suspected ambush from more than sixty warriors, the patrol made camp after the local people had deserted the area. All of the deaths which occurred with the spread of colonial control in Pangia are shrouded in uncertainty and ambivalent reporting. There is no doubt that the man's death was the direct result of the patrol's actions. His name was Peruma, and he was shot through the groin, the bullet emerging from his back. His body was on a pole because his comrades were carrying him from the fight and left him behind when the patrol emerged at the top of the cliffs. Did the kiap think that Tempikene people kept fresh bodies on hand in case they needed them for 'warnings' of what patrols could expect? Was the kiap actually aware of the fatality but misreporting it because of the administrative investigations that had to accompany any killing while on patrol? It seems unlikely that the kiap could have been unaware of the shooting as the warriors were in plain sight and a body being carried from the scene must have been noticed. The patrol was going to proceed 'even if it meant bloodshed', but all instructions were to fire over the warriors' heads in a civilized fashion. From the perspective of Tempikene, numerous warriors yelled at the *kapona* to go back because of the precedent for death set at Kaparoi. When it became obvious the patrol was proceeding, the warriors attempted to prevent its progress towards the settlement by firing arrows. Informants stated that two of the native police were superficially wounded by arrows which, if true, was not mentioned in the official account, suggesting that the reportedly restrained nature of the clash may have given way to panic and indiscriminate firing. There was another hostile consequence of this encounter in 1959, but first I will discuss an earlier patrol—the very first one into Pangia—for a different interpretation of Europeans.

Steel after Gold

The first Europeans to enter Pangia were the famous Leahy brothers, who in 1934 encountered Wiru in their quest for gold (see Connolly and Anderson 1987). It soon became apparent that Pangia was not gold country and the Leahys hurried back to their base in the Wahgi Valley, encouraged no doubt by the inclement weather, the perceived hostility of Wiru and their incomprehension of offers of trade for much-needed food:

the mountain natives had few shells and we saw no more steel axes. None of our interpreters could speak their language and once more we had to fall back on signs . . . we struggled over steep tracks that seemed to lead in every direction except north, we were drenched to the skin by almost constant rain and rarely had enough to eat. The natives, as is the case with bush country natives everywhere, were sullen and suspicious, and the women were kept out of sight. This hampered our trading for food, as the women are usually the gardeners and traders. (Leahy and Crain 1937: 227–8)

Leahy reports a markedly different reception from Wiru than that received from their neighbours, creating an impression of material and cultural differences, reflected in the protection of women (there were no relationships between them and carriers, with payment of shell valuables for 'services', Leahy and Crain 1937: 226), in the characterization of the indigenes as 'mountain' and 'sullen and suspicious', and in the difficulties of trade:

Unwilling to see the boys starve in a land of plenty, I took matters into my own hands at last, leading a group of natives to a flourishing garden of sweet potatoes and indicating quite plainly that we must have food. I spread out a generous amount of trade goods on the ground, which the natives accepted eagerly. But they still made no move to dig the sweet potatoes. 'Ah!' said I, 'there must be a good reason for such conduct. Perhaps the men in these parts have a taboo against entering the gardens. Clever of the lazy hounds at any rate'. I then told the boys to dig the sweet potatoes for themselves. At this there was a loud protest from the kanakas and they all stampeded for the village, to reappear presently with bows, arrows and spears. (Leahy and Crain 1937: 228–9)

I was not able to interview Wiru from each of the settlements through which the Leahys passed, but discovered at least three views on their identity, one of which was that they were *kapona*. They were travelling from the west and had indeed come from one of the major trade centres on the north–south trade route (Leahy and Crain 1937: 227), hence from one of the directions in which steel arrived. Consider this quote from Leahy's book: 'at each camp, two or three hundred kanakas would collect to gape at us and clap their hands together in amazement but when we offered them shells, knives, axes, salt and even cloth for food they brought us—sugar cane and bananas' (ibid.: 228).

When Europeans finally arrived in Pangia, bringing with them all the major valuables, the amazement of Wiru is partly explained by the fact that they were confronted, as were the Melpa, with the source and true owners of wealth. The amazement may also be explained, as a recent argument by Marilyn Strathern (1990) would indicate, by the fact that Wiru felt themselves in some way responsible for the Leahys' arrival, perhaps by their performance of a new cult. That is, Wiru were amazed at what they themselves had wrought.

The west was the direction from which the most recent cult had arrived—the *Aroa Ipono yapu*, Female Spirit cult—perhaps only a decade or so before this patrol. The Leahys were certainly linked to the earlier arrival of the cult because in some settlements they were thought to be *Ipono Aroane mana*, sons of the Female Spirit. Other Wiru perceived the Leahys to be spirits of the dead; by the late 1950s it was this perception of whites which came to dominate, although other views were by no means absent. It may only be because of a coincidence, the patrol arriving a relatively short time after the introduction of the Female Spirit cult, that the Leahys became its 'sons'. Whether an interpretation of the Leahys in cult terms would have been made regardless of this importation is now impossible to know. In one settlement, at least, the Leahys were offered a pig in apparent sacrifice to the cult deity they represented, although there was no consensus even within individual settlements and it is quite possible that many Wiru thought the offering was made to spirits of the dead (the Leahys appear to have been unaware of this offering as they left without it).

The gifts of banana and sugar cane, male luxury crops, were given by Wiru in recognition of the power, gender, and 'supernatural' status of their guests. It is a supreme irony that the Leahys thought that Wiru were treating them badly because of their refusal to exchange, while Wiru could not conceive of these creatures having any need to eat or engage in exchange of wealth for mundane sweet potatoes. Wiru accepted gifts but gave nothing in return (the luxury crops appear to have been not an exchange for gifts but a ritual placation of possibly hostile spirits, based on the techniques for making peace with enemies; cf. Radford 1987: 14–15; Crittenden 1991: 171). The characterization of whites as *Ipono Aroane mana*, together with their status as the source of wealth, set the scene for a similar perception of kiaps and missionaries from the early 1950s to 1960 and perhaps later. This certainly reinforced the perceived power of whites, as well as influencing a desire for their presence in areas which later came to have closer and more regular contacts with Europeans. Patrols from bases within the Southern

Highlands, the first in 1952, also came from the west, and increased in frequency after the establishment of Ialibu station in 1953.

To return to 1934, the Leahys continued their journey and camped in Laiyo, 'a small poverty-stricken village showing charred shapes of houses burned in recent wars. There was very little food here, and the people were too overcome to think about bringing any in' (Leahy 1991: 188). This was the third camp they had made in Pangia, and by now they were becoming irritated by their failure to trade for food. I continue from the quote where we left the Wiru with their bows and arrows, menacing the patrol.

Before they came within bowshot, we fired a few shots over their heads, at which they drew off some distance for a conference. It was now almost nightfall and had begun to rain. While our half-starved boys were trying to coax the fire to burn enough to cook the potatoes, there was a wild yell from the kanakas and several arrows landed among us. We promptly replied with a volley, firing blindly into the woods.

Throughout a miserable night of torrential rain the whole camp remained awake, the kanakas occasionally coming near enough to pelt arrows at us. We were forced to fire into the darkness . . . I think it was the rain which really saved us a fight. Long before daylight we had pulled down the tents and packed up for the road, and as soon as we could see the track, we moved ahead. (Leahy and Crain 1937: 229)

Their reception in Laiyo as *kapona* aggravated what was, from the Leahys' standpoint, a steadily worsening situation (this perception of the Leahys preceded their presence in Laiyo, as a man from their previous camp at Kumiane arrived, announcing that *kapona* were coming). They inadvertently contributed to the deterioration in relations by concluding that enough was enough, with Leahy instructing his 'boys' to dig up sweet-potato gardens. This served to compound Laiyo perceptions of the intruders as *kapona*; why else would people engage in such a hostile act as stealing from a garden? Laiyo had recently been partly destroyed by warfare, and it can be easily imagined that the patrol was hardly greeted with enthusiasm, even though Leahy records that they were still regarded with amazement (an emotion compounded by a demonstration of the power of a rifle on five stacked shields, which caused the people to 'fall over with fright', Leahy [n.d.], May 1934).

In Mick Leahy's account of their desperation to obtain sweet potatoes, digging up the gardens was the trigger for a series of skirmishes, with Wiru loosing arrows into the camp throughout the night, the patrol replying with volleys fired into the darkness. According to Laiyo informants these hostilities never took place. Leahy's diary account and his book contradict each other on this point; the diary, on which the book is based, makes no mention of an arrow attack, only the fear of one (Leahy's posthumous book [1991: 188] condenses his account to a few sentences, 'During the night a raiding party shot a few arrows into the camp, and from that moment forward no one had any sleep . . . the natives yelled and called and howled all night'). What happened that night after the gardens were dug up remains an enigma, more because it is unclear why certain events happened rather than whether they actually did happen. The expedition leaders seem to fade into the background in the events following the garden pillage, which are not referred to in Leahy's book or his diaries:

Had a bit of a misunderstanding with the kanakas last night probably cross over us just wanting a feed and at last going into their [word unclear] and taking it, instead of just standing about for them to gape at and clap their hands together in amazement. Two of them got bowled over I think and the whole camp were up all night through a night of torrential rain and watching for a rush from a big mob from the south whom they had sent messages to earlier in the evening. Happily we had commandeered all the bows, arrows, spears and shields we could find earlier in the evening so between my boys armed with guns and rifles and the Purari and Hagen kanakas armed with bows and arrows we had rather a formidable army, and this I think together with the heavy rain, which in turn swelled the streams the reinforcing mob would have to cross, damped their ardour a bit, but we had a hell of a night. (Leahy [n.d.]: May 1934)

It was in Laiyo, according to Laiyo informants, that some of the patrol's 'gunbois' engaged in particularly brutal acts of rape and violence, culminating in the shooting to death of two men, one of whom was attempting to rescue his wife from the carnal intentions of Leahy's 'police', and according to some informants the clubbing to death with rifle butts of two women who were either protesting against the 'gunbois' dragging women into houses to be raped, or who were themselves to be raped. I could only locate one person still alive who was an adult in 1934, a remarkable woman called Lariame (not her real name). This is her 1985 account of the patrol and the killing of her husband, providing a totally different perspective on the events of that night:

My husband [Porenge] had four other wives and I was the fifth, with two sons. He went to the village of one wife to bring her back home, I went to a bush garden to cook a possum. I left my pigs in my house with my little son to look after them. I came back from the garden and sat down at my house with my sons and then the black and white creatures [*lianea aketanea-kiri*] surrounded the house and a loud thundering noise filled the air. They were carrying a black stick with a shiny narrow end and a wide curved base that made a very loud thundering noise. The white creature broke a hole in the roof and peeped through to see me sitting in the dark room, he came through the door into my house while I and my two sons kept our face down and covered ourselves with pandanus rain mats. I gave him a whole possum that I had cooked in the bush, it was nice and warm but he refused to take it. I gave him a live small pig as well but he waved his hand and signed 'no' by turning his head. I gave him ripe bananas and some sweet potato but he refused these too. My husband came into the house but the white and black creatures grabbed his arms and took him outside. I also fought with them because at that time I was strong enough to fight the enemies. While I was struggling hard to escape the dog [Leahy's dog Snowy] was trying to bite my legs and the white creature kicked it and ordered it away. He showed me the sign by slapping his face that he wouldn't harm or kill me. But my husband never left me alone and kept creeping closer while we struggled. They took me by the hand into Porenge's *pokou* ['men's house'], with my two sons, and firmly closed the door [of the sleeping compartment] after throwing in some firewood. Other women who came back from the garden were locked up in the *pokou* too. We thought we were going to be killed so we killed a small pig and cooked it in the fire and ate it. They built their own house next to the *pokou* which looked like a tapa cloth house [*pue yapu*: a tent] and spoke a language that really puzzled us. They were talking and singing their strange language while going back and forth on the *poma* [ceremonial ground] making a loud sound like thunder. My husband was still struggling to get us out of the house but he couldn't because the black men with sticks wouldn't let him come close to the house. When he tried the black and shiny stick blasted with fire and smoke and thunder that broke the branches of the *kalipe* tree into pieces. But he didn't care about the firing stick, he was really worried about his family and kept coming closer telling the strangers 'they are my family', but they wouldn't listen to him because they didn't know what he was saying. He crept closer to us while they were not watching, my husband made a hole in the roof but a white creature saw him and chased him off by throwing cooking stones at him. I told him, 'I am going to be eaten or killed by this creature or taken away, I don't know so just go away quickly and don't come back. You are out there with other sons so wait and see what happens.' But he hadn't often left me alone so he came back again to the hole he made in the roof which the white creature had closed. At last it rained but Porenge did not go home to his wives. He broke the roof and made the hole again. He took away Lopeka's mother and another woman who was married to Kumiane while the creatures were in the *pue yapu* and not guarding the back of the *pokou*. There were some black men sitting in the front of the *pokou* while it rained. Kenai was a young woman who was kept in the house with me, and a young girl Einu, Mara's daughter, as well as Yambainu, Tawe's mother. I told my husband when he was getting people out through the hole in the *pokou* that you are one but I am three so see what happens tomorrow morning. He got my two sons out but was seen and shot by the white creature while he was trying hard to get me out. One woman who was with me dug into the ground by the side of the *pokou* to escape but she was seen by two black men who fired their thunder stick at two men who were trying to help her, killing them both. In the morning I ran out of the *pokou* but they didn't run after me or say anything, they were talking their strange language back and forth and then they pulled their *pue yapu* down and left. All the people had run away to their bush houses so I followed their tracks looking for Porenge and came to a place where men and women met together to see who was killed. A man called Mara from Kimbori group was killed while struggling to free his daughter from the creatures. They killed my husband. My sick sister who had to lie down fought with the creatures and was killed as well, and a woman who was Nora's mother. Five people were killed at this time. The creatures got two pigs from me and after killing them they carried the meat and food away, walking to Kaupena across the Tangue river where they built a very big fire. The brothers and groups of the men who were killed wanted to kill me because I was the cause of their death, I told them to kill me but they did not because I was still breast-feeding my little son. I am about to die in Lore hamlet. That is the end of my story.

In one of those strange coincidences of history, Lariame died not long before Danny Leahy in 1992. When I last saw her in 1991 she asked me if I was one of the men who had killed her husband. Her account of events is intriguing, not the least because she identifies one of the Leahy brothers as her husband's killer. Lariame tells of her three attempts to engage the white stranger in exchange, whose refusal to accept any of the proffered gifts betrays his 'enemy' intentions, denying his humanness. Her story recounts how, after surviving the terror of the night, she was nearly killed by the dead men's relatives, but makes no reference as to why she and other young women were locked up or why she was singled out for retribution. There is no mention of whether she or other women had been raped by any member of the patrol. Lariame was locked up for most of the events which happened and her narrative differs in some respects from an account provided by Aiye, the son of a man called Tipi who witnessed that night in 1934.

Aiye himself was locked up in a men's house by Tipi to protect him from the strange intruders.

Tipi was sitting on the wooden verandah pole of his *pokou* and was signed not to worry by the white men. They put up many tents. A short, fat carrier broke into the *pokou* and took a bow and arrows and salt. He tasted a bit and asked for it but Tipi kept his head bowed. The salt was put back but two other carriers and a policeman took it. The policeman signed with the bow and arrow 'do you shoot men?' A policeman found me hiding in the house and pulled me out by the arm and set me down near the whites in their tent on the *poma*, then I was put back in the *pokou* and signed to sleep. The dog [Snowy] was barking all the way through this and people were very afraid of the *kapona*. For some reason a Weipe man was laughing [from fear?], and he was hit in the nose and chest with a rifle butt, he ran away and hid in a *pokou*. A pig was taken by the policeman, first of all Kepalo's pig but this was rejected when its foreskin was pulled back and its penis was not fat [informants now claim to recognize this as a Simbu practice]. Porenge's pig was then taken because it was fatter. He said to people, 'Why don't you kill those creatures who aren't acting like people, they hit Weipe Kia and stole my pig. I have seen these policemen singsinging at Pokale [near Ialibu], they are tricking us [that is, they are human] so let's kill them.' Tipi replied that they are not our people so let them do what they want. There were some Auwa [Ialibu] people with the police who knew a little Wiru, they told the police what Porenge said to make him worried, and they locked up his wife Lariame in the *pokou* when she returned from the garden. Porenge took a stick that some pig ropes were tied to and hit some of the police, who beat him with their rifle butts. The police gave bananas to Porenge's sons, and told him to settle down and that they wouldn't kill him or his wife. The sign used was, 'When she opens her eyes she'll still be alive, we only want sex with her.' Weipe Kia and Tipi told Porenge to go to a bush hamlet called Poiyapini to stop him from doing anything to the police. Three women came back from fishing in Wera creek and were also put in the *pokou* by police, although one was rejected as too young and another female from a nearby *pokou*, Kenai, was abducted. One of the women's husbands, Piopo, fought police with a pig stick. The police pinned his arms behind his back and one of them ran to his tent and took out a black stick and was putting red things into it. This frightened Piopo and he pulled free and ran away to the bush. The police took Kenai to one of the whites and showed her to him, then they dug up a sugar cane garden belonging to Yari who, with his brother Kulako, was returning from the bush with firewood. When they heard what was happening they dropped their firewood and ran into their houses and came out with bows and arrows. They shot at the police but missed. The police shot back, aiming for Yari's chest but he turned and the bullet grazed him from one side of his chest to the other. Kulako was shot in the wrist. The police took the two men away to the whites, who put medicine on their wounds and bandaged them. The whites told them to sit down quietly. People had by now run away to their bush houses. The police broke into all of the houses and assembled all the shields, bows and arrows around a *kendo* [ceremonial mound], then they shot at them and broke them. Feathers, belts, pearl- shells and bailer shells were gathered and using the destroyed weapons, with broken arrows as kindling, they were burned using fence posts as firewood. Gardens were dug up all around Laiyo with a spade. Tipi fled to Wanowai but came back to fetch Porenge with him, who said, 'Those men are only tricking us, I will kill one and then come.' Around dusk the police gathered for sex with the captive women, Lariame yelled out that 'they are not treating me like Porenge does.' Porenge dug a hole under the wall of the *pokou* and managed to pull his wife's headwear out and tuck it into his netbag. The police proceeded to have sex with the women while others watched. Lariame told her husband to settle down or the police would kill her. At this point one of the police made a hole in the *pokou* wall, poked his gun out and shot Porenge in the chest, making a big hole. A man helping Porenge, Waiame Kimbori, ran away but police chased him and shot him through the stomach from hip to hip. His intestines fell to the ground and the whites' dog ate them up. A Wera Kambiri woman was in a nearby *pokou* and some police tried to rape her, she threw ashes in their faces and poked at their eyes with a smouldering stick. They clubbed her in the head and chest, breaking her ribs, and killed her. The police had to get bandages for their faces. When they left in the morning the patrol left a bundle of small knives, and the police entered every *pokou* and dug a hole in each fireplace and defecated in it, covering it with ashes [cf. Sillitoe 1991: 165]. Pigs had been shot the night before and thrown on the fire to cook. The best parts were eaten and the head, legs and much meat was left behind and wasted. The two wounded men got some salt, medicine for later use, and some pork. The patrol left us and walked towards Weipe.

Neither of these indigenous accounts refers to any organized retaliation by local Wiru to the patrol's actions; indeed, chaos and confusion are what come to the fore in recollections of the patrol's incursion into the lives of Laiyo residents. Its behaviour in the destruction of gardens, weapons, and wealth, could only have been seen as acts of destructive spirits or of war. These varying accounts relate to what Heider (1988) has called the Rashomon effect, where people bring different interpretations to events depending on who they are and their role in the proceedings. In some respects the accounts agree on details, such as firing rifles at the collected shields, but in others there is disagreement, such as who actually shot Porenge, and whether there actually was an arrow attack during the night (cf. Sillitoe 1991, who discusses a similar confusion of interpretation concerning the Hides patrol and the massacre at the Korpe defile). Kulako and Yari, angry at unexpectedly finding their garden pillaged, hardly constitute a wild group of arrow-loosing bowmen. The Leahy version does not even consider the actions portrayed in the two accounts just presented. It is as if the Leahys retire to their tent to contemplate a phantom conspiracy of vengeful savages, allowing their 'bois' to take over for the first time as major actors in the night's events, the playing out of another tragedy in the colonial heart of darkness.

Lariame's perspective is defined by her imprisonment and rape in the *pokou*, constructing her view of Porenge's courageous but ultimately doomed attempt to rescue his family. What are we to make of her account of Leahy's refusal to exchange, not once but three times, like Peter denying Jesus, and his killing of her husband? It seems clear from other informants that the 'police' were totally responsible for the actual physical violence, although non-intervention can also be bloody. Porenge, with his five wives obviously a man of some stature and ability, emerges as a more motivated character in Aiye's account, reacting to beatings and pig thefts, and to his anger at the deception of 'gunbois' whom he claims to recognize as human, spurring him to the rescue of his family when he may otherwise have intervened. From Aiye's account, it is possible that Lariame might not have escaped imprisonment and that the subsequent rapes and deaths might have been avoided if his plans to kill some of the patrol members had not been overheard. (If true, this could help to explain why Lariame was threatened with death in retaliation for the killings; cf. Sillitoe 1991: 160.)

What the Leahys were doing while all this activity was going on remains a major puzzle. Their apparent lack of control over the 'gunbois', which was very uncharacteristic of Mick Leahy, an extremely capable leader and a strict disciplinarian, hints at a possible motive—the Leahys were indirectly punishing the people, through their inaction, for what they understood as surly and inhospitable treatment from all Wiru encountered. Support is lent to this theory by the fact that Leahy's 'bois' were usually thrashed with rubber shock absorbers for sexual intercourse without Leahy's permission while on patrol (Leahy sardonically notes that the absorbers did not absorb much shock, Leahy [n.d.], April 1934). The inconsistency about the arrow attack in the book, diary and Laiyo accounts, and Leahy's understatement about the night of the incident—'Had a bit of a misunderstanding with the kanakas last night', which he still relates to the garden digging, as he does the deaths which he 'thought' occurred—suggest that his 'bois' were given their head to vent their own as well as Leahy's frustration on his penultimate expedition through the Highlands. The Laiyo incident reflects his changing attitude towards the thieving and treacherous 'kanaka' after several years of expeditions and little sign of gold, and his next and last expedition into Enga territory led to the massacre of people at Doi, an event which was perhaps foreshadowed by Laiyo; Danny Leahy described Wiru to me as 'very mean and nasty, as bad as the Wabags [Enga]' (see Connolly and Anderson 1987: 199–200). The alternative is that Leahy did not know what was going on, and could not control his 'gunbois', both of which I consider unlikely given his experience in the Highlands and the type of man he was (see Connolly and Anderson 1987).

Leahy writes of his hopes of discovering an El Dorado in the Highlands: 'This was the area we had conjured up in our imaginations on the strength of sunlight and blues skies over the ranges beyond [the] Goroka-Bena Bena valleys and the number of bodies sailing down the 'Marki' [Markham river]' (Leahy 1991: 47).

Myths of El Dorado inevitably conflict with local imaginings of the world 'over the ranges', and it is ironic that part of Leahy's construction of the romance of the Highlands valleys rests upon the image of dead bodies. Like Captain Cook on his third and final voyage into the Pacific, Leahy in his last patrols was more inclined to express his anger and frustration through violence, not for any irrational reasons but because the explorer was let down by the noble savage who, like gold, could not be found in any quantity.

That something happened at Laiyo is known all over Pangia, although in most conversations on this subject it is only the rape of a woman and the shooting to death of her husband which are reported. It was only in Laiyo that I was told that more people had been killed and injured, as the diary entry for the day supports— 'two of them got bowled over I think'. The Laiyo incident has become over time a mythical event, and certainly supplied a framework in which later interpretations of kiap behaviour were made. Murder and rape certainly took place at Laiyo, but has the imagination played a role in the recollection of this event to exaggerate the killings in line with its present status as a myth, or fiction, of aspects of the Wiru experience of colonialism? Did Leahy imaginatively recreate the events of that night as part of his self-construction as enlightened explorer, avatar of civilization, and recorder of history for posterity? Do Laiyo people have a better memory for what happened in their settlement, or do they have a 'mythical' account of it because of the death and devastation they suffered? From Leahy's perspective, was he fearful of an attack because of the savage actions of his 'bois'? We will never know, but the fascination and limits of oral and written history as 'true' accounts are revealed. By the time Leahy's book is written, a feared attack has become a real one, perhaps justifying in Leahy's own mind what took place, revealing the deception and violence at the heart of colonialism (and recalling the killing at the Iaro river in 1955). Laiyo was the time that Leahy forgot, a colonial amnesia by no means absent during the era of exploration. By contrast, Laiyo stories tell us more about Wiru attitudes towards the beginning of the colonial era than a more literal account ever could and, in this sense, they are fictional but true.[12]

In most of the settlements where I discussed the Laiyo incident, it was the Leahys themselves who were identified as the rapists and killers, mirroring Lariame's claim that it was a white man who shot her husband (even though she could not see outside of the house). By the time I was collecting stories about Laiyo and the 1934 patrol, the Leahys had become a sign in a myth of colonialism. The patrol was not historicized by Wiru as an event which led to later patrols, it was treated as a unique event, a 'mythical reality' (Sahlins 1981). Later patrols in the 1950s were seen to follow each other and to be somehow related; Wiru had by then visited Ialibu station and had some ideas that they were next in line for the European presence. The mythical status of the 1934 expedition is shown by the puzzlement expressed by many older men over why Danny Leahy

---

[12] That Wiru accounts of early (and late) patrols are fabricated is indicated by their reference either to Highlanders in the Leahy patrol who had some knowledge of Wiru, or to Wiru who understood Champion's Imbonggu carriers. This is despite clear statements from both Leahy and Champion that no-one in their party could speak Wiru, that Champion's Imbonggu guides refused to enter into Pangia, and that sign language was the only medium of communication. It may have been necessary to have had some oral communication in Wiru stories so that motivation could be attributed after the fact. In stories about Champion there is a Wiru character called Kapu who speaks some Imbonggu and makes Champion happy by proving himself useful to the patrol by obtaining food and leading them towards the Tua river. Neither the patrol report nor the journal article makes mention of Kapu or of any such assistance.

does not continue to walk the Highlands, instead confining himself to his plantation outside Hagen. They believe him to be a strong and young man, as he was
then.[13] Lariame's question as to whether I was one of the men who killed her
husband could also fit into this scenario. In a way, the Leahys had to be blamed
for the depredation: it was part of a logical working out of the implications of
kiap power, and of their sexual relations with Wiru women, during the colonial
period, and some younger Wiru have since transposed the events of Laiyo to the
1950s period of pacification in Pangia (see Paia 1977). Whether this explains
Lariame's claim that one of the Leahys killed her husband, or her query about
my role in his death, I cannot say. One thing is clear, however; Mick Leahy was
correct when he attributed the deaths to a 'misunderstanding', but not in the
facile manner he intended. It was a misunderstanding in terms of a structure of
the conjuncture, when world-views collide and more is at risk than obtaining
food through trade. When the story of what happened at Laiyo was passed on
from settlement to settlement, it was *kapona* who were blamed. The Leahys were
later said to have been the villains because they were, after all, consummate
kapona, providing an apt metaphor for capitalist penetration into the
Highlands—steel after gold.

Perception and Direction

One more perception of Europeans remains to be considered, and this relates to
patrols which entered into Pangia from the north, along the eastern flanks of Mt
Ialibu. Ivan Champion and Bill Adamson, in their historic l936 Bamu-Purari patrol,
consolidated and expanded the range of the Hides patrol of the previous year (see
Schieffelin and Crittenden 1991), and were also looking for gold (Sinclair 1988).
Walking from the west, they skirted north of Mt Ialibu and then dropped south to
the Poru plateau, naming it after the first Wiru settlement they camped near. They
proceeded in a southeasterly direction, without Champion's Imbonggu guides, who
refused to enter Wiru territory (Champion 1940: 249), along the eastern fringes of
Pangia until they met the Tua River, which they followed to the Erave before
proceeding eastwards to Mt Karimui. At some stage in the early 1950s Fathers Ross
and Krim, from the Catholic mission at Mt Hagen, entered into Pangia illegally
after crossing the eastern slopes of Mt Ialibu and proceeded westwards to mark
some settlements for the Catholics in preparation for the de-restriction of the area,

---

[13] Subsequent to his death, Captain Cook continued to be thought of by some Hawai'ians as the god
Lono, even after other Europeans came to be seen as human (Sahlins 1981). The Leahys and Cook
retained their mythical status because of their role in first encounters, and their importance in influencing the 'reality' which followed; they became mythical templates for an understanding of Europeans.
Perceiving whites as human did not mean that Highlanders were aware of a universal category called
'human', rather that they saw similarities between themselves and Europeans.
   Takuru Wiru also 'fix' Charlie Chaplin in the past. They were once shown one of his films and
could not believe he had since died as an old man. The film was treated as an unique event (which can
be repeated, like a ritual), existing out of time like a myth.

which did not commence until 1960.[14] They were stopped and reported by kiaps camping at Ialibu, but let off with a warning when the administration discovered the identity of their renowned law-breaker. Some Wiru thought that the priests were 'brothers' of Champion and Adamson. Others had no idea what these strange creatures could be; one man even told me he thought they were human because they ate and slept, but it was thought by many of those I interviewed that all these Europeans were *tuanango ipono*, spirits of the dead. Not one characterization of them as *kapona* or sons of the Female Spirit was encountered.

Father Ross's mission was certainly helped by this identification, as some believed the ancestors had returned to guide and help Wiru, in fact to 'tame' them (people were confused by Champion because he seemed to require nothing of them but food, and gave no instructions). Many of the settlements marked by Ross, who hung a rosary around the neck of Karia of Tindua, remained loyal even in the face of stiff competition from other missions many years later. Karia took this as a sign he was to be a 'boss' of his people, and later went to Ialibu station to become a 'Hanuapoliceman', eventually becoming the first president of the Pangia Local Government Council. Ross was fitted into stories about why the mission came to Pangia, and his patrol is widely remembered. While Wiru claim that Ross was given food for nothing, perhaps because of his later identification with the Catholic mission, difficulties of trade with Wiru were again encountered by Champion, if differently and less violently resolved. According to Champion, Wiru were willing to trade food for steel, but only for small piles of sweet potato: 'we asked the natives for food and they brought little bundles of potatoes for which they wanted axes' (Champion 1940: 250).[15] Assuming that a bargaining instinct is more developed with a well-defined trading route (cf. Hughes 1977: 55), it could be argued that Wiru were not as realistic in their expectations of trade as their neighbours. Champion remarks, dryly one suspects, that eventually 'we managed to buy a few pounds with calico and shell' (Champion 1940: 250). But the patrol members were seen as *tuanango ipono*, and Wiru did not see themselves as trading with Champion; rather they were expecting the ancestors to give them wealth. However, the next day the situation changed markedly, but only after Champion had made strenuous efforts to convince Wiru of his desire to trade valuables for food:

[14] A thorough search of Southern Highlands patrol reports and an interview with the late Bishop Bernarding in Mt Hagen failed to provide an accurate date for this journey, although there is a brief mention of a missionary entering into Pangia a year or so before the first post-WWII patrol in 1952 (Mendi PR5/52–53).

[15] Champion (1936: 98) noted the presence of many 'very old' steel axes, whereas less than two years previously the Leahys reported seeing no steel. It is tempting to conclude that it was only in the mid to late 1930s that steel in any quantity appeared on the Poru plateau, especially as the Leahys were further west of Champion and closer to the trade route. That the axes were 'very old' may indicate that they had been well used by previous owners and been a long time in the north–south trade route before being passed on by Kewa to Wiru. The latter were not in a strong bargaining position and received the older, blunter blades that were of less value to Kewa in their trade with Imbonggu and Mendi.

When I saw the exorbitant demands the men were making I told them that we could see that they had plenty of food and that I was willing to pay one tomahawk for a large swag bag of it. I told them in sign language that we would sleep here and if they did not bring food in the morning we would take it ourselves. If they fought us we would fight and I showed them the magazine rifles. They grinned sheepishly. This is the first time on the patrol that I have used threats of any sort . . . At 8 a.m. men and boys gathered around the flys [tents] but they made no attempt to bring any food, though they are quite friendly. We waited an hour and then Adamson and two police took three men and went over to the garden. Adamson showed them that he wanted potatoes and they dug them and filled a bag. When the bag was brought to the camp he gave the owner of the potatoes a large knife. At this several men asked if they would get a knife if they filled the swag, and being answered in the affirmative, went off and brought the bag back full of potatoes. Then they all brought potatoes. By noon we had half a ton bought with seven large knives and five plane irons . . . I do not think they believed us at first that we would pay a knife for a bag of potatoes . . . the difficulty was to get them started. (Champion 1936: 97–8)

These actions marked a gradual realization that if steel goods were to be obtained, the relationship with Europeans would have to involve the inconceivable trade of valuables for food, but for Wiru this did not seem to turn the whites into humans. Champion was less provocative in his patrol than were the Leahys; he brought a different personal history and motivation to contact, and handled the trade situation more sensitively by not forcing the destruction of gardens and demonstrating that the people themselves should dig up sweet potatoes. Stories of the clash with the Leahy expedition must have spread to the settlements where Champion camped, and if the men 'grinned sheepishly' at the display of rifles they must have had some idea of their power (this usually had to be demonstrated by killing pigs or people). Yet no outright hostility was shown by Wiru, and Champion apparently used threats—the first time on the entire patrol—only in frustration at the failure to obtain food and not because Wiru were being surly or unhelpful.

In Champion's case he was heading directly towards the land of the dead, located on the other side of the Tua river to the east of Pangia. This fact no doubt explains the reluctance of Wiru to accompany Champion and guide him in this direction (Frankel [1986: 11] records the trepidation that Huli felt towards Hides's 1935 patrol because it had come *from* the land of the dead). It was reported that Champion became very angry at following dead-end tracks and at people's reluctance to trade and to guide the patrol; he was said to have been shouting 'I am a man'. A few middle-aged men reported that, after the party returned from another fruitless attempt to find a track to the east, houses were broken into or burned by native police, and a garden pillaged and women molested, for which Champion left two pearl-shells. Given accounts of Champion's ability and temperament, it is possible that these claims are influenced by, or confused with events at Laiyo. People were still suspicious of these strange intruders and, given the violence which marked the Leahy patrol, it was perhaps only Champion's handling of the situation—and a fear of rifles—which prevented more deaths (although women did eventually bring food for trade on one occasion, suggesting that Champion had some success in convincing Wiru of his good intentions). These two early patrols were the first phase of a relationship with Europeans, but by the time Champion had departed, the trading relationship, as a context for reading or misreading motivation, had already changed. Yet the Leahy expedition, which foundered on trade or, as Leahy would phrase it, a misunderstanding, is remembered because of Laiyo, while the Champion patrol is largely forgotten and does not figure in Wiru narratives of colonialism, and is unknown outside of the settlements where he camped. A structure of the misjuncture indeed.

Patrolling whites perceived as *tuanango ipono* never experienced hostilities, unlike those seen as *kapona*, even though Wiru were ambivalent about the former and continued to avoid them. The point is, however, that when whites came from the north or east (like the Leahys) they elicited in Wiru a totally different perception from those they had of whites entering from the west or south (like Champion and Adamson). Because wealth, sorcery, and cults came from the latter directions, interpretations of whites as *kapona* and *Ipono Aroane mana* had dramatic consequences for the unfolding of Wiru history, especially as this was also the direction from which came pacification and control, missions and development. The perception of Europeans came to be influenced by the gradual spread of stories and rumours about *kianango* (red men), their power, and their willingness to trade, particularly after the Ialibu patrol post was established in 1953 and more frequent patrols were undertaken into Pangia.[16]

The 1950s—Spirits and Pacification

It seems likely that perceptions of Europeans changed as new information presented itself. As stated above, there was not always a consensus on what Europeans were, and events or discussion could always change people's minds. Wiru who thought the Leahys were spirits of the dead could have altered their opinion after the Laiyo incident, and regarded them as *kapona*. When the Leahys washed in the Polu river, people saw the greyish, soapy film floating downstream and concluded that they were dead, as the suds were thought to come from their decomposing bodies (cf. Connolly and Anderson 1987: 46). This activity of the Leahys could also have changed the perceptions of some Wiru as to their nature (similar bathing by Champion and Adamson confirmed their identity as 'dead', causing fear and consternation among observers).

---

[16] The importance of the direction from which whites came is evidenced by another reference to Tempikene. In 1952, before the Iaro river incident of 1955, a patrol arrived in Tempikene from the north and had a relatively friendly reception from 'unarmed timid natives', with enough food obtained in ten minutes (Mendi PR5/52–53). Unfortunately I was only in Tempikene a brief time and neglected to ask what perceptions were of this patrol but, in line with the argument, one would expect the kiaps to have been seen at least ambiguously, if not specifically as *tuanango ipono* or *Ipono Aroane mana*, and not as *kapona*. The reception of patrols at Tempikene after 1955 was, not surprisingly, 'decidedly cool' (Ialibu PR3/55–56).

The association of Europeans with the dead, water-courses, and the Female Spirit, had important implications for the decade of pacification in the 1950s, and links into my interpretation of the significance of *kapona* perceptions in the creation of a 'myth' of colonialism. The connection between whites, rivers, and a category of spirit not yet considered, water spirits (*uali*), now needs to be discussed:

> They [Europeans] were spoken of as *uele nekenea* 'coming along the water-courses'. This phrase likens, if not equates, them with the ghosts of the dead who travel in this way out of and back into local group territories. All their goods and wealth were held to have come by the same route, and their arrival was also in some way conflated with the myth of the Female Spirit . . . A white woman known as *Mis Aroa* (i.e. Mrs. Woman) was said to be trying to make her way into Pangia, but was stumbling on the rocky limestone paths. Songs were sung for her which were influenced by half-heard versions of mission hymns, requesting her to come . . . The general point here is that one way or another Europeans were associated with existing categories of spirit entities. (A. J. Strathern 1984: 20–1)

It may not be true that Europeans were only 'associated with existing categories of spirit entities' in so far as whites as *kapona* were linked to sorcery and perhaps cannibalism, categories of human action. If this linkage was originally based on the *maua* spirit, then Andrew Strathern's statement would be correct, with *kapona* later becoming an amalgam of spirit and sorcery beliefs. Regardless of association with spirit entities, the nature of *kapona*, as seemingly malevolent and/or non-reciprocal, like *uali*, could be explained in terms of the flexibility of the 'traditional' belief system.

This amalgam may be the reason why, despite a strong connection between Europeans, water-courses, and wealth, I never encountered a direct statement that whites were thought to be *uali* (a category of spirit only). One researcher, however, did manage to obtain a statement that whites were perceived as *uali*, whose skins would turn black if they remained in the sun (Barham 1984: 19). If perceptions of whites as *uali* were rare, examples of strong links between the two often occur in exegesis. My favourite concerns a Wesleyan missionary who, in driving along the road to Takuru, knocked an *uali* off his bicycle. The missionary stopped and removed its special netbag, *pindunu ka*, which contained its objects of power used to inflict sickness and death, and continued to the mission station at Takuru. The *uali* left some money on his pillow (shades of the tooth fairy!) in order to redeem its netbag. The two became friends and the *uali* lived in a pond close to the missionary's house (one missionary was mistaken for *uali* when he swam in the Polu river).

That a missionary entered into an alliance with an *uali*, a dangerous and, in Christian terms, 'evil' spirit, is very interesting but not surprising if one refers back to what was written above on the possibility of *ulo* being based on the *maua* spirit, which had the capacity to transform into *uali*. The alliance was another resonance of *kapona*, in the same sense that the sound of aeroplanes was compared to that of rushing waters, 'often taken as a warning . . . [and] likened to the sound of loud wailing by a group in grief' (Kerr 1987: 112). *Uali* are not entirely outside the moral order, for they may protect people who reside near their watery habitats (Kerr 1984: 6). In a sense, *uali* were, and perhaps in a muted sense still are, a source of Europeans' power and wealth. The precedent for alliance with a relatively benevolent *uali* existed before white arrival.

There are several indications of an association of whites with *uali*. One is that, prior to de-restriction, some settlements in the south of Pangia experienced collective outbursts of '*uali* madness' among young men, who became 'possessed' in the manner of hostile spirits (A. J. Strathern 1977: 138; Clark 1992). *Uali* could possess people to drive them temporarily mad, which later gave those afflicted power as ritual specialists (Kerr 1984: 6), and it may be that madness was a commentary on the experience of European power and its desirability (Clark 1985: 104–7; 1992), related to the wealth which 'flowed' along riparian conduits. Another indication is the conduct of mass baptisms in some settlements. During these affairs in Takuru, those to be immersed in pools wore long white shirts, supplied by the mission. Europeans were associated with the pale-skinned *uali* and baptism may be understood in terms of this connection; that is, the 'power' of baptism made Takuruns 'like whites' (see Chapter 3)—emphasized by donning white clothing—through a link to the power of spirits in a ceremony held in a typical *uali* habitat, small ponds. A Catholic missionary told me that people became almost hysterical if they could not get the right clothes for baptism.

To continue, kiaps were supposed to have put chemicals into the river which 'tamed' Wiru when they drank its water, and it was about this time that several sightings of white men suddenly emerging from the river were reported. White ghosts have also been seen driving trucks, an important symbol of power and wealth, which disappear into culverts and follow the river downstream, the direction of the land of the dead. The *uali* was riding a bicycle, another European symbol, which confirms again the connection made between whites, *uali*, and sources of power and wealth. While whites may have at one time been thought of as only one entity (as *kapona* for example), by the time Pangia station was established in 1961 it seems likely that many of these perceptions had combined. One can also see why, if whites were the sons of the Female Spirit, their presence was 'in some way conflated with the myth of the Female Spirit', and why it was that a *Mis Aroa*, a white woman, was attempting to enter Pangia.[17] If Europeans were white, then so was their mother. Some understanding of why Christianity is today practised as a cult is also obtained (see Chapters 4 and 6). That versions of prayers were said to entice the Female Spirit into Pangia indicated the initial (and lasting)

---

[17] Sillitoe remarks that Wola people attacked patrols because they thought that whites were spirits, and relates this to a belief in the 'malicious spirit of a white woman' (1979: 16, n.14). Unfortunately, no more is written so any connection to a 'Mis Aroa' type of figure or to a Female Spirit cult is unknown, as is the nature of the spirits with which whites were confused.

cult perceptions of Christianity (cf. Wagner 1967: 2, where he writes of Daribi performing rituals in order to attract Europeans to Karimui).[18]

There was another reason for the expectation of a white woman arriving in Pangia, which has to be related to the importance of prophetic dreaming in Wiru society. Dreams which promise wealth or predict events such as sorcery attacks, are sent by Akolali, who has a female counterpart, rarely mentioned, called Akolaroa (Kerr 1984: 7). Before whites pacified Pangia, Akolaroa appeared to certain men in dreams as a long-haired white woman (long-haired because kiaps were seen to have long hair). It seems the gender of the dream-sender was the result of a connection already made between whites and the Female Spirit. As a consequence of these prophetic dreams, a supremely metaphysical interpretation emerging out of a 'structure of the conjuncture', Europeans were identified with the future and with the true locus of wealth and power.

The rapid pacification of Pangia, and its equally rapid acceptance of Christianity, cannot be explained solely by the greater power and superior technology of Europeans (cf. A. J. Strathern 1984: 21–2). It was the resonances created between whites, spirits, God, wealth, and cults, which amplified the perceived power and prestige of Europeans, and accounted for Wiru fears and expectations of their presence. This was certainly a factor in the obedience shown towards administration and mission directives in respect of development and conversion. The point is worth making that in the colonial encounter the European perspective was based on racial distinctions, 'race' here defined by certain types of behaviour exhibited by 'kanakas':

Black skins are the hallmark of the sun and an evolutionary history in the tropics. Technology and culture cannot be separated, and the difference between the people of the sun and those farther away from the equator is the difference between the bow and arrow and the hydrogen bomb.

We were surviving [in Highlands exploration] by virtue of our presumed magic, superior mentality, and our firearms, in that order. (Leahy 1991: 244, 67)

For fringe and central Highlanders the criteria for differentiation were influenced, to varying degrees, by practice and myth cosmologies. Also, for Wiru, there was a spatial or directional dimension to the interpretation of the white presence.[19]

The Appropriation of the Colonial 'Other'

I will open this section by returning to Tempikene in 1959, when there was a sequel to the Iaro river incident of 1955. Tempikene with its allies, Puluparu and

---

[18] Daribi equate their culture hero Souw with God (Wagner 1972: 19), and the first Europeans with Souw, so it is possible to see why they performed rituals to attract whites, and how these perceptions would have affected the colonial and mission experience (see also Wagner 1979).

[19] Of the four early patrols into the Miyanmin area the only one attacked came from the south, the direction of Telefolmin enemies (Morren 1981: 52). Morren makes no mention of what people thought Europeans were. Wagner (1979: 142) states that the Karimui area was difficult to pacify from the south, the direction of Pawaiian enemies.

Mamuane, decided to attack the settlement of Pugi. In many respects this was a typical Wiru raid, to avenge a previous one by Pugi on Tempikene. The difference, however, is that this time the raiders decided to go as *kapona*; some of the men wound strips of steel from tin cans around their wrists, or wore whole tin cans as wristbands, prior to leaving for the attack. The raid was successful, many women were raped, Pugi was considerably devastated, and women and pigs were abducted and taken back to Tempikene. It was believed that if the men acted like *kapona* they would increase their power and become invincible, to which end steel wristbands were worn. This was for the same reason as the woven cane variety—they were indicators of 'powerful' men and as such could infuse the power of *kapona* into the raiders. Similar appropriations occurred in other parts of the Highlands:

The useless end of the matchstick . . . which the strangers had thrown away, was taken by the people, who said, 'These men from heaven threw this thing away so we must take it and eat it later, and we will become like them. And when we go to fight our enemies we will win because this thing is going to help us'. (Connolly and Anderson 1987: 55)[20]

The success of Tempikene *kapona* was short-lived. Pugi sent word to Ialibu station and a patrol was soon mounted to punish Tempikene and arrest those involved. A letter from the Assistant District Officer accompanied the resultant patrol report, stating that Tempikene people 'have a reputation for truculance [sic], having attacked Mr Corrigan's patrol in 1955.' The punitive expedition consisted of two kiaps, sixteen police, and fifty carriers. Following are daily extracts from the patrol report written by officer Q. Anthony (Ialibu PR4/58–59):

Patrol Officer Lucas with 5 police [walked] across valley to inspect devastated area. Considerable amount of damage done. Spoke to a gathering of Pugi natives, and commenced investigation into the raid and abductions.

Surprised and arrested two male natives on the track [to Tempikene]. Many others fled at the patrol's approach after watching our progress from surrounding ridges . . . Patrol Officer Lucas, 14 police, 1 interpreter and 3 Village Constables set out to make arrests after much vain shouting by the interpreters failed to induce the natives the patrol was seeking to surrender themselves. Three hours arduous chase resulted in only 3 more arrests. The rest of the group have fled across the deep gorge of the Iaro river to their allies the Puruparu [Puluparu] who shouted threats and insults across the gorge at the patrol. No sign of women or pigs.

Fourteen police sent out in two parties. Self spoke to the Purubaru across the Iaro river through an interpreter, pointing out the folly of continued resistance. Received in exchange lies, threats and insults. Police parties returned late afternoon with more prisoners.

---

[20] Compare with: 'Chimbu would pick up shreds and fragments of the white man: tin-can tops, pieces of metal and beads, rags, vests and paint were worn with pride' (Brown 1973: 7); 'They [Kuma] used fragments of European material culture—a bayonet, a cartridge, a piece of newspaper, a scrap of European cloth—as symbols of the power and wealth they hoped to gain' (Reay 1959: 201); 'Anything they [Europeans] touched would turn into a valuable . . . natives collected "whatever empty tins or bits of paper [were] left behind"' (Salisbury 1962: 114).

Self with 10 police and an interpreter climbed down almost vertical limestone cliffs into the gorge. All bridges destroyed by the Purubaru. Party ambushed by band of Tempikeni men in a narrow, rocky defile . . . attackers disappeared into the forest after a shot was fired over their heads at a range of fifteen yards . . . small groups of arrived men retreating slowly before the police party, shouting threats. Police surrounded several houses, but were able to make only one arrest.

Two strong police parties out all day. Returned late afternoon with more Tempikeni prisoners.

Police parties out again. Returned late afternoon with more prisoners . . . both officers remained in camp.

Two parties of 6 police sent ahead to try to make more arrests . . . At 1515 hrs report received that V. C. Iamuna and Const. Opehema wounded by axe and one native received bullet wound in the foot. Wounded carried in to camp shortly afterwards and attended to . . . Payment of compensation, pigs, axes, etc. made to Pugi natives in afternoon.

Tempikene informants stated that much of Tempikene was burnt to the ground and looted, a tactic of pacification practised in other parts of the Southern Highlands but one seldom mentioned in patrol reports. The fact that compensation of pigs and other valuables was made to Pugi suggests that houses certainly were pillaged by the patrol. The extracts indicate the alacrity and severity with which the administration methodically imposed its will, and tried to initiate peace through its own version of exchange. The resentment towards the patrol is clearly indicated in the patrol report.

Marilyn Strathern (1984: 21) states that 'a construction of otherness' was a feature of European penetration in the Highlands, with people acting out these constructions in an attempt to gain equivalence with whites. Being *kapona* was certainly an aspect of this 'construction'; to expand on the reasons for acting in this fashion, which were related to the resistance shown towards the Ialibu patrol, it was to increase their power and maintain their autonomy and control. The axe assailant told the Mendi administration that he acted as he did because 'he does not like the Government running his affairs' (letter accompanying Ialibu PR4/58–59). People wanted to appropriate the power of *kapona* but they did not want its presence. Tempikene and its allies were the only groups to put up such a spirited resistance to colonization, but eventually even they learnt that to be *kapona* was impossible; it was an attribute of Europeans which reinforced their power and led to the eventual acceptance of administration and mission authority throughout the Pangia area. Force was certainly a factor in the succumbing of Tempikene to an external and intrusive control but, as indicated above, this particular 'structure of the conjuncture' was such that Tempikene's resistance was only a postponement of an inevitable event. Force was not such a significant factor in the pacification of other Wiru settlements. They all came, including Tempikene, to actually *desire* the white presence as kiaps and missionaries. This desire accompanied the realization that Europeans and their power were more than *kapona*.

Acceptance of colonial control was a final confirmation of the direction from which power and wealth were flowing. It was as if Wiru, through their later

engagement in development and conversion, and by acting on various interpretations of Europeans, were ritually realigning themselves with the true source in the
same way as people who engage in cargo cults (cf. M. Strathern 1984: 21; A. J.
Strathern 1984: 21; Chapter 3). This realignment had profound consequences for
the ontological and structural conditions of Wiru society, which will be discussed
in other chapters. The letter from the Assistant District Officer which accompanied the report on the retributive patrol to Tempikene states that, 'As soon as staff
is available, it is proposed to establish a patrol post in the Wiru Division near
Kauwo. This should bring the whole of the Wiru Division to a complete understanding of the aims of the Administration' (Ialibu PR4/58–59). The colonial
years for Wiru were a struggle to completely understand what pacification and
submission to an external control entailed, even if they came to realize 'the folly of
continued resistance'.

Human, all too Human

So how did Wiru finally come to comprehend whites as human? Just as there was
no one interpretation of Europeans, there is more than one answer to this question.
The reasons given by the few men who thought Champion was human were sometimes advanced—closer observation of white behaviour and anatomy yielded the
obvious conclusions. But there was more involved here than a pragmatic empiricism as observation takes place in a cultural and historical context. For many, these
apparently empirical claims could be made only after the missionaries arrived,
living with the people and treating them as such, unlike the authoritarian kiaps who
maintained their distance from Wiru. It was the increasing interaction with all
types of Europeans that rendered them human, yet this construction was influenced by a cosmology founded on practice, generating its own myth of colonialism.

When I asked the question in Laiyo which starts this section I thought that,
because of their unhappy first encounter, I would receive a reply more revealing of
the perceived essence of change. However, I received a somewhat enigmatic
response: it was 'because their arms bend', or because the whites were revealed to
have elbows, *tuku*. The expression used is *yono-ka tuku kora tukuko*, 'hand elbow
there breaks'. *Tuku-* is also a verb, relating, among other things, to ceremonial
exchange (Kerr 1987: 105). It was explained that their arms were 'bent' because
they exchanged with Wiru, a recognition of humanness that was also extended to
native police and carriers. This expression is delightfully evocative of the division
of one into two, and of the complementarity and interdependence of two parts—
such as the upper arm and the wrist, with their connecting joint the elbow.
'Showing the hand' is another expression for gift-giving (A. J. Strathern 1984: 48),
extending on the 'elbow' metaphor. Hence Wiru, like Melpa, based their ultimate
perceptions on practice. If Europeans exchanged then they were human, and they
received more back than 'lies, threats and insults'.

The importance of origin stories for the reception of Europeans in Pangia is not to be discounted, but it is worth emphasizing the 'practice' view of Wiru in comparison with, for example, that of the Huli, who used the Bible to explain, with reference to their own mythology, why pacification and missionization had occurred (Frankel 1986: 23–6). Using the Bible as 'charter' is largely unknown in Pangia, where practice rather than myth informs behaviour and interpretation. The Wiru colonial world was understood more by acting in it than by reference to a mythological time although, as the text makes clear, these actions may help to construct myths. Understandings such as *kapona* or sons of the Female Spirit did not simply disappear when these observations were made. They continue to inform at a cognitive level the view of whites as creatures superior in power and wealth, not merely human but 'men of steel' (Glasse [n.d.: 23] refers to a similar view of European superiority among the Huli in the 1970s). It is worth stating once more that because central Highlanders and Wiru came to know whites in terms of a practice cosmology does not mean that they are more secular or pragmatic than fringe Highlanders. The Wiru case shows how interpretations made on this basis may actually help to create myths (or fictions) which can influence the course of development, even though there were no cosmogonic myths into which whites could be fitted.

Wiru now know Europeans as *kianango*, or 'red men', an appellation widespread in the Highlands (Finney 1973: 139; Newman 1965: 13). This term came into popular usage in the early 1960s with the increasing perception of whites as human. Yet Wiru describe European skin colour as white, and it seems that the use of red is less descriptive than metaphorical as, in common with other Highlanders, red is a colour associated with wealth (A. J. Strathern 1979–80: 162). 'Red men' may even continue to relate Europeans to ghosts, as both are described throughout the Highlands as red or light-skinned (Connolly and Anderson 1987: 6, 8). To reiterate, while Wiru came to acknowledge the humanness of Europeans, this interpretive change was not based on a purely pragmatic empiricism. All of the terms by which whites were and are known have their referents in (spirit and non-spirit) power, maleness, and wealth. The use of *kianango* merely reflects a more modern interpretation for the difference between Wiru and whites. For Wiru, even though they posit a radical disjunction between then and now, 'first contact' and the perceptions which followed are not relegated to what Westerners would call history. They continue to reach out from the past into the present, and extend their influence into the future.

First Contact, Again

Sahlins argues that the distinction between system and event (culture and history) is false (1985: xvii) because they are bound together in an 'indissoluble synthesis' (1985: 156). The use of the term 'first contact' illustrates this convincingly, for it implies, by suggesting that these encounters are historical events uninfluenced by culture, a disjunction between culture and history which is totally misleading.

Tempikene had twenty-six years after Kaparoi in which to reflect on the nature of *kapona*, which informed the hostile meeting when it eventually occurred. Culturally derived perceptions from the European side also influenced these first encounters. For example, the Leahy brothers' view of Wiru as a certain type of 'sullen and suspicious' native (Leahy and Crain 1937: 227) led them indirectly to create the Laiyo incident, in which up to five people died. A chance meeting perhaps, but one structured by cultural perceptions on both sides. Wiru, because they treated the Leahys with the respect and awe due to spirits, or the fear and distrust due to *kapona*, initiated a view of themselves as 'mean and nasty', reason enough for their death. A metaphysical experience clashed with Western prejudices and ethnocentric assumptions.

Marilyn Strathern (1990) assesses the notion of a 'structure of the conjuncture', and suggests that its mediation of the relationship between an event and system may not be applicable to Melanesia. She suggests reasons for the nonchalance which accompanied the amazement at the advent of Europeans. Hageners continually amaze themselves through their collective activities such as exchange and cult ceremony. Strauss (1990: 248), in reference to *moka*, writes, 'The "whole world" sets out and comes to this *kona* [ceremonial green] to look in amazement at the great numbers of things and animals—such a huge amount all in one place! To think that this is possible!' The rapid engagement of Hageners in mundane exchange with whites/spirits, whose arrival amazed them like a cult performance, is explained by Marilyn Strathern in terms of the event of 'first contact' already being contained within the artefacts and images created through such acts as exchange. The appearance of Europeans, although unexpected, was produced by people themselves. She discusses the readiness with which coastal Madang people exchanged with Miklouho-Maclay, but it is this example which points to the complexities of a pan-Melanesian explanation of events within images, for exchange with Miklouho-Maclay apparently did not detract from his perception as a local deity, whereas European exchange with Highlanders rendered both parties human. There are differences, of course, as Miklouho-Maclay's singularity and relative immobility engendered a perception of him as unencompassed by Madang contexts of human exchange. Yet there is something different about coastal interactions with whites, including the recurrence of cargo cults, and Highlanders' exchanges with Europeans, and the distinction made between fringe and central Highlands points to one of the ways in which this difference could be usefully examined (see Chapter 3).

Wiru were certainly amazed by the Leahys and their display of wealth, but they would not exchange with them, nor initially with Champion's patrol, and difficulties with trade continued into the 1950s. If people in the settlements that Champion passed through in 1936 thought that he was human after he finally made them engage in trade, then this news was not passed on to other settlements; Takuru people continued to think of Europeans as non-human into the 1950s. Exchange finally converted whites into men, but why did it take so long? It may be that the local particularities of exchange need to be taken into account in assessing the universality of Marilyn Strathern's claim (1990) for the European advent not being an 'interpreted happening', a mediated relationship between a chance encounter and system, but a potential within the performance of exchange or cult. Another factor may have been the competing interpretations of the nature of Europeans.

One way of dealing with Marilyn Strathern's observations is to make the concept of a 'structure of the conjuncture' both more general and specific. It was the various Wiru perceptions of the first Europeans, as events and categories, which set the scene for a later history of relationships with kiaps, missionaries, and development. Yet there was no one 'structure of the conjuncture' or, for that matter, 'misjuncture'. It was possible for successive patrols in the one area to be remembered (Leahy) and largely forgotten (Champion). The history of exploration and pacification in Pangia combined with changing perceptions of Europeans and power to produce a colonization experience and culture peculiar to the district. The 'interested action of the historic agents' (Sahlins 1985: xiv) spanned not one moment in time but a 'first contact' over decades, from Kaparoi in 1929 to the early 1960s. There was an accumulation of 'first contacts', as it were, with the 'structure of the conjuncture' changing and modifying over time with different dialogic encounters between Wiru, patrols, and contexts. The course of development and the nature of Pangia's dependency, before and after independence, cannot be explained without reference to the ways in which Wiru produce and understand their own history, out of rolling structure. This chapter has considered Wiru reactions to colonial power and knowledge, how they came to some 'understanding of the aims of the Administration', and it remains to be considered how power and knowledge acted upon them. In other words, how colonial history produces colonized culture.

PART II

3

'An Unsettled and Vicious People'

For one who first arrived in Pangia five years after independence in 1975, colonialism remains a difficult experience to imagine and write about. Many Christian missions were still operating in 1980, and indeed still arriving, giving a flavour of the colonial scene but nevertheless making it difficult to put oneself in the place of Wiru as they experienced its full onslaught. I remember walking through Gelote in 1992, an important Huli ritual centre once marked by a corridor of huge and majestic hoop pines, long since cut down by the Catholic mission for building purposes so that only their decomposing stumps remained. The area was totally overgrown and abandoned; the bridge across a creek which led to a sacred cave connected to the root of the earth was no longer there, and the tree which joined all the rivers and channelled their flow to heaven, from which water returned as rain, had broken in half. I tried to conjure up in my mind what this place would have looked like when various rituals of sacrifice involved the participation of Huli, Bosavi, and Duna men in large-scale fertility ceremonials. Quite simply, I could not do it; all I could see was the rotting supports of colonialism, the rubbish of the West thrown in my face, to paraphrase Lévi-Strauss in his search for the authentic primitive.

Similarly, to imagine colonialism (and 'tradition') is for me barely possible; I was not there to witness the authoritarian and almost feudal rule of the kiap and his native police (or, for that matter, the practice of elaborate fertility spirit cults). All I can try to do is paint a picture with the few colours in my possession, creating a broad sweep of canvas but missing many of the finer features of colonialism, such as the ontological changes accompanying the Wiru experience of pacification and evangelism, and of involvement in development projects. The colonial past had disappeared by the time I arrived in Pangia, and the present was already leaking into the future, creating a jarring sense of discontinuity. In writing of this past I envisage my role as akin to that of a piano-tuner; it is to be hoped that I make it sound good, but whether the experience of music can be produced is left to the reader to decide.

In this chapter I want to consider the discourses of colonialism, at least as they manifested themselves in Pangia, to try to understand their logic and momentum, as well as the coercive appeal of colonialism to Wiru. To do this I will present a range of quotes from patrol reports, with commentary where necessary, and examine what they reveal about the nature of colonial power/knowledge and its deployment. Pacification took place within the context of Australia's colonial mandate to control, develop, and improve the lives of its Papuan subjects. There was an inevitability to this project, and I doubt that many kiaps reflected critically upon their mission, succumbing to the rhetoric of development as a kind of manifest destiny.[1] Anthropology played its role in this project, as many of the young men who became kiaps were trained at the Australian School of Pacific Administration (ASOPA), where notions of social structure, kinship, local politics, and so on, were taught by anthropologists. It is no accident that sections in patrol reports around the time of pacification in the 1950s are labelled 'anthropology' and are usually concerned with leadership and land tenure, promptly disappearing once the subject is sufficiently 'known' (that is, colonized) to engage and control his or her body and labour in development.[2]

What also becomes colonized is the landscape, by patrolling, mapping, and census-taking, an institutional trilogy suggesting the fantasy of a colonial panopticon. The construction of roads, bridges, census districts, and so on, are also related to what Anderson (1991: 163–4) calls the imaginings of the colonial state in respect of its creation of, and control over ethnolinguistic dominions. Road-building is the end of colonial romance and the start of a new construction of the 'other' as a productive subject in a terrain transformed by colonialism, as the 'unknown' spaces in early maps were gradually filled in. The census completed the project of the map, giving political content through name, counting, age, and gender to its formal topography (Anderson 1991: 174), and enabling a more efficient surveillance and regulation of the population. Earlier patrol accounts, especially of first meetings with savages, referred to the 'Native Situation', and often allowed a hint of romance with descriptions of mythology and savage practices. The postwar period marked a different kind of colonialism in Papua New Guinea, no longer one of exploration, possession, and rule but of development and self-government (perceived by many Highlanders as an abandonment). While kiaps were rudimentarily trained in anthropology, the position of government anthropologist in Papua—a romantic appointment emblematic of another era and a different valuation of knowledge about the 'other'—had disappeared. In his memoirs of life as a patrol officer in the 1930s, J. K. McCarthy (1963: 15) writes that 'those were the days before "colonialism" had become a dirty word.'

Colonialism is an inherently paternalistic endeavour, couched in terms of duty and responsibility; but New Guinea was also Australia's nearest land mass to the north, a buffer zone against Asia, with strong possibilities for white investment. The rate of pacification and control in the Southern Highlands would undoubtedly have been different if its gas, oil, and gold deposits had been discovered earlier

[1] Very few of the kiaps actually wrote about their experiences in the Southern Highlands. One exception was Jack Hides, who had a romantic turn of mind; perhaps not coincidentally, he reflected on the long-term influence of pacification: 'We will have to give them a lot if they are not to be disillusioned; for if industry cannot be brought to them by the wealth of their land, then I do not see how we are going to give it to them' (quoted in Schieffelin and Crittenden 1991: 111).
[2] The negligible power of Pangia leaders was a worry for some of the early patrol officers, who knew the vital role of strong government appointments in consolidating control (Ialibu 2/54–55).

Timbu cult, after its removal from the cult house, on the ceremonial green where the kiaps would camp, at which point the cult emblems of fertility were paraded and attached to the pole, and it is quite likely that flag-raising was to some extent understood in terms of their own cult practices. Wiru were not too far from the mark when they confused an animate flag 'boss' with an icon of the power of the colonial state. Just as Wiru were controlled by kiaps, the latter were controlled by the flag.

Interestingly, the above quote was written by the same kiap who wrote the preceding patrol report extract, exemplifying the ambiguous and mystified nature of colonialism to those who promoted it—as a friendly but powerful force intent on achieving its aims with or without native consent. The reason for the eventual failure of colonialism in Pangia was due to a misrecognition of the abstract and material benefits that Wiru thought they would acquire from development. How, after all, could the administration know that Wiru wanted to be Europeans? I have written in Chapter 2 about the Tempikene men who went on a raid as *kapona*/Europeans, but there was a strange sequel to this affair. About a year later some Wiru men from south of the Iaro river, in company with Kewa men and led by a village constable and a medical orderly, raided Tempikene, tied up men— including the Tempikene village constable with his own chain of office—stole pigs, entered houses and broke bows and arrows, and raped a woman. The remarkable thing was that they did this armed not with weapons, but with the canes that marked the status of the 'bosboi', a European mission appointment that exerted a powerful attraction in Pangia (Ialibu PR10/59–60).[5] Tempikene, intimidated by an administration retributive patrol of the year before, seems to have offered little resistance to this small army of 'bosbois' because of its government overtones— the cane was emblematic of colonial power. What is indicated by this event is that the idea of 'being' European developed early in Pangia's colonial history, eventu- ally becoming a transformation attempted through human labour. I will return to this topic after discussing administrative attitudes to Wiru and their labour in development.

It is undoubtedly true that by 1961 the majority of Wiru were welcoming of the prospects of external control and acquiescent to the 'right' of the administration to interfere. To a large extent, they were unusual in this attitude: 'I was struck by the marked contrast of attitude between these people and those of, say, Mendi. The Wiru speakers are cooperative, keen and certainly not afraid of doing a bit of work [but] they are not really aware of the outside world' (Pangia PR3/61–62). Many Wiru visited Ialibu station in the 1950s—on special occasions such as the arrival of visiting dignitaries a thousand or more would turn up (Ialibu PR2/58–59)—and voluntarily participated in the building of station infrastructure for payment in

---

[5] The administration was concerned about the proliferation of 'bosbois' in Pangia, a practice that they regarded as assuming 'ridiculous proportions' (Ialibu PR2/58–59). The cane-carrying 'bosbois' were another emulation of European power, one that the kiaps could not understand.

paint, beads and salt (some finding employment as domestics at the Bible mission in Ialibu and Tambul).

The Wiri-Taru are a very cooperative people and they have pitched in with a will and are doing a very good job on the [Ialibu] roads. (Mendi PR3/55–56)

The attitude of voluntarily seeking contact demonstrates a keenness and a willingness on behalf of the natives themselves to accept Administration control ... It was, in a way, surprising to note that even in areas which had never been visited by a patrol before there appeared to be a widespread acceptance of the Administration and the system of law and order which the Administration is endeavouring to introduce. (Ialibu PR2/58–59)

I doubt if there is any [other] area in the Territory [of Papua] where the entire population is in agreement with the Administration's aims. (Assistant District Commissioner, cited in Pangia PR4/66–67)

And, from the Director of Native Affairs, 'excellent contact over the past decade has had its results of amicable relations and unusual cooperation from the people' (Pangia PR1/61–62). After complete de-restriction in June 1962 the administration saw a bright future for Wiru if the levels of hard work, self-help, and government assistance were maintained:

I predict within 10 years the area will be really moving and prosperity will result. (Pangia PR4/66–67)

Wiru are a keen progressive lot who are on the threshold of a great leap forward both economically and socially. (Pangia PR4/66–67)

the Pangia area is poised on the brow of the hill and once over should gain momentum rapidly. (Pangia PR3/71–72)

The patrol reports are littered with these kinds of positive comments about Wiru—almost an administration 'cargo cult'—many of whom helped build the road between Ialibu and Pangia that facilitated the eventual establishment of Pangia patrol post and airstrip. A cursory reading of patrol reports from other parts of the Southern Highlands reveals that Wiru were quite exceptional in terms of the reception they gave to colonialism: 'It seems that at last we have found a Southern Highlands group which is prepared to cooperate enthusiastically with the administration. It appears that climate, population density and the attitude of the people are such that the Wiru area could be developed quickly and become the showplace of this District' (Ialibu PR6/60–61). And, as reported in the very first patrol from Pangia station: 'Even before the patrol arrived at Pangia, the local people on their own initiative had cleared the topsoil off a section of the airstrip site some 1500' long by 300' wide' (Pangia PR1/61–62).

Clearly, something unusual was happening in Pangia that related to 'the attitude of the people', but what exactly? Wiru were in a relatively disadvantaged position in terms of precolonial trade, and were receptive to new cults and innovation (Clark 1985). 'The people want the road as quickly as possible so that 'their plantation' can be started and hence prosperity and development will follow' (Pangia PR8/65–66).

Prior to the establishment of Pangia patrol post the propaganda tours of the administration promised peace and development, appointing village constables to ensure such things as the upkeep of resthouses and the provision of food—'visible reminders to all of the Administration's interest and authority . . . appointed to assist in the just and proper administration of the new system of law and order' (Ialibu PR1/56–57, PR2/58–59). Roadwork actually commenced around Kauwo settlement in 1955, and road camps were established and manned by native constabulary, reportedly having a settling influence on the Wiru (Ialibu PR1/56–57); the Ialibu-Pangia road was only several miles short of completion in 1960 (Ialibu PR5/59–60). Medical patrols gave over 10,000 anti-yaws injections, and the rapid results of this intervention must have impressed Wiru with the power of the administration. Warfare was actively suppressed, with large numbers of men being sentenced to three months' hard labour for riotous behaviour. Rumours of a new cult accompanied these patrols, and at least two missions had illegally entered the area, one to entice young men to leave Pangia for 'education' at mission stations in Kaupena. Wiru society was in a disordered state as the 1960s approached, with wandering patrols demonstrating the power of firearms and forcing enemies to make peace through exchange;[6] returning mission evangelists speaking of a new cult; visits to Ialibu station revealing a different world of airstrips, missions, and European wealth; the influenza epidemic and its link to perceptions of a dramatic increase in *ulo* sorcery; all undoubtedly contributing to a readiness to embrace the colonial order and its vague promises of a rosy future (cf. Frankel 1986 for the Huli).

Sinclair, one of the few kiaps to write of his experiences in the Southern Highlands, comments (1981: 8) on the lack of an adequate plan for the administration of PNG by the Department of District Services and the Department of Native Affairs: 'The result was the development of a largely unco-ordinated, compartmentalized system of administration. Personalities doubtless played a part.' This view was undoubtedly valid for the Southern Highlands, and certainly applied to Pangia as its kiaps pursued their own development initiatives with little liaison with other areas or District headquarters; their concerns were with Pangia, not the Southern Highlands as a whole. Two kiaps played a significant role in Pangia's particular colonial history: Brian O'Neill, who established Pangia station and whose intention was to turn the region into a 'showcase', and Peter Barber

---

[6] In just one patrol report the 'suggestions' of the patrol, hardly likely to be interpreted as such by Wiru, included that: 'To date there has been no report received that the Poreio's have made the compensation payments recommended. Should they ignore the advice given them the matter will be pursued by the next patrol to visit the area.' The patrol was able to effect a settlement of the matter and . . . the men concerned in the killing made a compensation payment to the relatives of the deceased . . . in the presence of the patrol's officers: 'At the suggestion of the patrol some of the Porogo concerned in last year's murders have paid compensation to the relatives of those who were killed' (Ialibu PR2/58–59).

who, for over a decade during which he rose to the position of Assistant District Commissioner in Pangia, planned and forced its development through his single-mindedness and strength of personality. For good or ill, Barber was responsible for guiding Pangia through an intensive decade of development and self-help schemes. He is remembered by Wiru as a domineering and forceful character, for the most part in a positive sense although many people resented his coercive and aggressive approach to involving Wiru in his plans for Pangia's future.

Wiru, in a sense, had development thrust upon them. The technique for administering this colonial desire was known as the 'kiap system' of hands-on development, which basically meant that people 'must be politically, economically and socially adjusted' (Pangia PR1/70–71; PR3/71–72)—in a word, social engineering. Initiative and direction came very much from the top down, and this had obvious consequences, not the least of which was the creation of dependency among Wiru. Many of the patrols were to outline and reinforce administration intentions and its promises for 'a better way of life' based upon the rhetoric of self-help:

The people were told (a) that we had started in the dark and progressed along a 'road' of law and order, developmental roads [of] economic growth towards a clearing where the people could see that the 'road' was good, straight and indeed the only one possible if they were to progress; (b) that they could now continue along this road in sunlight and see where it would take them; (c) that Australia had controlled Papua New Guinea in the past but had aimed at training and teaching the people in order that they could run their own affairs. (Pangia PR 3/71–72)

It is not difficult to imagine how such speeches would have been received by a ritually oriented people, metaphysical as the propaganda is in references to roads, wealth, light and darkness. What to the administration was a straightforward statement of intention became for Wiru almost a 'cargo cult' prophecy of future prosperity. People engaged in roadwork and other self-help schemes because it was believed that through their labour, similar if not equivalent to the activities and preparations necessary for cult performance, a transformation into powerful and wealthy Europeans could take place. As Wagner (1979: 148) states in reference to the Daribi, ' "progress" and pacification ideologies are as mystical and hyperbolic as anything a native is likely to hear'. The fantastic notion of a road leading into a sunlit clearing is evocative of the colonial space in which new relationships between time, space, and being, and ultimately transformed subjectivities, came into being.

As early as 1961 the patrol reports indicate the major purposes behind colonization and propaganda in Pangia:

it is to the energetic younger generation that we must look to for our major support in developmental programs and acceptance of our aims and hopes. For success obviously our aims, hopes, etc., must become theirs.

To this general purpose talks were given to each group dealing with overall need and necessity for improvement, aims, policy—general Administration propaganda—these talks were extremely well received and in every case the people claimed the desire to progress and even stated that, while sometimes the actual needs and loftier ideals were somewhat obscure to them, all the Government had to do was direct the activity and they would provide it . . .

The several patrols to this area have pointed out that work, work and more work is neces-sary if any headway is to be seen . . . they have received some pay, trade, plus the thrill of seeing planes land on the strip and so on, but this alone will hardly be enough to maintain enthusiasm . . .

The point of all this is that if we want to show real headway in this area we have the perfect opportunity *now*. With a positive economic development plan and the appearance of schools, aid posts, etc., there is no reason why Wiru should not surge ahead . . . It was the government who stopped them fighting and told them if they heard the good word we could show them a better way of life and help them achieve it. (Pangia PR3/61–62)

Implicit in the 'kiap style' of development is that a fair amount of coercion was involved to make people engage in 'work, work and more work'. Wiru may have been initially enthusiastic but sometimes they had to be forced into following the administration's 'aims and hopes', and many people were jailed for not turning up for roadwork, planting enough coffee trees, or building latrines. Fear was an element in the Wiru response to colonialism, especially of beatings at the hands of native police. This coercion was partly due to the necessity of catching up with other areas, but it was also seen as an efficient 'developmental technique' (Pangia PR3/61–62) in its own right:

Half-hearted stabs at it [development] are not good enough—could result in frustration and loss of interest . . . A well-planned, fullscale assault, with clear policy as to crops and full support from the Agricultural Department is the answer. I believe anything falling short of this is nearly a waste of time. (Pangia PR3/61–62)

The military language indicates the 'take no prisoners' style of administration and the strength of its commitment to Pangia's progress; there was even talk of a five-year development plan (Pangia PR5/69–70).

For the most part, Wiru engaged in a ritual response to 'development', and it was this ritual predisposition rather than any simplistic 'relative deprivation' model that accounts for their enthusiasm and co-operation, although it also set the scene for a colonial tragedy of failed expectations and disillusionment. The development era in Pangia lasted from 1961 to the early 1970s, little more than a decade, and while the administration had clear priorities there was an almost complete lack of understanding of what development meant or offered to the Wiru. The kiaps assumed that Wiru had a Western understanding of 'development', encouraged by an initial enthusiasm for hard work that was readily (mis)understood by Europeans, while Wiru expectations of the process were varied and beyond the comprehension of the administration. For Wiru, work and its delayed promise of 'cargo' could ritually transform them into the equivalents of Europeans; Christianity and road-work were part of the same cult response to colonialism. In the early 1960s at a performance of the Timbu cult, one of the *timbu wara* fertility emblems, usually of anthropomorphic design, took the shape of a Norseman aircraft (H. Kerr, pers.comm.), a new embodiment of power related to Wiru labour on their own initiative to clear the pegged-out airstrip site.[7]

Development presented a series of structures of the conjuncture—a clash of 'cargo cults' if you like—in which Wiru and kiaps continually misinterpreted each other's intentions and motivations. For example, a Takuru man who was later appointed village constable and councillor was arrested for a revenge murder of a Mele man in 1955 and sentenced to several years in the Ialibu 'calabus'; because of his extensive prison labour he later claimed to have built Ialibu station with his own hands. The account of the aftermath of his arrest makes for interesting reading:

Some time later his relatives staggered in dragging a pig which would have left a native storyteller gasping for superlatives. The pig was tethered near the prisoner and a conical piece of sewn bark stuffed with human hair was attached to it. The hair was that of the prisoner's relative, killed years before by the Mele people. (Ialibu PR3/55–56)

The conical bark seems to have been a *kange* death compensation hat, presenting the kiaps with a reason for the murder despite the interdiction on fighting, and the size of the pig (unfortunately the report makes no mention of its fate or acceptance by the patrol) indicates as much an attempt to compensate the patrol for the return of the killer, as an offering to the spirits/*kapona* for their good will. A complex message was sent to the patrol about perceptions of European power and the substitutability of pigs and humans, the pig standing for the dead man as well as the prisoner. The message was angrily received as bribery, revealing a typical misunderstanding of Wiru motivation. These types of mutual incomprehension inevitably led to frustration on the part of the administration and confusion and disappointment for Wiru, contributing to their characterization as mercenary (Pangia PR10/71–72), and eventually as requiring spoon-feeding (Pangia PR 1/80). So much for an enthusiastic people creating, with adequate intervention and encouragement, the showplace of the Southern Highlands (see Clark (1985) for an overview of development schemes and their problems in Pangia). The notion of a Wiru 'cult' of development needs to be further explored at this point.

A Cult of Work

Participation in cargo cults or the embracing of plans for economic development are often viewed as alternative responses to colonialism and the intrusive effects of new power relations. It could be suggested that coastal Melanesian people, because of their longer contact history and generations of indentured labour, together with the alienation of land for European plantations and less enlightened missionary regimes, experienced a greater degree of cultural dislocation and structural change

---

[7] As argued in Chapter 2, steel was a complex metaphor for what Wiru desired of the European advent, and the hard work they were prepared to do is literally and metaphorically captured in the successful efforts of some men to file patiently a steel axe in two with an abrasive stone (Ialibu PR3/55–56).

than Highlanders. Kiaps in the Highlands were less likely to treat people as a labour pool of inferior 'kanakas' to be exploited by traders, planters, and the like. Many coastal peoples did not have the advantage of a more considered interaction with Europeans, as did their Highlands counterparts who were not 'discovered' until the 1930s, at which time relatively more humane policies for dealing with newly contacted peoples were in force (cf. Lawrence and Meggitt 1965: 3). Development in the Southern Highlands, at least, was supposed to be in the indigenous, not expatriate interest, and directed towards independence. Thus, an existential and epistemological crisis was believed to underlie the proclivities of coastal peoples towards cargo cult activity.

I will suggest that the perceived difference between development and cargo cultism is not as stark as one would at first suppose, at least for Pangia. In their comparison of Highlands and coastal or Seaboard religions, Lawrence and Meggitt (1965: 21) write that '[Seaboard] cargo cults have been far more prevalent and longer sustained than those in the Highlands.' It seems debatable that cults occurred with greater frequency on the Seaboard (Finney 1973: 141; but see Walter 1981: 94), but what may have some validity is their latter claim. Cargo cults persist and recur on the coast whilst Highlands cults, in the main, had their heyday at a certain point in colonial history—the time of pacification and development. The last Highlands cult seems to have occurred in 1970–1 (A. J. Strathern 1979–80), while on the coast cults continue to be reported by anthropologists and in the media. Finney attributes the lack of cult appeal in the Highlands to the earlier and greater involvement in cash-cropping and local business (1973: 144). This relates to another statement made by Lawrence and Meggitt (1965: 23, my emphasis):

except in a few places such as Kainantu, where there has been pronounced cargo cult activity, the contact situation [in the Highlands] has never been such as to make the people self-conscious about or reliant on any religious ideology. In this context, the people's response seems to have stressed *physical effort, aggressiveness and mental astuteness*—'life values' most likely to commend themselves to middle-class Europeans trying to promote their welfare.

These arguments are attractive but I shall present some evidence from Pangia which questions their underlying assumptions.

I am not the first person to suggest a connection between development and cargo cults, although Walter maintains that this distinction is made and at the emic level, that villagers themselves make a distinction because development *works*. Finney (1973: 144) makes a similar distinction, although he tends to confuse the matter by implying that cults and development are antithetical and then stating that: 'Business for the Gorokans has been . . . a cargo cult that works. Coffee growing and other commercial activities have given the Gorokans what cargo cults promise but cannot confer—status as active participants in the modern world.'

These emic distinctions do not necessarily imply that the ideological basis and hopes for development are different from those of cults. To distinguish between spirit cults and Christianity does not preclude the aim and ideology of both being similar, if not the same (Clark 1985; cf. Josephides 1985: 77–8). To reiterate, the period during which Highlanders came under colonial control, together with the early emphasis on business and development, are the factors which are commonly presented to account for the low profile of cargo cults in this region. This explanation relies too heavily on the notion that participation by Highlanders in development is secular, rational, and pragmatic. It neglects the extent to which work, ritual, and morality are interconnected (cf. A. J. Strathern 1979–80), and to which people engage in development in terms of beliefs associated with cult activities and expectations.

In his discussion of the Kaun cargo cult in the Duke of York islands, Errington (1974: 264) states that there is no expectation that cargo or money will come to Karavarans through the intervention of a deity, only that 'business is necessary to make money for the order of cargo'. Yet business is seen as a ritual and secrets are involved of which the Karavarans are ignorant, and which Errington suggests they attempt to purchase from Europeans (ibid.). Karavarans engage in business to become 'like whites' because business is what whites *do*. Wiru attitudes to development are in many respects similar to Karavaran cargo cult beliefs. It has taken me many years to appreciate fully the significance of the development era for Wiru, partly because I was not present during the heady decade of development in the 1960s, and partly because I assumed, like Finney and others, that Wiru adopted a secular and pragmatic attitude to development.

Wiru identify their origins with the world to the west, which is the source of the wealth and cults that flow into Pangia. This identification facilitated the acceptance of kiaps and missionaries—who also came from the west, bringing promises of wealth, health, and Christianity—and gave their directives legitimacy and force because of the close correspondence between promises made by Europeans and traditional expectations about cults and the source of power and fertility. Changes to the line of power with colonialism helped to create development in Pangia as a component of church ritual activity. There are no mentions of cargo cult activities in Pangia patrol reports or in any of the Wiru ethnography, and for a long time I did not consider the possibility that participation in development, along with engagement in the Christian cult, in many respects resembled features of cargo cults—especially the Kaun cult. The administration was so obsessed with the dangers of cargo cults, especially as possible outcomes of fundamentalist revivals, that they immediately initiated labour-intensive development schemes involving the whole district. It is ironic that, in their efforts to prevent anything like a cargo cult emerging, the administration, together with the missions, initiated and encouraged a Christian work cult. (In humorous 'confirmation' of this link between development and the church, a Catholic missionary once told me that there was no need to go to church in Pangia on Sunday because A. D. O. Barber *was* God.)

The development and missionization experience of Wiru led to an organized and concerted attack on tradition, along with an emphasis on 'hard work' for Wiru to achieve their desires (during the colonial era Pangia sold more coffee than the rest of the Southern Highlands districts combined). This was very different from the colonial experience of many other Highlanders, and this led to a closer connection in Pangia between Christianity (ritual) and development (work). The 'physical effort, aggressiveness, and mental astuteness' which Europeans admired, and which Wiru applied to development, actually masked the 'cult' aspects of development from the administration and observers. What are the grounds, then, for viewing development as part of a cult approach to the new values, requirements and expectations of colonialism?

'Cargo thinking' was certainly in evidence in the early days of colonial control (cf. A. J. Strathern 1984: 27), and Wiru enthusiasm for work cannot be interpreted solely as compliance with administrative directives as the kiaps were surprised to see the effort with which Wiru voluntarily commenced activities such as airstrip construction. By itself this piece of information is not conclusive as many societies, in their first experiences with European control, manifested symptoms of 'cargo thinking'. Many of my informants perceived development, in conjunction with Christianity, as inaugurating a new age (cf. Sorenson's [1972: 362] discussion of the Fore interpretation of the Australian presence in millennial terms. Like Wiru, Fore were exceedingly enthusiastic in aquiescing to administration demands). The past, however, has first to be disposed of and in Takuru, the fieldwork site, it was reported that the patrilineal spirits became very angry and went about cutting people with their axes and urging the destruction of cult houses. This story clearly embodies the tensions and contradictions between the past and a promised future—the anger of 'tradition', expressed by spirits, and the necessity for its destruction to herald the new world, also expressed, paradoxically, through spirits. In some settlements Europeans were confused with spirits of the dead, and as such their urgings may have been interpreted as a legitimation of cult abandonment and acceptance of the Christian cult (see Chapter 4).

Millennial notions are certainly present in Wiru society today, at least in fundamentalist settlements, and are continual themes of Christian revivals, except that the emphasis now is on the end of the world rather than a new beginning.[8] Wiru view colonial change as dramatic, involving the total transformation of society. They describe themselves as existing like 'wild pigs' before the arrival of Europeans, and often express their amazement at how they could have behaved as they did before pacification. A new social order was initiated by Europeans in Pangia, with Takuru Wiru viewing their past lives as sinful and composed in large part of 'greed, violence and untrammeled self-interest' (Errington 1974: 257). Karavarans engaged in the Kaun cult to make themselves the moral equivalent of

---

[8] There is no reason, of course, why the end of the world need not signify a new beginning, but many, if not all Wiru are terrified of such a development. For them it is very much a case of 'new heaven can wait'. The final transformation to whites that would have enabled Wiru to enter heaven without fear did not take place. Also, all exchanges have to be finished before the end, otherwise how would people start again, even in heaven? The link between exchange, morality, and a new order is here made clear.

Europeans and Wiru, I would argue, engaged in development for a similar purpose. Colonialism was a process during which whites 'tamed' Wiru, by putting chemicals into river water or through yaws injections, to make them suitable for the new order, that is, domesticated like Europeans. Chemicals and medicine were given the magical power to transform Wiru into a human state closer in equivalence to Europeans.

To a certain extent Takuru Wiru view this engagement as successful. Pangia is called the 'home of peace' or the 'place of love' to indicate a sense of discontinuity, of transformation from a Hobbesian primitive state. Andrew Strathern comments that when he talked to people about precolonial life he received the impression that 'the past had been suspended, if not abolished', acknowledging that Wiru were aware of 'the huge transition between "then" and "now" ' (1984: 99). Another element in this disjunction was made clear to me by many older informants. In response to my queries about traditional activities, the reply was often, 'Don't ask me anything about customs before because I don't know.' This was because an active effort had been made to forget a past now seen as sinful. The intensive missionization and development experience in Pangia may have entrenched such a notion in a more emphatic manner than occurred elsewhere. A denunciation of the past is one thing, but many fundamentalist Wiru feel strong shame about their 'heathen' ways, as evidenced by their stated amnesia about life before Christianity. A rejection of the past was similar to phases in cargo cults, for instance the Vailala 'Madness', where cults were abandoned to bring about a new world.

Expectations of development were not, however, completely fulfilled. Wiru did not become 'like whites' who, in the 1980s at least, were often viewed as superior creatures in terms of morality and wealth. For example, the moral purity of this ethnographer was enough to keep Satan out of the settlement in which I lived; the educated young believe that jails and poverty do not exist in Australia, where the absence of bridewealth practices was cited as evidence for a higher form of society. It is not surprising that after regular patrolling was established in Pangia, whites were viewed with a considerable amount of trepidation, wonder and expectation. If Europeans were in some sense like spirits, then it is not surprising that a 'cult' interpretation of their presence was evident. This encouraged a ritual orientation to European directives about the necessity for conversion and development:

Their [the Wiru] whole attitude to change was itself ritualistic, as if by total involvement in patterns of work they would achieve desired results. And this of course was what government officers endorsed, since wealth could only come through 'hard work' . . . Wiru hoped the white man's power would come to them. They had to become 'like the white men', and that meant they should *replace* their previous practices with those appropriate to such an aim. (A. J. Strathern 1984: 42, emphasis in original)

Wiru requirements of development were based less on secular, pragmatic concerns than on their 'hard work' creating a moral equivalence with Europeans.

Participation by Wiru in development and church ritual was, I suggest, in terms of a Christian 'work' cult, in which Europeans were the leaders and Wiru the followers. Development work and church ritual are both described as *kongono*. Activities such as prayer and work were not so obvious as the more exotic behaviours found in many cargo cults, and it was the Western features of the 'work' cult that obfuscated my appreciation of it in ritual terms.

At the risk of repetition, let me state once more that 'ritual and work may be seen as types of "work", and both may be considered essential for success' (A. J. Strathern 1979–80: 90). Wiru for work is *pupu toko*, but after Europeans arrived a new word was adopted for the 'work' requirements of the administration and mission. This was *kongono*, the Imbonggu and Kewa term for 'work' (Melpa *kongon*). The Ialibu area controlled the entry of shell and steel valuables into the major Highlands valleys, and its inhabitants were regarded as in some sense superior. The desire to be 'like whites' was a continuation of a cultural logic about the outside world. In so far as whites also came from this world, they were the apotheosis of what Highlanders represented to Wiru. The adoption of the term *kongono* suggests that the labour requirements of Europeans, especially road building, *ka kongono*, were seen by Wiru as a special kind of work, in a context in which work was rewarded by money, which soon became the prime valuable and the aim of development. As in the Melpa Red-box Money Cult, sometimes called *Wok* (work) *Bembe* (A. J. Strathern, pers.comm.), money for Wiru was made the 'supreme object of value' (A. J. Strathern 1979–80: 174). To paraphrase Marx, a new man was the aim of production. A senior church official, in response to the question 'what is the most important thing in life?', promptly answered 'money'. This was not because he was mercenary but because money is a crucial feature of the church/work cult, and part of the meaning of being Christian.

I have written 'church/work cult' but at this point it may be analytically useful to distinguish between work and labour in terms of their correlation with *pupu toko* and *kongono*, that is, a proportion along the lines of

pupu toko : *kongono* : : work : labour.

While these sorts of proportions often take on the form of total explanations (cf. Sahlins 1985: xvi) and tend to mystify the material social processes underlying transformations, they do have analytical value if used as a description of, not a mechanism for processual change. Labour for the white man, for any activity involving money, or in non-traditional forms of socio-economic relationship with other Melanesians, led to a transformation in the social context of production. Work featured in the social relations of production determined by kinship, such that what was produced embodied the producer. This is the demon which drives the perpetual motion of Wiru life-cycle exchanges, yet its exorcism is threatened by *kongono*/labour. If kinship did not necessarily underlie production, what was produced could become detached from the producer. Money is the prime symbol of this detachment, or alienation in the Marxist sense (cf. Taussig 1980), a theme taken up in more detail in Chapter 6.

If aesthetics can be defined as a cultural appreciation, and perhaps celebration, of the value of signs, then money may have an aesthetic which quantifies by mediating social relations with a thing. Traditional wealth does have an aesthetic which qualitatively mediates between people with something—pigs or pearl shells, for instance—that represents them (Clark 1991). Money celebrates the mediation of difference, and creates difference, in a way unlike traditional wealth. It is used in terms of a system of ideas which gives a particular dynamism to the redefinition of social relations, particularly those between Wiru and Europeans; money has the potential to commodify social relations. Varying appreciations of money and traditional wealth occur as part of an ongoing process which could be summarized by the following proportion, which is not presented as a static model but one in which the relationships between the terms are still being negotiated:

pupu toko : *kongono* : : work : labour : : gifts : commodities.

It is the potential of money to be both gift and commodity (Gregory 1980: 649) that provides the dynamic for this negotiation, a dynamism which in the years of development took the form of a cult.

I am reminded of Sahlins's argument (1981) about the transformation of Hawai'ian culture, which was related to the move from a ranked society ritually constituted to a class society constituted by material pragmatism, from differentiations based on myth and *tabu* to those on wealth and property. Wiru society is not about to disappear, but the way in which it is culturally constituted is changing. Internal distinctions are not always based on kinship and exchange but on money and commodities, a change mirrored by, and a product of what I have called the movement from work to labour. If ritual can be described as work, Christianity and development can be characterized as labour. Ideas about the socio-religious world had to change in accompaniment to this shift. *Kongono* is becoming the ubiquitous term for all productive activities, in the everyday and religious domain. It is because of this that I propose to call the Christian 'work' ritual complex—the 'special kind of work' now referring to labour—the Kongono cult.

This constitutional change has not been 'a simple empirical *sequitur*' (Sahlins 1981: 24) of a development project insensitive to the problems facing a recently pacified society. It is the result of people using ideas about the relationships between categories to respond to the event of change, thereby actively transforming society in its reproduction. The explanation of social change in terms of a revaluation of the categories of work and gift is a case in point, and is influenced by Sahlins's account (1981: 37) of the 'historical stress' imposed by a European presence on the 'scheme of social distinctions, together with its cosmological values', which ordered Hawai'ian culture. The way in which ideas were used to respond to events was not determined by these categories, nor did this use imply intentionality on the part of Wiru. Rather, the categories of Wiru culture provided a framework within which various responses to colonialism were possible.

'Cargo' metaphorizes what cultists understand to be European 'culture' (Wagner, 1975: 32). For Wiru, 'cargo' was money, and its possession fuelled their desire to be 'like whites'. Kongono was a means by which Wiru ritually realigned themselves with the new source of power and wealth (A. J. Strathern 1984: 21). To do this they had to respond to European directives about beliefs and practices, evidenced by their enthusiasm for labour or business and an obsession with Christianity and money. Events do not have to be as dramatic as the killing of Captain Cook (Sahlins 1981) to initiate structural transformation. They can appear relatively benign and unspectacular, such as the engagement of people in road construction and the payment of money for labour—the commodification of 'work'. Yet the 'pragmatic revaluation of categorical distinctions' (ibid.: 37) accompanying the movement from work to labour was enough to initiate a transformation of Wiru society. The cultural use and interpretation of money is constituting a different society.

Marilyn Strathern (1984: 21) states that, 'In many contexts [of white penetration] people acted out their interpretations in terms of cargo cults (Wagner 1975), setting up specific structures to capture cause-effect relations. Contained within these acts was a construction of otherness.' The 'capturing structure' for Wiru was participation in Christianity and development through Kongono, a cult aimed at constructing the 'other' in order to assume a moral equivalence with Europeans. Marilyn Strathern suggests that for Melpa ' "becoming European" or . . . "remaining Hagen" . . . were choices between domains of personal efficacy' (ibid.: 17). I would suggest that Wiru, for historical and cultural reasons, did not feel a choice was being offered. To become 'like whites' was a matter of real urgency, reflected in the almost total rejection of tradition. Perhaps this was one reason why a cult solution was an early feature of Wiru attempts to deal with colonial change, but was relatively absent in Hagen until the 1970s. That is, the contact situation in Pangia did make Wiru self-conscious about cults and reliant on religious (Christian) ideology (cf. Lawrence and Meggitt 1965: 23, quoted above). For Wiru the sense of self was more threatened or colonized, and the self did become problematic (see Chapter 5).

To refer back to a point made in Chapter 2 about cosmological differences between Highlands and fringe societies—a difference that can be extended to the Highlands and Seaboard: Kongono could not have been conceived as a 'cargo cult' on the Seaboard because it was based upon practice and exchange rather than myth. Wagner (1979: 142) refers to a Daribi 'cult' of the early 1940s which he calls the 'Talk of Koriki', belonging to a 'self-prolonging dialogue between Daribi and Westerners, in which each side chose to understand the other in ways in which this 'other' did not choose to understand itself. The dialogue began, perhaps, in 1930 [when Europeans were identified with the culture-hero Soux], and continues to the present day.'

The Talk of Koriki shared some features of 'cargo cults', as they are commonly defined, and in many respects it led to practices and beliefs similar to those of Kongono in terms of its preoccupations with the interpretation of experience, starting with Europeans as *kapona* or sons of the Female Spirit, and the invention of cultural forms—what Wagner (1979: 160) calls the 'creative anticipation of the future'. One of the later consequences of the Talk of Koriki was an attempt 'to combine the Administration's road-building propaganda with native cosmology in a sort of anticipatory syncretism' (ibid.: 150), leading to visions of a beautiful underground world full of money and motor vehicles of all kinds.[9] These visions were based upon Daribi mythology, whereas Wiru hopes for development and road-building, if no less fantastic, were much more 'practical'—even if they were still a reaction to an epistemological crisis—involving the engagement of Europeans through ritual and exchange. This is the last of the points I wish to make in support of my claim that Christianity and development, in the context of what I call the Kongono cult, were not exclusive in terms of ideology, membership, and ritual/work requirements.

The Failure of Development

The great hopes that Wiru and the administration held for development were not to be fulfilled because of misunderstandings about the nature of labour. The kiaps also had only a limited time in which to carry out their plans, although positive expectations for development continued well into the 1970s: 'The Pangia subdistrict with continued good administration will remain one of the most stable and productive areas in the Southern Highlands if not the whole Highlands region' (Pangia PR9/72–73). Still, there were occasions on which this colonial optimism (or self-deception) was replaced by a more realistic appraisal of the situation: 'Pangia may be considered to be ahead of most Southern Highlands areas but, if it is, the reason is simply continuity [of staffing] rather than any real self-help or local drive or ambition' (Pangia PR3/71–72). And kiaps realized that the wider context and demands of colonization provided stumbling blocks to their plans for local development schemes that were 'wholly dependent on cheap, intensive labour' (Pangia PR2/70–71), as the following quote about the inequity of the Highlands Labour Scheme indicates: 'History may well condemn a system which permitted such a stripping of undeveloped rural Papua New Guinea to the detriment of the home area and, probably in the long term, the country as a whole to assist already developed areas' (Pangia PR3/70–71).

Under the colonial regime, the notion of self-help, understandable as it is from a Western perspective, becomes something of a sham, although its incomprehension by Wiru met with criticism rather than understanding:

---

[9] Christian revivals are discussed in the next chapter, but it is worth noting a statement by one man who ran along narrow church rafters while possessed—'It looked like a beautiful big road to me' (Harvey 1973: 191).

The theory of self-help . . . seems a little absurd to these people as they are only interested in the money they can get in their hands, not in some nebulous figure which includes the self-help component. At present the people will work for 20c. a day . . . not through any self-less motives of self-help, but merely because it's a cash wage. When they refuse to work for 20c./day no appeals to their patriotism or the advancement of Pangia will make them work. (Pangia PR16/71–72)

By the early 1970s some of the glow from the heady decade of the 1960s was starting to wear off and disillusionment was setting in on both sides; Wiru had laboured mightily and still no European company had come to deliver them from their darkness. The cult of development had failed to satisfy people's expectations, and eventual independence in 1975 merely signalled the *coup de grace* of colonial desire. All the propaganda in the world was unlikely, in the space of a decade, to educate Wiru in the complexities of Western notions of the individual and the work ethic, and the kiaps, well intentioned as they may have been, failed to understand the ethnocentrism and limits of their project. Wiru were instead blamed for perpetuating such things as the 'cult of the pig' (Pangia PR5/73–74), for a counter-productive dependence on the destructive forces of tradition. From the point of view of the administration, Wiru could not stop being 'primitive'—reactionary, unmotivated, and mercenary—and responsive to the loyalties of the tribe rather than the demands of the state.

For the administration, the purpose of the development era, although it would not have phrased its aims in such terms, was to create a particular kind of colonial subject through the imposition of new regimes of power/knowledge. The 'kiap style' of coercion, control and 'calabus' (jail) was a colonial technology that worked on the bodies of tribal primitives to turn them into docile and productive Christian peasants. This transformation in subjectivity was to be achieved through discipline and the character-building process of hard work, designed to move people up to the next rung on the ladder of evolutionary types and human consciousness. Primitivism provided a central pillar for the support and practice of colonial discourse. To this end, patrols were a means of administration surveillance in a context in which Wiru had to be 'politically, economically and socially adjusted', a process that the Comaroffs (1991: xi) call the 'colonization of consciousness'. Census-taking was one of the earlier attempts by which the subject could be known for purposes of later adjustment. What was attempted was an Orwellian colonial experiment in producing receptive and willing converts to the virtues of work and self-sacrifice. To this end, the administration was not averse to interfering in matters of 'custom', such as enforcing hours spent in garden work, telling people to increase the size of gardens, regulating marriage practices and the timing of pig-kills, abolishing food prohibitions, and so on: 'only when there has been a sensible land tenure system imposed on the people will we get any real order and planning into rural development. The brawls and upheaval will be great but once done there will exist a system conducive to rapid development . . . The present system . . . is a severe handicap to any semblance of unity within the area (Pangia PR3/71–72).

The same patrol report stated the desirability of the complete extermination of the pig before any real progress could be made.

The chapter so far has demonstrated that, for Pangia, 'the goals of an encapsulating power alone do not determine the *content* of the linkages forged by pacification. Each episode of pacification occurs in a particular historical context that affects the course of subsequent events (Rodman 1979: 22, my emphasis).

I have presented several factors here, and in Chapter 2, that help to account for the direction and content of Pangia's colonial history, such as kiap personalities and ambitions, the timing of the *pax Australiana*, a previous history of patrolling, including the linkage of Europeans to *kapona* and sorcery, and a ritual response to change. I cannot fully explain Wiru motivation in respect of kiap directives or their reasons for engaging in work as a kind of ritual—the cult dimensions of development. There were obvious shifts in power/knowledge under colonialism, and engaging in self-help schemes can partly be explained in these terms, as attempts through work to access European power/knowledge and seek equivalence. The alacrity with which most Wiru came to embrace colonialism is related to earlier claims about Europeans becoming a new symbol of the cassowary—the external source of power and wealth once located along a major trade route or line of power into the Highlands (although Wiru retained their autonomy in precolonial dealings with the Highlands). Europeans came from the direction of Mbuna, the ancestral home of Wiru and the locus for the most recent fertility cult of the Female Spirit, with whom Europeans were identified.

Kiaps misapprehended Wiru desire for catching up with other more developed areas as motivated by a kind of indigenous economic rationalism

there is a universal cry for money which is found from one side of the division to the other . . . the realization of the value of money has produced almost a pre-occupation, at least while in the presence of 'white men', about complaining of their limited access to economic advancement (earning money). The people are more than willing to allow a European, be he a Mission representative or the lauded, almost mythological 'Company Master' to establish himself permanently amongst them. (Pangia PR6/63–64)

'Economic advancement' for Wiru meant accessing money as a powerful substance associated with European power, and the reference to the need for a 'mythological "Company Master" ' reveals the nature of this desire in decidedly non-economic terms. It was a product of one of a series of structures of the conjuncture, and understandable only in relation to a cultural context generated out of this structure at a particular moment in time. Simply put, mutual misapprehension arose out of a clash between two different 'cults' of development based on exclusive cultural logics. The administration wanted to create a 'farming peasantry' (Pangia PR1/70–71), while Wiru wanted to re-create themselves as Europeans.

In all of the patrol reports seen by me there is only one reference to the possible unforeseen consequences that a period of intensive development may have had on Wiru as a whole:

the change and development of the area has been rapid and very satisfactory for so short a space of time. No doubt there have been quite remarkable stresses and strains to the society unknown, unnoticed by us . . . bordering on the traumatic. Without question there has been quite an upheaval to the traditional existence and maybe the excellent conditions prevailing here are to some extent due to the nature of the people but largely to good fortune . . . [and] a prevailing cooperation and willingness to work together by people and administration. (Pangia PR5/69–70)

I will discuss in Chapter 5 some of the consequences of the 'stresses and strains' of development, including fears of male emasculation and outbreaks of madness and Christian revival 'hysteria', and confine myself to observing that there were indeed traumatic consequences to a 'very satisfactory' colonial experience in Pangia, and that there was a general anomie at the eventual failure of Wiru hopes for development (cf. A. J. Strathern 1984). With hindsight, these consequences were entirely predictable but, given the ethnocentric model of development and its style of implementation, it would have been impossible for the kiaps to have conceived exactly what it was that Wiru desired of development and why they gradually lost interest in contributing their labour to the project. Pangia never made the 'great leap forward'.

As Hughes (1978: 318) comments on colonialism in Papua New Guinea, 'with every new initiative on the part of an official . . . a measure of indigenous autonomy was lost'. The 'kiap style' used to accelerate the rate of progress in Pangia meant that kiaps had to become very authoritarian in their imposition of a rigid discipline of work. It is not surprising that as early as 1966 a report stated that 'the most insignificant quarrels and problems are brought before the patrol for arbitration' (Pangia PR9/66–67); children were sometimes brought in by their parents for punishment by the kiaps. Yet the kiaps did not see this tendency for what it really was, a shift in the locus of power relations that created a dependence on the administration for motivation, direction, funding, and leadership:

so long as the present system remains no real sense of urgency will drive these people forward as they consider the benevolent government—as it now exists—will provide and will protect. (Pangia PR3/71–72)

they would rather earn a regular wage and sell their resources to others than develop their own land and become entrepreneurs themselves. (Pangia PR4/73–74)

There is an irony here as kiaps wanted Wiru to become like Europeans in their economic behaviour, a transformation that was a signal failure on their part, while Wiru wanted to become European at an ontological level of personhood.

The failures, in the last analysis, were obvious ones, an almost complete neglect of the importance of the cultural context in developing strategies for change, and an inability to recognize the problems of a 'cocooning' effect in the administration approach to development that encouraged dependency, expressed in a fear of what would happen when Europeans left at independence:

It is perhaps a natural sentiment as this area has had to take the leads and examples from expatriates in government and mission organizations in the relatively short time that the area has come under European contact. They still rely heavily on the presence of these expatriates for direction, advice and the opportunities to earn a little cash. This strong reliance . . . hasn't made it easier to develop a confidence in the ability of themselves. (Pangia PR 10/72–73)

When cults were imported in the past, specialists had to be paid until people had learnt to take on and perform the cult themselves. Wiru never learnt the true secrets of the cult of development, of how to become European, despite its early promises of prosperity and power. This inability was blamed by the kiaps on the lack of a 'mental ability to keep pace' (Pangia PR8/70–71) rather than on the internal contradictions of colonialism. As Thomas (1994: 16) notes: 'the gaps between projection and performance are frequently betrayed by the anxieties of their texts, which reveal the gestural character of efforts to govern, sanitize, convert, and reform.'

Wiru eventually lost faith in development, leading to a moribund state of affairs after independence in 1975.[10] It is only through a close examination of colonial discourses that their assumptions can be revealed and the reasons for the failure of development comprehended. What is also revealed is the nature of power, deception, and coercion under colonial regimes, and these issues will again be taken up in the next chapter that deals with Christian missions in Pangia, their role in colonialism, and their relations with the administration.

---

[10] Disappointment accompanied changing attitudes to Europeans, as it did among the Daribi, 'from awe to anticipation, resentment, and finally, perhaps, opposition' (Wagner 1979: 150).

4

Waiting for the Word, Walking in the Light

The majority of Wiru were aware of the existence of Christian missions before Pangia station was established in August 1961, and were also aware that, like their own cults, there were different varieties. Christianity remains to this day a plural experience in Pangia. At this early stage of colonial history Wiru were unsure of mission requirements and aims, although they knew that mission churches had similar concerns to local cults because of their talk about a spirit and its ability to enable healthy and prosperous lives. The missions had been hovering like bees over the honeypot of Pangia since the 1950s—as one of the last densely populated areas ripe for conversion in the Highlands—and illegal forays had been conducted into the restricted area by at least the Catholics and the East and West Indies Bible Mission (later the Evangelical Bible Mission). Many Wiru had been exposed to missions on visits to Ialibu station and Kaupena mission, and as many as two hundred boys had been entered into mission school at Kaupena by the late 1950s. Boys and men were sent back into Pangia as forward scouts or 'bosbois' in order to establish beachheads for the missions pending de-restriction, and some settlements knew their Christian denomination before even sighting a missionary or Bible.

The interdependence between missions and the district administration was attested to by the fact that some missions were allowed into certain areas in Pangia after the first of November in 1960, before the station itself was established and prior to full de-restriction in 1962. These missions were welcomed into settlements at the same time as their inhabitants were concluding what were probably the last performances of the Timbu cult cycle, which is interesting as missionaries were seen as cult-bringers themselves, although at this stage their often violent opposition to pagan cults was largely unknown. The Ialibu administration purposefully used the missions for their 'general settling effect on the people' (Ialibu PR3/60–61) before commencing its own efforts at promoting change. Missions and administration *were* colonialism in Pangia, and to some extent they shared a common discourse about the primitive and development. The colonization of territory was as necessary for saving souls as it was for finding subjects for development. Although seen as in some ways different because it was known that they lived apart and one group sometimes had families, missionaries and kiaps were initially indistinguishable to Wiru in terms of their perceived aims. While the two were later distinguished, notions of the transformative powers of Christianity and development to Wiru came to be inextricably related, as in the Kongono cult, even if their proponents were often at loggerheads. Colonialism had a coherence for Wiru—both missions and the administration used the metaphor of seeking light in their respective propaganda—that it never had for kiaps and missionaries, who had different plans and priorities for the savage (bearing in mind that different missions had different discourses and agendas; Andrew Strathern [1984: 37] reports, with some scepticism, that Catholics claim never to have directly told people to destroy their cults).

The changing attitude of the kiaps towards the missions paralleled that of their attitude to Wiru over time, although it moved from enthusiasm to disappointment more rapidly as the emphasis on spiritual development clashed with the economic priorities of the administration: 'missions must be convinced that they should contribute to the growth of the economic and political Pangia and not simply remain with their churches and schools . . . missions are failing to support development' (Pangia PR5/69–70). The administration was soon disabused of the opinion that religious and socio-economic change could proceed hand in hand, as if colonialism was a unitary project with the aim of creating a productive Christian peasant. Both kiaps and missions came to change their initially positive thoughts about Wiru, in strikingly similar terms, as we shall see, just as Wiru themselves came to reconsider the colonial Janus.

Invention and Abandonment

The influenza epidemic and the failure of indigenous ritual to stop the ensuing deaths contributed to the Wiru acceptance of missions, even to their active seeking out by some settlements. In Takuru, people said that they went to get the mission in an attempt to bring to a halt the depredations of *ulo* sorcery, its spread and scale an artefact of the pathogens of colonialism. The litany found in patrol reports about Wiru enthusiasm and co-operation has its echoes in mission accounts of Wiru receptivity to the Christian message: 'When we went to New Guinea, I sanguinely expected that it would take ten years to establish a viable Christian community. We saw God do it in as many weeks' (Ridgway 1976: 81). The response was not universal as some isolated settlements had not experienced the promises of mission 'bosbois' or other representatives, and people sometimes refused access to the Evangelical Bible Mission (EBM) because of its reputation for burning down cult houses (Pangia PR3/62–63). In the main, though, the Wiru response to missions, as it was to kiap propaganda about development, remained highly positive. Very quickly, within a year or two, there was a wholesale abandonment of ritual and cults, reflected in the desire of Takuru people to bring the EBM *because* they knew of its reputation for burning down cult houses, although I suspect that this may be a retrospective explanation, despite the fact that many Wiru eventually did collaborate in this destruction: 'The people themselves burnt their spirit houses and swung clear of their old idolatries and superstitious beliefs. They eagerly walked in the light' (Ridgway 1976: 86).

This abandonment of an established cosmology was more than another instance of Wiru receptivity to new cults, as in precolonial times older indigenous cults were not displaced or destroyed in favour of a new one. Wiru remained committed to the long-established Tapa ancestor cult when Timbu arrived from the south (possibly traceable to the fertility cults of the Papuan coast), and loyal to Tapa and Timbu when *Aroa Ipono* was introduced from the Highlands in the first decades of this century. An earlier anthropology would have viewed this colonial abandonment on a par with F. E. Williams's pronouncements on the Vailala Madness, as a kind of cultural self-destruction at a time when people were not aware of what they were doing. This would be an erroneous conclusion because Wiru were not passive respondents to colonialism and actively (if not always strategically) engaged with the trajectories of its agents. Wiru burnt down their own cult houses and destroyed or buried their cult stones not just because missionaries told them to, but because a new age needed to be inaugurated. What was being repudiated, according to Thomas (1992: 220),

was not indigenous religion, as an anthropologist might have construed it, but the particular array of practices and beliefs that the encounter had made constitutive of heathenism. (Needless to say, when Christianity finally was adopted, this usually took place because of a new congruence with indigenous strategies and imagined futures, rather than because the missionary agenda was accepted in any simple sense.)

Wiru played a significant part, along with missionaries and kiaps, in creating 'colonialism's culture' (Thomas 1994), an 'invention of culture' similar to Wagner's (1975) usage, except that in this case it was colonial agents, not anthropologists, who with Wiru constructed cultures out of their interactions, desires, and misunderstandings.

From their own perspective, although this is based upon accounts given in the 1980s, Wiru were engaging in exactly what Williams (1976: 323) suggested of the Elema—'the wholesale destruction of native practice and tradition'—although it is difficult to write about the awareness that Wiru had of their motivation in the 1960s as I imagine that the situation was much more complex and bewildering than it became with hindsight. Certainly people did not destroy cult houses only as a strategy for initiating a new order; in a sense Wiru had no choice but to abandon their cults given the demonstrated superiority of Europeans. The 1960s were a time of stress and confusion, and decisions people made about cults were influenced by the general state of disorder at the time. There was obviously also an emotional side to conversion, but recovering traces of emotions in explanations of behaviour decades after the event proved almost impossible. Their embracing of the missions is now, and perhaps was then, seen as a giving up and denial of the past or 'culture', especially in fundamentalist settlements where culture became equated with 'sin' (giving up cults as sinful can only be a retrospective explanation as new experiences of difference allowed for the reification of culture [Thomas 1992]; giving them up for a new order makes more sense, despite its implication of intentionality).

In this respect the coming of Christianity was radically different from the introduction of previous cults, having as much in common with so-called 'cargo cults', many of which were opposed to tradition, as it did with the cults of fertility it replaced (which were not essentially millenarian in outlook). A factor in this difference was the mission habit of giving 'presents' of blankets, axes, and sometimes shells to settlements to obtain and ensure their adherence, actions that had consequences for the long-term perceptions of Christianity, especially as previous cults were purchased and their exporters did not come to stay: 'There is no doubt that material gain, or the belief that it will ensue, is the major Christianising influence . . . The art of playing one mission against the other is well known to the local people' (Pangia PR13/72–73).

The preceding quote is from the 1970s, but the *Diary* of the Catholic mission reveals a saga of bribery, duplicity, and hostility from the early 1960s, when missions vigorously and ruthlessly competed with each other for settlements and souls. The *Catholic Diary* (n.d.), makes clear the extent of Wiru indecisiveness about the best mission, and documents many instances of gifts being returned once another mission had made a more substantial offer. People did play off the missions but it is a misunderstanding of Wiru motivation to label their actions as mercenary. New cults were evaluated in terms of their ability to produce the goods, as it were, and the more generous a mission was with presents the more likely it would be accepted. As remarked above, Wiru were no doubt surprised not only to have a new cult brought directly to them, but also to have its acceptance solicited by gifts, and the novelty of this situation contributed to their labelling as 'mercenary'. The situation was more complex, of course, as much of the fundamentalist appeal lay in its claims of apocalypse and a new age, appealing messages to a people with a sense of dislocation and a desire for a moral equivalence with Europeans: 'At the same time as the old order was declining, the missionaries were presenting a new one . . . The mission, in effect, initiated cultural dislocation . . . then seized the opportunity . . . promoting large-scale conversions to Christianity' (Robin 1982: 337).

A vigorous critic of missions in the Southern Highlands, Robin tends to underplay people's own agency. Wiru were not forced on to reservations and made to deny their own culture and language, as was the fate of many other colonized peoples, even if in their active collaboration Wiru had surrendered something of their autonomy, of their control over processes of cultural reproduction. Colonialism, as indicated in the previous chapter, had created new dependencies, unlike the imported cults that Wiru appropriated and adapted for their own purposes. The movement of cults, including Christianity, along lines of power created the history that generated culture and supported cosmological beliefs. The innovation of culture proceeds differently, however, under the hegemony of colonial power, a process in which Wiru were made subject to the gaze of its agents. Wiru may have been interpreting Christianity and Europeans in terms of continuity with previous beliefs, but their lack of autonomy led to a marked discontinuity in cultural reproduction. Wiru did not have the choice they thought, for their voluntary act of giving up their cults and labour to 'development' did not satisfy the desires that had been engendered. One writer on development in Papua New

Guinea comments that people were to be 'missionised and exhorted, until in the fullness of time they should by some magical means become European in all but colour' (Hastings 1969: 55). This captures precisely the desire that Wiru themselves had of development, although this desire remained unsatisfied because Wiru were not free to act under colonialism as anything but its subjects; and neither, perhaps, were the kiaps, who had to toe the line of government policy—alluded to in the Wiru misreading of the power of the Australian flag—albeit sometimes reluctantly and manipulatively.

Government and Evangelism

District and territory administrations generally had a good relationship with missions, which were often well connected politically and moreover fitted into the 'big picture' of development. One of the objectives of Paul Hasluck, as Minister of Territories, was 'to replace paganism by the acceptance of the Christian faith, and the ritual of primitive life by the practice of religion'; pagans, evidently, did not have any form of religion:

The missions have been an especially important and influential force in the Southern Highlands Province . . . [which] relies heavily on the contributions of missions to provide health and education services . . . missions have been permitted to settle anywhere and to propagate such religious doctrines as they have seen fit. Missions have been regarded largely with favour and have been permitted to proliferate. (Robin 1982: 323)

Kiaps on the front line, however, rapidly became ambivalent about the consequences of evangelism, as this quote about the initial entry of missions into Pangia indicates (echoing in miniature the scramble of European nations for whole continents): 'the ensuing scramble for the plum spots, however undignified, no doubt provided all groups with sufficient of their "own territory" to even satisfy them' (Pangia PR3/61–62).

The Pangia administration tried to inform people of their right to freedom of religious choice, despite the earlier strategic use of missions as a settling influence: 'it is each individual's right to choose between one or another mission or traditional form of worship; that headmen or missionaries have no right to force anyone to attend any particular mission; that if they wanted to keep their spirit houses it was entirely up to them' (Pangia PR1/62–63). The concept of choice would have had little meaning to Wiru, and paradoxically accentuated the administration's fears that confusion of choice could lead to undesirable 'cargo cult' activity. Besides, the Mendi District Office was actually worried about the mission response to interference in their activities: 'To advise people of their rights of choice could easily lead to more confused thinking by both Papuan locals and European missionaries. It is quite possible for your advice to be construed as anti-mission and if that did occur, with the type of people with whom you are dealing, then the Administration work in the area would be hampered' (cited in Pangia PR1/62–63).

The administration was clearly powerless in its dealings with missions, and when kiaps became worried about social disturbances caused by revival activity, they were told, in a note from the Director of Native Affairs:

It is really a matter of basic 'conversion', and that is hardly a matter for Administration officers . . . I hope your talks with members of the mission have some effect, but I doubt it, and in the face of this belief it is probably impossible to deal with their native adherents'. (Memo from Director of Native Affairs, Mendi District Office, 31/6/1964)

As early as 1935 the Melbourne *Age* reported the views of Jack Hides in respect of the evangelization of the Highlanders he had recently 'discovered':

he was merely expressing the fear that a type of inexperienced missionary might go among these new people, disrupt their social system, and cause such disintegration of native life as would bring disaster in its train [by an] unholy rush on the part of some bodies to occupy the territory . . . Missionaries who go to these primitive people should be thoroughly equipped for their delicate task, and should be aware of the danger of breaking down a long-organized past without having carefully thought out plans for future development. For old interests, if a change had to be made, there should be substituted new and worthier ones. (*Age*, 16/10/1935)

Hides's reasonable request for government regulation of mission activity, and some kind of training requirement for missionaries selected for the 'delicate task' of proselytizing 'new people', was ignored because of the interdependencies between mission and administration. Hides perhaps overstated the disaster that could befall inexperienced attempts at conversion, although evangelism did have serious consequences in Pangia and elsewhere. His concern about an 'unholy rush' of untrained missionaries was well-placed for the Wiru. The behaviour of many missionaries provoked derision as well as concern among Pangia kiaps:

By the time the particular Bible lesson comes to the ears of the Wiru people one wonders if Genesis becomes a football match . . . the final result is very different from the original. (Pangia PR1/62–63)

There is quite a degree of cheekiness towards, and lack of any real respect for, some American missionaries. This may be due to the fact that quite a few are unable to speak Pidgin or Wiru and some appear to have difficulty with English too . . . [when he is accepted] the locals will endeavour to milk him of his last penny . . . [missions] are generating petty jealousies and lack of understanding through a general—with one or two exceptions—and total inability to communicate. (Pangia PR5/69–70)

None of the missions in the area have any respect for another's work in so far as each one is willing to go into a village and break new ground on an already established set-up run by another church organization. (Pangia PR2/76–77)

Colonial Romance, Colonial Rationality

The historical period in which missionaries entered into Pangia was different from other moments of mission activity, in New Guinea and elsewhere. The evangelism of much of Africa occurred during the Industrial Age and the rise of modernity, and cannot be understood apart from this background (Comaroff and Comaroff 1991). While the mission impetus was in some respects unchanged over time, the context for evangelism had been transformed by the 1960s, at which time the mission project appears strangely anachronistic in Pangia—the conversion of the savage occurring in the same decade as the Beatles were making their first appearance on the world stage. Knauft (1993: 17) writes of an earlier time:

Missionaries' religious interests, knowledge of local customs, and logistical support had a significant impact on nineteenth- and early twentieth-century Melanesian survey ethnography . . .

Intellectually, missionaries and early scholarly observers shared literacy, education, and an Enlightenment vision of Melanesians as savages capable of improvement.

It is not surprising that scholarly works such as those produced by an earlier generation of missionaries, including the German Lutherans at Mt Hagen in the 1930s, rarely appear after the 1950s. Pangia certainly produced no missionary scholars, unless Harland Kerr of the Summer Institute of Linguistics (SIL) is considered (and SIL is theoretically not a mission organization). Missionaries in the 1960s rarely shared the education, literacy, or Enlightenment concerns of their predecessors, for the *Zeitgeist* had changed, and they now inhabited a post-industrial world veering towards the postmodern. Non-mainstream, non-intellectual and fundamentalist mission sects had also proliferated by the 1950s, and were allowed more or less complete access to unevangelized populations. More than a superficial knowledge of the cultures they were proselytizing no longer seemed necessary, even for the Catholics and Lutherans (although for the Pangia Catholic mission this knowledge became important again in the 1980s). Certainly there was no systematic or scholarly writing about Wiru by any of the Pangia missions.

Anthropology was not seen as particularly useful knowledge to facilitate conversion, even in the 'know thine enemy' sense, especially when, as remarked above, some missions regarded 'culture' as sinful. The 1960s had shifted to a postwar pragmatism, a non-intellectual and decidedly unromantic mode in which the savage was known and constructed as a subject in a different way from the savage of the post-Enlightenment period. There was an epistemological shift in the nature of colonialism under modernism, as kiaps worked to prepare people for eventual self-government and independence. Wiru would become Christians because, once shown the light, they would realize the inevitability of their conversion. They did not first have to be known in their pristine and savage state; their pagan nature was assumed and did not have to be understood to enable proselytization. Patrol reports from the 1920s to the 1960s reflect the same shift towards a utilitarian view, as well as a gradual 'disenchantment' with the savage, transformed from a warrior/killer/sorcerer in an unknown landscape containing pearls or gold, as described in Brewster's *Pearls of Papua*, to a potential labour source in the mundane world of development (this shift is also indicated by a comparison of

Brewster's map (Map 2), depicting an extensive and mysterious savage terrain, with administrative maps concerned with creating bounded and known districts as colonized entities). Even when anthropology was considered important in Papua its major purpose, according to Sir Hubert Murray in 1922, was in 'its application to practical administration' (cited in Sinclair 1988: 250). In 1980, ex-kiaps involved with the Southern Highlands Rural Development Project treated anthropologists mostly as an irrelevance, if not a joke, and one in particular delighted in inquiring about my 'holiday' in Pangia.[1]

The historical background to the operation of missions in Pangia in the 1960s has been sketched, and implicit in the account is that Wiru, who once perceived Europeans as sons of the Female Spirit, accepted and were drawn to Christianity as a new form of cult (the influenza epidemic and the extent of social disorder also have to be considered as factors in this acceptance). Different church denominations were known as 'X "lotu" *yapu*', where X refers to the denomination, 'lotu' to church, and *yapu* to the cult house, as in *Tapa yapu* and *Aroa Ipono yapu* (see Clark 1989). Christianity promised health and prosperity, messages that were readily understandable to Wiru, and Europeans were interpreted in terms of the line of power that connected Wiru to the Highlands and the coast. This is not to suggest that one cult, Christianity, simply replaced others, as the aim of evangelism was the creation of a pagan *fin de siècle* and took place in the context of a concerted attack on 'tradition'. Attitudes to labour in development schemes suggest that Wiru also understood the kiap propaganda message in cult terms, but again the nature of colonialism transformed and decentred a ritualized cosmology; these sorts of issues will be discussed in more detail in the next chapter.

Mission Discourses in Pangia

What I want to do in the rest of this chapter is consider some of the writings of missionaries about their evangelical project, and contrast their discourse about savage potential with that found in patrol reports. Unfortunately, the only missionary books written about Wiru are by adherents of fundamentalist sects, for the most part because such books played an important role in fund-raising among congregations in Australia and North America.

Read this book. Be blessed and support missions. Offer to God your children, your money and your time for the propagation of the Gospel. (Harvey 1973: 6)

---

[1] A few anthropologists later became involved in other World Bank-funded development projects in the Highlands, such as in research on the resurgence of 'tribal' fighting, or on the connections between land systems, people, and nutrition. A belated recognition was made that some input from the 'people' was needed, or even that the 'people' themselves might be a factor in implementing development plans. This relationship between anthropology and administration was of a different kind to that which existed in F. E. Williams's day, more influenced by the idea that the 'people' of an independent state may need to be consulted regarding their own development, or by the fact that they may present an intractable social problem for development by engaging in such activities as fighting, drinking, spreading sexually transmitted diseases, and so on.

those of you who have helped support this work have invested your means in a far better way than you could have had you put it in a bank to draw interest. Praise God, we're drawing interest which pays more than one hundred per cent on the principal. (Bustin n.d.: 10)

Lutherans and Catholics, whose Wiru converts make up the bulk of Christians in Pangia, were financially supported by large church and mission organizations in their home countries and did not need to publish popular texts for funding. The sort of books written are by no means ethnographies; rather they tell of money well spent and are in the evangelical style of 'how we saved them from sin and led them out of darkness'. The willingness of Wiru to convert is a theme, even if it is interpreted differently by the administration:

the bane of the mission organizations, the reason for [their acceptance] does . . . not ascend higher than the simple strategy of importing the means of acquiring greater material wealth. (Pangia PR6/63–64)

The early attitude of respect and awe for the missions by locals has died and become somewhat mercenary. There is a fair amount of disappointment that missions have not helped in the economic field as was hoped. (Pangia PR4/70–71)

The 'disappointment' expressed here seems to be as much that of the administration as of the Wiru, who would not have divided their colonial experience, or indeed their actions in road-work or church attendance, into economic, political or religious domains. Again we meet the characterization of Wiru as 'mercenary', and rebut it for the same reasons given above. Just as Wiru experienced disillusionment with their ritualized expectations of development, it is clear that similar cult expectations about the missions—at the level of church participation as well as mission commitment to development—met with disappointment, accounting in part for the appeal of new Christian sects in Pangia today, and their high turnover. Administration reductions of Wiru motivations to economic behaviour do not account for the 'religious' aspect of participation in church services, for a belief in 'the almost magical significance of baptism' (Pangia PR2/72–73), or for the 'respect and awe' accorded the European cult-bringers.

A better insight into motivation is revealed in a reference to the activities of the Pentecostal Full Gospel Movement (FGM) in the early 1970s, which had been showing 'miracle films' as a new medium of evangelism: 'People have been quick to accept belief in this kind of power and the appeal is instantaneous. It is believed by most that the F.G.M. can do a lot for the area in a short time and the people . . . believe that the F.G.M. is coming to stay and bring with it all the "benefits", material and otherwise, in order to cater to their wants' (Pangia PR4/73–74).

It is interesting that the administration phrases Wiru hopes in terms of its own hopes for development, whereas Wiru had their own notions of what development (including Christianity) entailed, in 'material and otherwise' terms. It is the 'otherwise' that is neglected in European interpretations of Wiru desire. To label Wiru as mercenary is to misunderstand not just the continuing appeal and vitality of Christianity in Pangia, but also the attraction of new sects/cults. Many Wiru are still searching for the cult that works and, while they may also want some form of 'bisnis', it is the church that has greater salience in their lives and ambitions.

The relevant missionary texts are *Four Years with my Savage Brothers* [*FY*], by Gerald Bustin (n.d.), *Out of the Shadows in New Guinea* [*OS*], by Lily Harvey (1973), and *Feet upon the Mountains* [*FM*], by Kingsley Ridgway (1976). The first two authors were based at the Evangelical Bible Mission at Mele, and the last was a Wesleyan missionary at Takuru (who in 1963 had taken over and purchased for $2,300 the mission station set up by the overstretched EBM). The books are littered with biblical quotations, making it clear that these missionaries are doing God's work; the language used often has an old-fashioned and biblical tone, as captured in the titles. No doubt is ever expressed that Satan was responsible for cult practices, and that conversion was not a choice but the only avenue for the heathen to enter into the world of God (read Europeans). The similarities between the books make close attention to all three redundant, and I concentrate on *Four Years with my Savage Brothers* as an exemplar of its kind.[2] A more realistic account of the early days of evangelism is recorded in the *Catholic Diary* for Pangia, its straightforward narrative style often providing a relief from the sanctimonious tenor of the published books. The *Diary* clearly reveals the bickering and insults traded between the various missions (and also the absence of a single mission discourse).

Many of the American missionaries came from the mid-West Bible-belt area and some, like Bustin, were themselves the children of missionaries. Their biographies often depict a struggle against sin, childhood revelations combined with intense emotional experiences, and the need to do something for God, often expressed in terms of his personal call to take up mission work:

[My mother's] passing made an impression on me which the Lord used to bring me under conviction—it made me death-conscious. The Lord really began dealing with me concerning my need to accept Him as my Saviour. I had done things which I knew I had to confess should I get saved . . . The Lord dealt mightily with me until I became so afraid of dying that when bedtime came I would lay on the bed wondering how much chance I had of living all night long . . . in the prayer meeting that followed I confessed all my sins, pleading the Blood of Christ. My heart was flooded with a joy so deep and peaceful that I felt like shouting the rest of the night. (*FY*: i)

The author was prepared by the Lord through his 'steps' and 'stops' to be the one to undertake the development of this field. Missionary work had lain heavily on his heart and occupied much of his prayer time for several years. When the time, place, and purpose seemed

---

[2] Harvey's book is different from the other two in that part of it purports to be a biography of the life of one of the first Wiru EBM pastors. There are many emotional moments of prophetic dreaming and divine revelations of Heaven and forgiveness along the way. In many respects it is an odd book, bordering on the fictional, recounting dialogue between Wiru decades before the missionaries arrived and often with a distinct American cast to it, as in this example where a man is explaining to his son the reasons for taking a second wife: 'Oh well, you see, son, it's like this. Hardly any first wife likes the idea at first, but they get used to it. And it gives your mom help with the garden and the pigs' (*OS*: 31).

in providential agreement God's clock struck and the doors of New Guinea opened. (*FM*: 7)

The Harveys ran a sawmill but always thought that God had a higher purpose for them, eventually enrolling in Transylvania Bible School to train as missionaries called to New Guinea (*OS*: 5). The psychological and cultural background of missionaries is obviously important in understanding the type of people heeding God's command to undertake the Great Commission.

The significance of this background emerges in explanations of the particular colonial experience of Wiru, which was different from the majority of other Southern Highlanders. Consistent administrative staffing, in conjunction with a coercive and propaganda-based, military-style assault on Wiru practices and beliefs, were used to initiate and maintain a planned development programme (development was rarely such an early priority after pacification in other parts of the Highlands). The missions were also well organized and in some cases had years to plan, from established bases nearby in the Highlands, for their entry into Pangia and the conquest of heathen souls:

Waiting for the opening door . . . Word came to us one day . . . that the Widu [Wiru] Valley would soon be opened for missionary activity. It was a well-known fact that some other missions were making plans towards going into the valley with the intentions of proselytizing some of our followers. Some of these missions have a form of godliness but little or no power . . . [for Catholics] evangelizing consists of hanging a small medal around the neck of the people and writing down their names. With that they are considered a church member. (*FY*: 3)[3]

To protect our interests in the Widu Valley, we felt it necessary to build some houses on the border of this area and prepare to enter it as soon as it was declared open. (FY: 8)

Wiru were not oblivious to the intentions or rivalries of missionaries, and actively encouraged missions to set up in Pangia:

the natives from across the border were constantly coming to us and asking when we would come to their villages. We would explain . . . that we were ready as soon as the doors were opened. They would then ask how many missionaries we had ready to go in . . . [and] where we were going to be located.
Many of the natives were disappointed because those two places [Mele and Alia, selected as mission stations] didn't include their villages. They offered us land and told us they would help build the houses if only we would come to their places too. (*FY*: 10)

Given that the great majority of Wiru would have had little or no knowledge of Christianity at this time, a ritual basis for the desire for missions is indicated. The

---

[3] This characterization of the Catholics is unfair. Unlike the fundamentalists, they discouraged early or mass conversion, requiring many years of education in Catholic principles before baptism into the church was allowed. Conversion was meant to be as much a rational as an emotional decision. Bustin (n.d.: 54) writes of 'Catholicism, heathen religions, and Christianity', giving some idea of his view of Catholics in the scheme of things.

enthusiasm for Christianity shown by Wiru even before de-restriction must have surprised even the missions:

The natives wanted us to come or send another white man to go and teach them about God . . . We were temporarily blocked from going, but we were led to send for several boys and young men of school age to come to our station at Kaupena to be taught.

When word got out among the people of the Widu Valley that we were enrolling students from their area, they started flocking in by the dozens . . . When you get a group of nearly 200 wild, savage, untamed boys together you have nearly 200 problems together too . . . The Lord helped, however, and while there were many moments of trials and discouragements, still it was through those same boys we were able to reach the natives of the Widu Valley. (*FY*: 3)

Occasional fights would break out among the students, at which time 'their faces resembled those of raving bull apes instead of humans' (*FY*: 3), the racist underpinnings of some missionary activity becoming visible as animal-like blacks are shown by European example the path to righteousness and civilization. The roadshow of the pagan/Christian dialectic, playing itself out over millennia and relying on a certain kind of essentialism which made pagans 'bad' and Christians 'good', had finally arrived in Pangia—although time, space, and culture generated a specific colonial history of evangelism.

A key metaphor through which these missionaries constructed Wiru was that of darkness and light—'Surely the entrance of His word bringeth Light' (*FY*: 7)—readily taken up by the people themselves in their description of living like wild pigs in a time of darkness before conversion. Harvey's book title captures this metaphorical usage and, along with *Four Years with my Savage Brothers*, establishes the connection between darkness/blindness, savagery, skin colour, sin, and a kind of spiritual death. Harvey opens her book with a quote from Matthew 4: 16:

The people that sat in darkness
Have seen a great light,
And they that sat in the land and shadow of death,
On them light has dawned.

Fundamentalists used the Bible as a master trope for understanding their own motivation and the sorts of messages about sin and redemption that they had to impart to Wiru to ensure their conversion. Things happen because of prophecies and the miraculous intervention of God, in a not too dissimilar way to the importance of prophetic dreaming and spirit intervention in pagan life. Many missionaries lived in a world fully as 'magical' as the one they imagined Wiru to inhabit.

Like the kiaps' attitude to development, missionaries believed themselves to have a right and duty to evangelize, and furthermore, that their work was for the good of the savage. The right to do the work and the rightness of the message is justified by drawing upon another trope:

[This book] reveals the strategy of the Holy Spirit in missions as he calls workers, opens doors for them that would otherwise remain closed, and provides the necessary resources in

God's way at God's time. There are marvellous lessons for all readers in how the Holy Spirit reveals the sinfulness of the human heart, and the need for repentance, confession, and restitution. (*FM*: 8)

Invoking the Holy Spirit removes any need to reference individual agency (their own or that of the Wiru) or to demonstrate any kind of cultural sensitivity. Evangelism can then take place in a kind of cultural vacuum, and missionaries become simply the agents or conduit of the Holy Spirit or God:

I yielded my all over to the Master Planner and sincerely told him that I was taking my hands off. He could run my life as he pleased and use me as He saw fit. (*FY*: ii)

To break down the firm belief of the natives in spirits would have taken years if at all possible by any other way save through the power of the Holy Spirit. (*FY*: 16)

Such a deterministic and politically naive view reduces the entirety of Wiru culture to 'sin' in so far as this state defines the absence of God, and the Holy Spirit rather than the historical and colonial context becomes responsible for motivating Wiru in their responses to Christianity (people never stopped believing in the power of the spirits, they were merely re-consigned to the category of 'Satan'). When one considers the political views of some missionaries, Hides's warning about the dangers of unleashing the untrained and unsophisticated missionary on Highlanders seems even more poignant:

New Guinea, isolated as it may seem, is right now becoming so caught up in the communistic plan for world dominion, that many authorities fear that it too, shall soon be closed to the Gospel. One authority stated that if New Guineans were given their independence right now (that's what the communists in the United Nations are pushing for) the chaos resulting from such a move would make the Congo seem like a picnic. (*FY*: 54)

Not only is there an absence of God, but

They have no pots, pans, spoons, forks, dishes, clothes [!] or shoes. They had no true doctor to help their sick; there were no charity organizations to feed their hungry. Worst of all they had no messenger to give them the 'Bread of Life'. (*FY*: 1)

Wiru are defined by absence—and their nakedness inferred despite their own traditional dress—not by the content of their culture and practices. They are denied any integrity as members of a functioning culture, and become passive ciphers in a narrative about conversion and victory against Satan. It is inconceivable to Bustin that Wiru would convert for reasons other than the intervention of the Holy Spirit. Wiru conversion then appears as a 'natural' consequence of evangelism, and the colonial context of changing power relations and attempts to access European wealth is entirely minimized ('To the people we appeared inordinately rich, though we thought of ourselves as having less than the minimum for comfort' [*FM*: 25]). Encouraging people to condemn their cults is justified because they offer 'no Saviour of mankind, no God of love, nothing but confusion and fear for a while and then an endless eternity of torment and pain' (*FY*: 1).

Akolali, the 'man on top', who was a vaguely benevolent deity, became a Wiru term for God.

Bustin describes a scene involving a cult house that has no doubt been repeated numerous times in the history of Christian evangelism, but which is nonetheless revealing of mission ethnocentrism and arrogance:

> The natives seeing us go into the very building which they entered only when they had a peace offering to give the spirits, came running and told us that we would all die if we remained there. I told them that we had no fear of the spirits ... When they saw that they couldn't remove us by appealing to our fears, they told us that the tribe of that village would die as a result of our desecrating the spirit's dwelling place ... I explained to them that the God I served was able to keep them from any harm which their supposed spirits might try to inflict upon them. (*FY*: 15)

No opportunities were missed to disparage and condemn people's beliefs, such as those associated with ritual curing (*FY*: 17). Non-Wiru mission evangelists from Hagen and Ialibu went to even greater lengths to denigrate cult houses and the power of the spirits, including smearing excrement on cult stones—'the logic was irresistible, especially as it mimicked the demonstrations of strength employed by the kiaps' (A. J. Strathern 1984: 35).

The *Catholic Diary*, at least, reveals the politics of human agency in conversion and the pettiness of the competition for souls. One Protestant missionary would arrange for men to cut grass outside churches while the Catholics were at Mass (he also fired his shotgun into cult houses, and the kiaps eventually had to get rid of him after he ran a man over); another would distribute anti-Catholic literature, sometimes directly to the fathers themselves; and another would not buy food from Wiru Catholics or allow them treatment at the Wesleyan aid post. People were told that followers of the 'Father' would go to hell—'In all accounts the Blessed Mother is always attacked. How they fear Mary!' (*Catholic Diary* [n.d.], 19/5/63)—and that Jesus was coming soon and people had to convert to the EBM if they wanted to enter heaven. The Lutheran Master would reportedly hit natives and literally put the fear of God into them to make them stay Lutheran:

> We appear in danger of losing a few places I thought we would get [presents were returned and Lutherans accepted instead when they gave extra pearl shells] ... The Lutheran Master did his work well and seems to have scared the natives ... Perhaps he has the right approach—put fear into the natives. If so I can't imitate him for that isn't my nature. I'll have to keep plugging away at the idea of respecting their freedom and perhaps some will come to us in that way. (*Catholic Diary* [n.d.], 9/3/63)

A letter was sent by the Lutherans to the Catholics containing 'various wild charges, accusations and insinuations' (*Catholic Diary* [n.d.], 8/8/63). Bustin also felt grievances against the Catholics about the freedom of choice of pupils to enter the EBM school (a freedom that the administration was not willing to assert, as indicated above):

'Our Catholic teacher tells us,' they said, 'that if we should leave his school, we and our parents will be put in jail. He says that our names are written down on the books at the Government headquarters and the government will not permit us to change.'

I informed them that the government upheld freedom of religion . . . [and] that if the Catholic teacher beat them . . . I personally would see to it that he was sued in court for it.

Once or twice some of the natives would come running and tell us the Roman Catholic teacher was down in the village with a club getting ready to beat them . . . but while we have seen him pulling them by the hand, we have never caught him beating them. (*FY*: 9)

It is indicative that Bustin never thought of extending freedom of choice to pagan religion, but what these quotes and others indicate is the half-lies and accusations, and the bribery, coercion, and intimidation that accompanied the missionization process. The Catholics did not permit their converts to marry outside the 'true faith', and were keen to keep their flock in the face of Lutheran domination of the field. While I doubt that children were beaten, it would not be surprising if veiled threats of jail and divine punishment were used by some missionaries as a technique of control (the EBM did in fact cane some of their flock for misbehaviour (*OS*: 171)). These were desperate and competitive times, and given the territory and number of souls fought over, it was sometimes thought necessary to resort to 'dirty tricks' (the Catholics were ambivalent about giving 'presents'—of red handkerchiefs, red paint, knives, paper and tobacco, and salt—but they knew that other missions resorted to bribery, so in effect they had no choice if they wanted to win souls; the greater success of the Lutherans may have been largely due to their practice of gifting pearl shells). It seems that Wiru also provoked antagonism between missions, particularly as their initial expectations were disappointed and another mission was tried. The first Christian settlements were heavily contested:

[The Lutheran missionary] said that we were trying to grease the natives. I pointed out that the Tunda 'bosbois' had approached me. [One man said] I sought him out and gave him money even though he wanted the Lutherans. At Kalue they showed him a tin of money I supposedly gave. I pointed out that I hadn't given so much as a penny . . . I don't think Rev. Hertle believed me. We went on and on and each of us had different stories from the natives. We both deplored the fact that some natives play one mission against the other to get pay. (*Catholic Diary* [n.d.], 15/3/63)

It hardly needs repeating that the process of missionization was very complex and cannot be reduced either to the actions of the Holy Spirit, or to 'economic' motivation on the part of Wiru. Besides, Wiru know the Holy Spirit as Yakili, a vengeful figure who punishes people for breaches in kinship morality when humans invoke the power of cursing. The bitterness and denigration between missions was obvious to Wiru, and extended to conflicts between themselves as they became caught up in mission and 'bosboi' machinations for territory and dominance, and it was not surprising that some of them exploited these divisions.

The attacks made between missions were not based purely upon competition, as a certain amount of demonization of the Catholics took place:

While the children needed to be taught in English and their own language, he was teaching them songs and prayers in Latin. (The songs they were taught were actually chants and sounded fully as weird as their own pagan songs.) While the children needed to be saved by the blood of Jesus Christ, he had not had that blood applied to his own heart. While the children needed to be taught a form of government built on freedom and democracy, he was denying them the freedom of religion. While the people needed to be taught good morals, he himself was immoral. By teaching them how to play cards and to gamble, and by . . . taking part in the sensual dances and courting ceremonies in which foul and suggestive language was prevalent and immorality the ultimate outcome, he was propagating the things of the devil rather than fighting them. (*FY*: 9)

The ethnocentric and judgemental tone reveals that Catholicism is equated with (or seen as worse than) Wiru paganism, and that Bustin is more than willing to believe stereotypes of primitive 'sensual dances'—I do not know of any sensual Wiru dances—and Catholic gambling and licentiousness. In fact gambling was at this time punishable by jail, and the Diary reveals that many catechists were dismissed for playing cards. Bustin's 'freedom and democracy', revealing his own American biases, were certainly not extended to Wiru or Catholics; for what sort of freedom is involved in intimidating people with threats of hellfire and brimstone? The Catholics were not above projecting their own constructions of the devil's work and, during an EBM-inspired revival, Catholic settlements were sprinkled with holy water to keep its evil influence away, and people were also exorcised if they came under the sway of 'Holy Rollers' (*Catholic Diary* [n.d.], 6/8/63). The language used by missionaries reveals the inherent paternalism in their construction of the 'black, savage, heathen New Guineans' (*FY*: 53) as naked and childlike, needing European guidance:

I can still see a small group of men sitting beside the road planning a big pig feast, trying to be prepared, but yet lost . . . because the Bible says without Christ there is no salvation. I can hear them yet, as they ask what they must do to avoid Hell and to make it to Heaven. I can see them as blind men groping for the wall, with no one to help them. It seems I can hear another voice, more powerful . . . saying 'And ye shall know the truth and the truth shall make you free.' But how can they know the truth unless we tell them? (*FY*: 52).

There is certainly not one truth as Bustin implies; truth is contextual and produced by the operation of colonial techniques of control upon savage and immoral child-like bodies. Truth emerges out of biases and deceit as power is exercised in the attempt to create the docile subjects necessary to justify the evangelical endeavour. Christianity was indeed 'true' for Wiru because of European power and wealth, just as for one Fijian chief the white men's muskets were true, so that 'your religion must be true' (Sahlins 1985: 38). And the 'freedom' that this truth entails is certainly not the liberal, rose-coloured version of the mission, but a freedom with costs and limitations for autonomy and cultural expression.

Duplicity is demonstrated in the subversion of the restricted-area decree by sending for Wiru students, and in the presentation of Wiru testimony about their conversion, manufactured for overseas consumption (for some missionaries this is not deceit but justifiable behaviour). These reports come from the first years of evangelism at a time when the missionaries had few or no language skills, relying upon second-hand translation:

Last Sunday I gave my heart to Jesus. When I prayed, I told him that I would give up my spirit worship if he would save me. Jesus filled my heart with joy when I told Him that and he washed all my sins away. Yesterday, I completed my vow by tearing down my spirit house and burying the bones that were in it. (*FY*: 16)

Missionaries of a certain persuasion may talk like this, but Wiru in the early 1960s most certainly did not, and rarely do so today, with the exception of some pastors ('as nearly as I can remember, this is what he said').

The destruction of cult houses was not quite so straightforward. The Catholics record that first they had to be blessed, and holy water sprinkled around the site and places of burial of stones and bones. Crosses were often planted where the cult house had formerly stood (*Catholic Diary* [n.d.], 16/1/63). The spirits still had a power that had to be nullified and contained by the superior 'magic' of prayers and holy water, and planting the crosses suggests that their power was somehow incorporated into Christianity. Holy water was sometimes stolen and rubbed into pigs to make them grow and to obey their owners. At least the Catholics had the grace to admit to some uncertainty in these procedures: 'One fellow said he wanted to "bury his tambaran house" and asked me to bless it . . . In absence of exorcism and holy water, I composed a short prayer . . . Hope they are sincere about it all—I wonder if they know what it's all about. I wonder if I know what this is about!' (*Catholic Diary* [n.d.], 1/3/62).

Skin Christians

It was Wiru, of course, who were accused of being mercenary and duplicitous in the early (and later) days of missionization; an interpretation of such behaviour as a reflection of experiences of missionary motivation and actions was less acceptable. These accusations sit uneasily with the 'respect and awe' of Wiru towards missionaries, as recorded in patrol reports of the 1960s. From the Wiru perspective, respecting the power of the cult of Christianity while playing off its evangelists for greater wealth were not antithetical responses to the missions, and such actions do not compromise the argument for a ritual attitude to proselytization. Otherwise it becomes difficult to explain the abandonment of cults, whose spirits were still held to be powerful, in favour of the church, whose spirits were yet more powerful—

One of the early victories on the Wiru field was the destruction of the village spirit house at Takuru. There were housed two stone fetishes . . . [that] were the last of such stones in the village, and apparently the people were somewhat fearful about destroying them. They sent for our leading national Christian to come and take away the stones for us to destroy them, which [we] had great pleasure in doing! This act of renunciation of the old spirit-worship practices gave an impetus to the work there . . . God had famished the gods of the Wirus! (*FM*: 75)

It was not God who destroyed cult houses, unless he is understood as a metaphor for a superior European wealth and power. Wiru were complicit in this destruction, even if they did not have Bustin's much vaunted 'freedom of choice' over their actions. Their decision made 'cultural' sense to the extent that a cult was imported to deal with new alignments of power, but it compromised Wiru independence and autonomy in cultural reproduction by taking on board a debilitating and restrictive sense of sin about their past and traditions, such that cults were displaced and devalued rather than complemented. This time there was to be no accommodation with the past, and what Thomas (1992) describes as an 'inversion of tradition', a negative evaluation of a (by now) objectified Wiru culture located in the time and space of darkness, came to define certain aspects of colonial and postcolonial Wiru identity.

I talked to several missionaries who were demeaning of the Wiru commitment to Christianity, calling them 'wishy-washy', disloyal, and even grasping. The Wesleyans had another station in Tari, and unfavourable comparisons were often made in the early 1980s between Wiru and the 'Holy Huli' (although I doubt that the Huli could sustain such a description today):[4]

One Wesleyan missionary [interviewed in Takuru] who had resided for many years in both the Tari and Pangia Districts praised the Huli's outward cooperativeness and apparent acceptance of Christianity. But when referring to the Pangia population, he displayed disenchantment, frustration, and some anger towards their general unwillingness to follow the gospel. Other missionary residents have expressed similar sentiments . . . lamenting the propensity of the local people to shift from mission to mission according to expectations of goods and material rewards. (Robin 1980: 91)

These missionary criticisms of Wiru are a classic example of the 'blame the victim' syndrome, in this case of a particular type of evangelical process. Harvey (*OS*: 209) even projects them on to the pastor of her biography, in her description of his fall in terms of going back to Satan: 'His wife was a Christian, his parents were saved. Hundreds and hundreds of his Widu people were now in God's family . . . But in spite of all this he still felt uneasy inside . . . Something within him keenly desired material things until he felt that they were almost gods to him.' This

---

[4] It is interesting to speculate upon the reasons for these early differences between Wiru and Huli responses to Christianity, which I would relate to differences between systems based upon ritual and mythology respectively. The working synthesis that Huli forged between their myths and those of the Bible ensured a much greater acceptance and commitment to the message of Christianity, whereas Wiru had a greater commitment to its ritual praxis and were more likely to be disappointed earlier. Also, Huli had ritual leaders who exercised considerable control over the population, and when these men were won over to Christianity, allowing missions to do such things as fell the sacred groves, the 'authority' of conversion and Christianity made a stronger and more lasting impression (C. Ballard, pers.comm.). Huli displayed more of an initial resistance to the message of Christianity because of their commitment to a more encompassing mythology and its 'earth spell' rituals, and this may be what endeared them to the missions once they finally converted.

misreading of desire once more points to the connections Wiru make between 'material things' and cults, rendered sinful by Harvey despite the EBM's own message, so appealing to Wiru, of the link between Christianity and prosperity, between valuables and 'gods'. This explains the disappointment with, and continuing attraction of Christianity, which obviously 'works' for Europeans, encouraging many Wiru to persevere in their efforts to attract new Christian sects and churches.[5]

The activities of missionaries in an unusual colonial context helped to create the Wiru Christian, not the Holy Spirit, despite the ecstatic and positive pronouncements made about the extent and fervour of the first conversions during Holy Spirit-inspired revivals. The early hopes that missionaries held of Wiru, and their later disappointments with the superficiality of their Christianity—I have heard missionaries refer to Wiru as 'skin Christians'—compares with the administration's disillusionment with the Wiru commitment to development, their failure to become peasants. It is not to the mercenary or shallow nature of Wiru that these European sentiments must be traced, rather it is to the nature of colonialism and its construction of the knowing and productive subject. The next chapter will consider how Wiru constructed themselves as agents and subjects through two separate but interrelated responses to the twin messages of development and Christianity, but it is worth concluding with this plea from the Ialibu Assistant District Officer in 1955:

If the [Pangia] area is derestricted, please do your best to ensure that the missions operate in separate spheres of influence, and warn them that tactless or over-zealous evangelizing could have markedly adverse effects on native attitudes which appear to be at present satisfactory. (Ialibu PR2/55–56)

---

[5] This interpretation is not meant to deny the emotive appeal and support of Christianity to many Wiru, especially to women, or its meaning to them in their everyday lives.

PART III

5

Shrinking, Colonialism, and the Wildman

The previous two chapters elaborated upon the consequences of 'contact' and pacification presented in Chapter 2, and examined and displayed the historical trajectory of colonialism in Pangia through the discourses of the missions and administration. These chapters set the scene for a more in-depth consideration, initiated with the analysis of the Kongono cult, of Wiru responses to development and Christianity. Undue emphasis on the discourses and practices of kiaps and missionaries tends to deny agency to the colonized, glossing over the entanglements and misunderstandings between Europeans and Wiru that produce the particular characteristics of colonial and colonized culture. For Thomas (1994: 16), the former

includes not only official reports and texts related directly to the process of governing colonies and extracting wealth, but also a variety of travellers' accounts, representations produced by other colonial actors such as missionaries and collectors of ethnographic specimens, and fictional, artistic, photographic, cinematic and decorative appropriations.

It should be clear from previous chapters that Thomas's notion of colonial culture, as it existed in Pangia, cannot be considered separately from or as impervious to Wiru culture, and vice versa. Interactions between the administration, kiaps, mission headquarters, missionaries, and Wiru transformed both cultures (explanations of the culture of the prison, hospital, or school cannot assume the passivity of the inmates in the construction of cultural forms). Out of Wiru accommodation to the propaganda and praxis of colonial agents, a culture of collaboration, misunderstanding, and opposition arose in the imaginative space between colonizer and colonized (Taussig 1984).[1] This is the 'space of colonialism', an area of overlap between colonialism's culture and Wiru culture where, in the partial eclipse of certainty and meaning, new images of Wiru and Europeans, and of the relationships between them, are generated. Wiru culture transforms into a colonized culture and, in the dialectical process, transforms aspects of colonial culture itself. Despite inequalities in power, wealth, and knowledge the hegemonic control of Europeans was not total and unrestricted, as is indicated by the

---

[1] My argument is indebted to Taussig's notion of the 'space of death' in the Putumayo region of South America: 'The space of death is pre-eminently a space of transformation: through the experience of death, life; through fear, loss of self and conformity to a new reality; or through evil, good' (Taussig 1984: 468). The colonial space I refer to was less lethal for Wiru than it was for the Indians of the Putumayo, but it was no less transformative of subjectivity.

120*Shrinking, Colonialism, and the Wildman*

gradual slide from optimism about the native's potential to disappointment with his recalcitrance and dependence.[2]

The responses of Wiru to colonialism take the form of a series of 'histories' of the European encounter which, written on and through the body, read very differently from the accounts presented in Chapters 3 and 4. I am not referring to oral histories of the type discussed in Chapter 2, which approximate to a Western sense of history that Wiru are quite capable of reproducing (cf. Neumann 1992), but rather to idioms and beliefs that display an experiential reflexivity about changing alignments of power and knowledge (accounting for the androcentric biases of this chapter, as women seem less compromised by colonialism and talk more positively about its benefits; see also Clark and Hughes [1995] for Huli women). This sense of embodied history is distinctly non-Western, at least until recent feminist theorizing, and is less a critique of colonialism per se (cf. Taussig 1980) than a way to make sense of a rapidly changing world. This 'making sense' is not at a level Western common sense would label as 'rational' or 'intellectual', as history for Wiru is far from a process of imposing order on events through a linear, cause and effect paradigm. In writing this, it is not my intention to belittle Wiru historical understandings of the ways in which fundamental assumptions about reality are challenged and re-conceptualized. Change is imagined through metaphors that utilize the body as a vehicle or idiom for the interpretation and expression of experience and, as a way of making history; it is not determined or constrained by a mythic mode of thought, as it involves a relationship between consciousness and understanding that invokes the body as hermeneutic. The movement from Wiru culture to colonized culture is what Wiru history 'describes', producing the major discontinuity that I had so much trouble understanding as a callow fieldworker. I can better demonstrate these assertions about history writing itself through the body, rather than select individuals writing it for the consumption of others, through ethnographic example. But first a brief theoretical interlude.

The phenomena of mad and shrinking men will be analysed from a Foucauldian perspective, namely for the way in which new regimes of power and knowledge are inscribed on the body (Foucault 1979).[3] Using Foucault to present a Wiru history may appear to undermine my claim that accounts of madness, for instance, are examples of indigenous history-making, but some resort to Western theory for explanation is unavoidable and Foucault does less violence to the cultural categories through which Wiru conceptualize processes of change.[4] Reading Foucault

---

[2] Taussig's point is that paranoid images of Indians as cannibalistic savages legitimated appalling acts of savagery by the rubber collectors themselves, whereas in Pangia the initial images of Wiru were of a hard-working and eager Christian convert, prospective members of a 'showcase' district. The Western biases and misunderstandings that created these images helped to transform them into views of Wiru as mercenary, requiring 'spoon-feeding', and as 'wishy-washy'.

[3] Following Foucault, my use of 'body' always refers to an entity that is historically located and culturally constituted.

[4] I am aware that claims of representing the 'other' can demonstrate what Taussig (1987: 135) calls 'the ultimate anthropological conceit'. I am also aware that this monograph is an attempt at an anthropological history and is not a 'Wiru' history as such.

I am struck by the aptness of his language for describing the Wiru colonial experience; I do not use him because of fashionable postmodern preoccupations with the body and inscription, but because Wiru themselves 'think' through the body and use it to image discontinuity. The early years of development amongst the Wiru will be discussed using Foucault's account of discipline and punishment in the European penal system, although the theme discussed for colonial Pangia would be better expressed as pacification and conversion. The difference between a study of the prison and of colonialism is, to paraphrase Sahlins (1985: x), one of different bodies, different historicities, yet inscribed in both is a 'truth' produced through the deployment of power on the imprisoned/colonized.

Foucault confined his history of the body to Western society, and his treatise on the emergence of a disciplinary society mainly concerns France between the seventeenth and nineteenth centuries. In his work on the 'birth of the prison', Foucault (1979) demonstrated how changing attitudes to the body and its punishment underpinned the movement from torture to confinement. This transformation reflected a discontinuity within the social logics of French justice and morality. The numbered and individuated prisoner was delivered from the maimed body of the tortured; the womb of pain gave way to the cell of the soul. Instead of terror, the confined experienced an alienation produced by the rules and practices of discipline, and these new technologies of power were given the mystified form of serving rehabilitative and humanitarian ends. A departure from Foucault, in scope if not in analytical style, is in the way I represent the body—as do the Wiru—as the fulcrum around which a colonized culture emerged. Like Foucault, I am concerned with the historical processes by which the body becomes subject to, and is constituted by new regimes of power and knowledge. My aim is to describe how the Wiru body became the focus for an encounter between cultures, and between epistemic moments in a historically developing society (although Foucault's analysis in *Discipline and Punish* will be modified to take into account the historical specificity of colonial regimes of power in Pangia, and the fact that Wiru inscribed altered states upon their bodies as much as did the colonizers).

My argument will be developed by presenting an ethnohistory of the body, which takes 'into account the people's own sense of how events are constituted, and their ways of culturally constructing the past' (Schieffelin and Gewertz 1985: 3). This focus on the body is appropriate given its central role in Wiru thought, particularly in relation to the life-cycle exchanges which reproduce Wiru society (Clark 1991; for Melpa 'the body is the person himself' (Strauss 1990: 100)). The body was culturally constructed before its engagement with 'the experts in normality' (Foucault 1979: 228), namely patrol officers and missionaries who, through technologies of power I gloss as 'development', imposed regimes for the discipline and punishment—in the 'calabus' (jail) or hell—of the body. Indigenous constructions of the body influenced the interaction of Wiru with colonial structures of power. Out of this encounter emerged new subjectivities and identities, all mediated by the new bodies which the colonial order was producing.

There are two strands to the argument that I am attempting to weave together; the first involves the claim that the Wiru response to colonialism was a ritual one, and the second is that changes experienced under colonialism were interpreted through and productive of an embodied ethnohistory. Precolonial links between cults and the body are indicated by actions such as men tying vines between their scrota and the stones of the Tapa house, known as the 'ancestor's testicles'; and the decoration of their own bodies by using the same designs and colours as those found on certain cult stones—an embodiment of cult power. Wiru lived in what Wagner calls a 'cult world', and continued to do so during the development era:

The only way to awaken from the dream is to dream one has awakened: a cult world does not 'awaken' or 'adjust' to a superordinate reality [such as colonialism]; rather, under the impress of event, it adjusts to itself and negotiates commensurate realities of its own. (Wagner 1979: 148)

Ironically, missionaries described Christian revivals as 'awakenings', but certainly there was no 'awakening' in Wagner's sense, as we shall see. The Kongono cult, like revivals, was part of an attempt to 'negotiate commensurate realities', to make a new and more relevant cult world, but things are only 'made' through actions of the body, whether it be pearl shells or enhanced fertility of the ground. Wiru madness was an interpretation of colonial power, later acted upon through Christian revivals to achieve the new world promised by development, while the notion of shrinking men was an interpretation of the failure of this world to appear.[5]

Madness and Colonization

In Chapter 2 I discussed how the body figured in early reactions to colonialism by reference to the desire of some men to become *kapona*, through the wearing of steel, in order to appropriate the power of Europeans; the later wearing of white clothes at baptism demonstrates a similar desire.[6] Chapter 3 indicated that, through the intensive labour of their bodies in *ka kongono*, people believed that they would become 'like whites'. Elsewhere I have considered Wiru procreation beliefs that underpin constructions of gender and the logic of exchange (Clark 1991), which I will briefly summarize. The Wiru body is entirely created by

---

[5] Wagner (1979: 150) comments that 'failure is what makes cargo cults', and suggests the notion of 'history as failure'. In Pangia it would be more appropriate to discuss development in terms of 'failure as embodied history'.

[6] Franklin (1972: 135) records for the Kewa a similar belief in the 'magical significance of baptism': 'The head water [used in baptism] is the blood and water of Jesus which was collected in bottles by the white men when Christ died. When the water is poured on the head it goes inside the stomach where it guards God's talk. It cleanses us from bad talk and helps us do good work. Its power is reactivated through eating the food [communion].'

The stress on baptism as a bodily transformation through the ingestion or rubbing in of sacrificial substance is clearly indicated. Communion food is known by Wiru as *yomborono*, traditional medicine used in curing.

women, said by men to do all the 'hard work' in pregnancy, birth, and nurturance. Semen is viewed as triggering foetal formation only, playing no part in bodily constitution. As a consequence of this, persons are indebted for their bodies to matrikin, which involves them in lifelong exchanges of pearl shells for pork rib-cages. Pearl shells represent the achievements of their owner, and acts of exchange create the pearl shell donor as a subject, a personalized and socially recognized body, or rather a body plus skin. The skin displays an external 'maleness', for women also, and is a metaphor for the personality and affectivity of the body it contains—the body is gendered in surface and depth. Wiru experience and *create* the world through their own bodies, reading social relationships and meaning into the perceived body, such that procreation beliefs reflect an ontological dimension in the achievement of personhood.

Europeans brought development and Christianity to Pangia from the world identified in origin stories as the source, and gender constructs are refracted into this logic, thereby linking Wiru to this world. Wiru were enthusiastic to obtain what Europeans represented, but were indebted for the 'gifts' of development. There was a ritual exchange of work, including prayer and church attendance, for the 'new' Christian body promised by development. But the parameters of power within which the body was constructed were no longer solely Wiru. Europeans had entered into this construction, much to the initial desire of Wiru, but deprived Wiru of autonomy in the creation of personhood and in cultural reproduction, which was only gradually recognized or, perhaps more appropriately, 'felt'. Masculinity had to be compromised as men, once warriors, followed the dictates of colonial authority or suffered the consequences. The recognition of compromise and loss of autonomy was expressed through the belief that men were physically shrinking, experiencing a bodily detumescence in the face of colonial control (see below).

History came to be mapped on to the body as Wiru attempted to interpret their colonial experience. The way in which notions of the body influenced people's reactions to colonial power will be demonstrated, first by considering 'wildman' and Christian revival behaviour. At first sight, the only thing which these two phenomena have in common is that both involved bouts of madness (described as *leau* by informants, or 'long long' in Melanesian Pidgin). Wildman behaviour involved young madmen threatening others in their travels; Christian revivals involved men and women of all ages directing their enthusiasm and aggression more against themselves than towards other people. Both forms of behaviour were triggered by an encroaching colonial presence and novel experiences of power; both involved a 'loss' of bodily control which was highly meaningful to the observers and participants.

In the early 1960s many young Wiru men of the southern Pangia district went 'mad'. They experienced a wind which closed their ears, after which they carefully decorated themselves as warriors. The afflicted individual often ran from settlement to settlement stealing food, threatening physical violence to the men and children he encountered, and sexual violence to the women. The madness was contagious, and sometimes gangs of young madmen would gather together and aggressively wander around, destroying gardens and property, and inviting any woman they met, irrespective of age and kinship, to 'show us your vulva' as a prelude to rape. They broke into houses and defecated on the floor, the hearth, and sleeping areas. Madmen from different settlements sometimes fought each other, or clashed with similarly afflicted men they met on their travels. After weeks or months, the madness burnt itself out like a flame; the wind died away and the madmen returned to normalcy, their ears unfolded and their faces no longer covered.[7]

If the activities of the young madmen are shorn of their exoticism, they seem little different from acts of vandalism common in Western society—the destruction of property, defecation in houses, theft, and so on. The labelling of wildmen as 'mad' has to be questioned; madness represented not arbitrary behaviour but was to some extent culturally channelled; it was how young men who go 'mad' were expected to behave.[8] Madness was the method through which resentments against the established—or soon to be established—colonial order were expressed. The area in which the madness was most prevalent was the last part of Pangia to be pacified. To summarize points from earlier chapters, administration patrols were arresting homicides and warriors and arranging compensation between enemies by making them kill pigs together. This was the only area where a fatality had occurred during government patrolling, and where settlements had been burnt and looted by kiaps. Wiru were openly resistant to the new order, with warfare continuing until 1960 (it is highly unlikely that Wiru in this area had been contacted by missions). People were aware that a patrol station had been established at Ialibu (some had even visited and worked there), and that it was soon to be their turn for colonial control. The madness occurred at a time when epidemics of European-introduced diseases such as influenza were claiming many lives, and when patrolling had been stepped up and plans for the establishment of Pangia station were well advanced. Southern Wiru felt threatened by these events, and their lack of co-operation with the administration demonstrated their apprehensions about the approaching colonial embrace.

In some areas the deaths from disease were linked to the new type of *ulo* sorcery, possibly associated with Europeans. It was also believed that patrol officers had

---

[7] This account is a summary of events described in A. J. Strathern (1977).

[8] Clarke (1973: 207) quotes Devereux in respect of the cultural directive: 'Don't become insane, but if you do, you must behave as follows . . .' McCarthy's accounts (1963: 101) of fainting among the Anga in reaction to his presence also come to mind, as in the example where an 'unconscious' man firmly kept a grip on the steel axe McCarthy had just given him when his companions attempted to take it. Harvey's account (1973: 186, 201) of the revival suggests that 'hysteria' was often emulated: 'A young boy was rolling on the ground nearby. The leaves in his bark belt loosened. Quickly he stopped rolling and tightened them by pulling them up. The girls, too, were modest as possible with their skimpy grass skirts. It was rather comical to see a woman jump then remember that she did not have a cloth tied around her. Mrs Harvey knew that the Holy Spirit is clean in everything that He does.'

special or magical techniques for 'taming' Wiru, especially young men. This involved the introduction of substances into the river system and water supply, which people later drank. This brought on fits in some young men, and the madness in the south was also directly related to Europeans (A. J. Strathern 1977: 138). Wildman behaviour has been explained as a response to highly emotional conflict situations (Robin 1981; Clarke 1973). Young Wiru men 'coming under the pressures of the exchange system, of adult society and its possible accompanying rivalries' (A. J. Strathern 1977: 133, my translation), were more susceptible to an uncertain future. These men, with warfare suppressed and aggression punished, were lacking in ways to constitute their masculinity socially. According to Clarke (1973: 208) wildman behaviour in Highlands societies 'fulfils for a time the cultural ideal of being an aggressive and dynamic man,' in a situation where the achievement of male adulthood had become increasingly problematic. Andrew Strathern (1977: 139, my translation) suggests that

What the white men were bringing with them was a new system of control over ownership, behaviour and power. Wiru could not avoid subjugation to this control . . . Policemen, guns, labour, rules and regulations, all these together must have given rise to the image of powerful control. If this is the case, the reaction of madness was reversal; to put one's self 'out of control', thus giving a powerful temporary 'answer' to the whites' arrival.

Andrew Strathern's description of the entailments of colonialism reads very much like one of Foucault's disciplinary regimes, although I am not so sure that madness was an answer to anything. Wiru, in a similar fashion to the Paiela of Enga province (Biersack 1990), do not entertain notions of a Cartesian mind–body duality; one's self was also one's body. I would suggest that the madness, far from being a result of anxiety or just a reaction to powerlessness, was the internalization within the body of the alienating presence of whites. Men felt themselves alienated from the control of their own bodies, and became mad. Like physical attacks upon patrols, this behaviour was to some extent a form of resistance—a politics of the body directed against its colonial control (cf. A. J. Strathern 1977: 143). Madness occurred after some men had attempted to bodily transform themselves into *kapona*; they were arrested and taken away for imprisonment. More than resistance, madness, a loss of bodily control, provided a metacommentary, a lucid acting out of a dilemma experienced by everyone, namely the loss of autonomy which colonialism entailed. Clarke (1973) has commented on these theatrical aspects of madness, suggesting that it provides a context for people to reflect upon the human condition as well as to experience amusement and stimulation. He sees madness as adaptive in bridging transitions (cf. A. J. Strathern 1977: 143), and as offering an 'escape' from role confusion and boredom for young men (Clarke 1973: 211).

While I would question the adaptive and escape functions of madness, it is useful to consider the condition which people reflect upon through madness, which is that of animality. Madness was a form of 'deep play' (cf. Geertz 1973 on the Balinese cockfight), and its portrayal presented for contemplation some cultural themes in a colonial context. Madmen ate raw food and slept in the bush (A. J. Strathern 1977: 134); they were 'wild', undomesticated, which is why they were deaf, indicating a lack of comprehension and an inability to communicate (*leau* translates as 'wild', a condition outside the domain of human society, an absence of culture. cf. Herdt 1986). This can also be a stage in spirit possession, a stripping down of the person to the 'wild' body unaware of the codes of conduct of kinship and sexuality, so that revelations of power and knowledge can be made available to the possessed (the link between power/knowledge and sexuality, so important for Foucault, will be returned to below). The possessing spirit then creates a body *ne plus ultra*, such that madness can be an apotheosis, a communion with the divine, another realm of experience (Stephen 1979: 13, 14). While Wiru madness was often related to spirit possession, the outbreak in the 1960s was believed to be spread by Europeans, as an informant of Andrew Strathern's relates: 'it was the white men who were sending the madness . . . it was the white men who were mad and were making us mad and ill like them' (1977: 138, my translation).

Wiru associated white men with river spirits and watercourses, along which wealth and the ghosts of the dead travel, and in which kiaps had put 'taming' substances. These spirits cause sickness and were described as white in colour, with the torsos of men and legs of the cassowary (recall the attribution to Europeans of 'cassowary' status in Chapter 3). Andrew Strathern (1977: 138, my translation) argues that 'to attribute the cause of the fit to the strange intruding Europeans is, in a way, culturally equivalent to attributing it to evil spirits.' There are similarities between this aspect of madness and the trance or possession states common to cargo cults, which attempt to reveal and appropriate colonial relations of power/knowledge. Wildmen were to some extent acting like whites by behaving arbitrarily and causing disorder (A. J. Strathern 1977: 143), which was another version of the transformation attempted by the *kapona* men. The young madmen were perhaps not putting themselves 'out of control' but displaying the nature of this control to themselves and others. The body as stage creatively presented an attempt at dealing with new configurations of power and knowledge, to understand and perhaps capture them—as Kongono later attempted. As Turner (in Kapferer 1991: xxv) states, play and entertainment create a 'threshold between mundane spaces and times . . . where all is magical possibility'.

Wildman behaviour then, was not pathological in origin, a fact recognized long ago by Salisbury (1966: 106), who viewed it as 'appropriate behaviour [in] abnormal circumstances . . . a social responsibility'. Andrew Strathern's account (1977: 133) of the madness extends this argument by suggesting that the stories he collected, several years after the events to which they refer, may have been largely, if not purely fictional. My research was conducted in an area north of where Strathern worked, and none of my informants knew of outbreaks of madness further south. Missionaries whom I interviewed, who had been in Pangia in the early 1960s, had also never witnessed or heard tales of this event, implying that madness may have been an act of the imagination, fabricated out of a particular experience of pacification. Wiru madness was different from accounts of similar phenomena in other societies in that wildmen spoke, could be reasoned with, and afterwards clearly remembered their activities. Madness was a narrative which Wiru 'told' through their own bodies, and elaborated upon in the retelling so as to understand their part in the colonial encounter. Tales of madness, as distinct from the madness itself (if it actually occurred), were the result of 'a need to assimilate and integrate their continuing historical experience from the crucial moment when Europeans established their administrative station among them' (A. J. Strathern 1977: 143, my translation).

As part of the technology of development, patrol officers imposed a regime of labour and discipline to serve new social, political and economic ends (see Chapter 3; A. J. Strathern 1982b). To put people to work, to divide days into tasks, to census populations, were constant refrains of administrative reports. Andrew Strathern (1978: 81) reports an instance in which many of the men of a settlement were taken off to jail for failing to maintain latrines. Random police checks, which could result in arrest, beatings, and imprisonment, were made to ensure people's compliance with administrative directives. Informants recounted the uncertainty, resentment, and awe they felt towards the heavy-handed and intimidating behaviour of patrol officers— 'people lived in fear and anxiety of being caught without an excuse for absence from work' (A. J. Strathern 1982b: 93).[9] They told stories of women being made to line up while an officer walked along with a stick, lifting up their grass skirts to expose their vaginas, supposedly to check for scabies. Kiaps were said to select women to sleep with them while they were out on patrol. The threat of imprisonment was continually present if people did not present themselves for government work days or were lazy if they did, if they did not turn up for census, or if their latrines did not pass the 'kick test'.[10] It may be that some of these accounts of patrol officers behaving as wildmen are fictional in the same sense as that discussed for madness, but nonetheless they do capture in narrative form the Wiru experience of colonialism as a technology inscribed upon their own bodies and the spaces they inhabited, as the following song about the powerlessness felt by Wiru towards Europeans demonstrates:

Yesterday, white men, you came from Ialibu.
And here at Pangia you made
A house of metal and barbed wire around it.
I'll jump inside it now.   (Paia and Strathern 1977: 29)

The disciplinary regime created a colonial space in which different alignments of power, knowledge, and time were experienced, resulting in transformed

---

[9] Josephides and Schiltz (1991: 279) quote a Kewa man, from an area bordering Pangia, on the sort of training received by a *luluai*, an appointed village leader: 'Becoming a *luluai* was no easy matter. First they would seize a man and beat him up thoroughly, then put him in a uniform and give him good food, soap, and loincloths. Then he would come back and tell us how good they had been to him, and urge us to obey the government.' These 'techniques of coercion and dressage applied to the bodies of individuals' (Patton 1987: 235) were also reported in Pangia.

[10] Kiaps noted that in the early days of colonialism some settlements built fake villages at which they welcomed patrols, believing that the administration encouraged a movement towards more centralized settlements (Pangia PR7/62–63).

subjectivities and what I refer to as colonized culture. Fabian (1983: 144) states that, 'colonialist-imperialist expansion required Time to accommodate the schemes of a one-way history: progress, development, modernity (and their negative mirror images: stagnation, underdevelopment, tradition).' The cogency of this statement is demonstrated in Chapter 3, but the point is that there is often a new experience of 'time' for the colonized with the imposition of work days, Sunday observances, and so on. It is no accident that one of the first icons of European power to be fetishized by Wiru men was the wrist-watch, soon the most desirable of items of dress, even if it had long ceased working—in 1980, one of the wealthiest men in Pangia demonstrated his grief at his father's death by smashing his wrist-watch. The watch was first known in the vernacular as *lo pine*, the base/cause of the sun, a celestial body held to be 'boss' over men—particularly their labour—and while I doubt that Wiru actually thought that it caused the sun to rise and fall, it does indicate the connection made between Europeans and their power to control the 'time' of Wiru, creating new interrelationships between time and subjectivity that were captured through embodied histories. The Wiru equation of time with the sun could be read to imply that time continued to be circular, but as a term, *lo pine* seems to have dropped out of circulation, and with the imposition of government work days, Sunday observances, plantation labour, and so on, it is likely that a linear sense of time gradually emerged, perhaps co-existing with a circular sense when epochs rather than events are considered (cf. Harkin 1988: 125, n.28).

The Joy of Jumping

In 1963, two years after the establishment of Pangia station, the fundamentalist missions were encouraging religious 'revivals' amongst their recently acquired congregations. Administrative reports and missionary accounts of the period contain many references to outbursts of strange behaviour—the most exuberant forms being displayed by men—caught up in the excitement and fears of conversion to Christianity. Men hit themselves and rolled around on the ground, their bodies 'writhed and twisted in seeming torments' (Harvey 1973: 190). Gymnastic feats were attempted, people hung upside down from church rafters and climbed over church buildings or jumped off rooftops. Injuries were reported, along with violent head movements, vomiting, and lapses into unconsciousness (for similar reports from the Tari area, see Robin 1981: 155). The *Catholic Diary* (n.d., 4/8/1963) reports that in one settlement people removed their clothes and engaged in a 'naked frenzy' and, at another, people tied their houses to the ground in fear of the end of the world.[11] Visions of bright lights, heaven, and Jesus, particularly of

---

[11] Revivals did not always proceed as their propagators hoped: 'Satan tried to get in and he counterfeited the work of the Lord in a few instances. But God gave His native leaders discernment and anything unclean was sharply rebuked' (Harvey 1973: 203). Missionary observers were certainly aware of the potential for sexuality to emerge with loss of bodily control—'I watched carefully lest there be any scandalous behaviour' (Ridgway 1976: 82)—indicating the power and extent of the colonial gaze.

his crucifixion, were experienced during apparent states of trance. It was believed that people were possessed by the Holy Spirit (see also Clark 1985, 1989). The administration was very concerned about revivals and J. K. McCarthy, by this time the Director of Native Affairs, decried the 'extremist views' of fundamentalist missionaries:

[Hysteria] can be more dangerous in this Territory than in most places, because the whole social system is going through a period of great change and consequent strain, and unbalanced views can therefore lead to considerable social disturbance and trouble. (Memo from the Director of Native Affairs, in Pangia PR4/63–64)

Christian missions played an important part in establishing, through the practice of their own rules of discipline, a colonized culture. The regime of power/knowledge associated with Christianity also impinged upon the body and transformed subjectivity. These claims will be investigated by considering the revival which occurred in 1963 in settlements with fundamentalist and evangelical missions, and involved over 2,000 Wiru at its peak. The fundamentalist mission attitude to heathens was to convert them as groups rather than as individuals. The aim was not to bring people to an intellectual appreciation of Christian philosophy and morality, but to create a psychological climate in which the Holy Spirit could move among the people and convert them *en masse*. The emphasis was on an emotional conversion, and the style for inducing this state was hellfire-and-brimstone proselytizing. Unlike the madness, the revival 'hysteria' was actually promoted and given form by Europeans through claims such as the impending end of the world and the necessity to confess sin to enter the European heaven, and was not a totally indigenous response to the colonial presence.

The similarity between revival behaviour in Pangia and the Western world was not due to the actions of the Holy Spirit but traceable to similar techniques used in achieving conversion (Robin 1981: 161). This included causing people to reflect on their previous life-styles, and to reject them as sinful, as a prerequisite to accepting a new order—an acceptance based on promises of reward and threats of punishment. It is, of course, problematic to write of notions of sin in another culture, but it is undeniable that missions succeeded in creating a tremendous sense of 'shame'—in the Wiru sense of improper or immoral behaviour—about precolonial life. People spent many hours, often days, deprived of food and sleep, whilst engaged in repetitive prayers and hymns in church: 'they flocked to the churches to pray day and night. Gardens were neglected as the people sought the Lord' (Ridgway 1976: 85)—and they were continually exhorted to give up their heathen ways or be condemned to an eternity of suffering in hell.

It seems that conversion techniques did create susceptible psychological states in which stress and anxiety were experienced. I remain reluctant, however, to reduce revival 'hysteria' to an explanation in pathological terms. The revival was experienced within a new structure of power which sought to control the bodies of the colonized. To call what happened 'hysteria' is to rob this behaviour, as a drama

Fig. 1. The Fate of Sinful Pagans

played out through the bodies of its participants, of its cultural specificity. It could be that people lost bodily control, became 'possessed', to gain knowledge of the power used against them—possession here being a culturally appropriate way of producing a 'new' truth (cf. Stephen 1979). The sorts of behaviour demonstrated in revivals were not without precedent in precolonial Melanesia, and Wagner (1979: 146) describes some of the Daribi actions associated with the Talk of Koriki in strikingly similar terms to revivals in Pangia: 'some men and women had fits and were unconscious; after they revived they climbed around on houses and trees, danced, and jumped down. The talk from [Koriki] said that if people did this they would be able to understand Pidgin.' What is interesting about the Daribi cult was not just that it was meant to attract Europeans but that participation would impart knowledge to people through the ability to speak pidgin, the language of colonial hegemony, rendering equitable Daribi communication and exchanges with Europeans.

It is instructive to compare the different ways in which the concept of 'wild' related to the colonial process. Young men in particular had to be tamed by kiaps and this sometimes 'caused' madness, a condition known as *leau* (wild). A common Wiru perception of themselves before colonization was that they were like wild pigs. In this case, wildness was not a result of European control but a causal factor in its acceptance. Wiru bodies had to be domesticated in order to receive the benefits of development, just as pigs have to become subject to sociality (cf. Herdt 1986: 358–9). It is this perception that came into play in revivals. The wild aspect of Wiru, particularly their uncontrolled sexuality, had to be repressed, and their experience of shame at the hands of missionaries lent new meaning to the concept of 'wild'/madness. People were encouraged to let the Holy Spirit enter into them, to *possess* them and exorcize their wildness and the past.[12] An ethnohistory of the body takes this sense of agency, of Wiru attempts to make themselves more like whites through madness itself, into account.

For the Wiru, possession involved returning a person to a 'wild' state, out of which knowledge may be revealed through divine communion, such as the view of heaven in trance. Some people talked about their revival behaviour in terms of the Holy Spirit fighting with their Wiru/wild/animal nature. They associated their 'traditional' bodies with the rule of Satan, who became known as *ipono* (the term for spirits and ancestors). The body became a battle ground in which *ipono*, representing the past/'sin', fought for possession with the Holy Spirit, the spirit of the new. The object of revivals was a metamorphosis of the body, achieved through creating a new locus of power and knowledge for the new world (the approaching millennium promised by the missions). To do this, the 'old' body had first to be destroyed. This was at a time when missions were encouraging washing, shaving

---

[12] The idiom for possession is being 'hit' by a spirit. Harvey (1973: 185, 188) records the start of revival behaviour in people as: 'He was struck down as with a heavy blow on the head'; 'When I came in the door of the church, something hit me.'

and the wearing of clothes, the covering of the savage/sensual body of the heathen being crucial to its transformation into that of an obedient Christian—'When I first saw the white men, they gave me a towel, soap, and a razor' (Pastor Wendeka of Takuru, in reference to his encounter with missionaries as a young man).

F. E. Williams compared the extravagances of the Vailala Madness, which he explained as 'a product of religious zeal and boredom' (1944: 140), to a religious revival. If the Eurocentric bias of the term 'revival' is discarded, the Vailala cult can be regarded as a revival of the precolonial religious system. It was an attempt to make this system meaningful again by changing its emphases and adopting new insights and practices, making it more relevant to the colonial situation. Cultural continuity in religious understanding and the flexibility of ritual systems have been cited by many authors to explain cargo cults (Lawrence 1964; Stephen 1979). Christian revivals in Pangia may also be viewed in these terms although, as stated earlier, continuity in belief can itself lead to discontinuities in colonized cultures:

With the intrusion of the white man, guidelines from the ancestors as to how to deal with the new and devastating force were sought through the usual channels, in some cases resulting in only minor modifications of existing ritual and social practice, and in others, the development of full-blown religious and social revolutions, depending on the circumstances of contact and the ideological adjustments made by different cultures. (Stephen 1979: 20)

In Pangia, advice from the ancestors was no longer a viable option as they came to occupy the terrain of 'sin', which itself became mapped on to the bodies of pagans. I have argued above and elsewhere (Clark 1989) that Christianity was received and practised as a cult, yet the 'adjustments' required of Wiru in a system of asymmetrical power relations seemed to require a dramatic change to their lives and, if not a 'revolution', at least a major discontinuity. Parts of Christianity were dynamically synthesized into indigenous cosmology, although for fundamentalist Wiru, facing demands to replace the old pagan order almost violently, there was less room for compromise. This demand and urgency was enacted in the bodies of those experiencing revival, and to demonstrate this some of the features of revival need to be examined in more detail.

Over a period of several months, there were many revivals of varying scale and intensity. The conditions which precipitated these events have already been discussed; eventually they culminated in large-scale revivals involving, in different settlements, hundreds of Wiru. Consider this mission account of a revival in Takuru:

Such singing! And such praying! . . . people could not discern the noise of the shout of joy from the noise of the weeping of the people. Under conviction [of God's truth] some trembled and cried aloud, *confessing their sins* and beating their breasts, even smiting their mouths as they were convicted of lying or cursing. Then as they grasped in simple faith the promise [of forgiveness] there came a light of joy upon their dark faces, and they arose from their knees to give joyous testimony that God had pardoned and delivered them from their sins. They literally leapt for joy [and] joined those already on their feet, jumping for joy. What a sight! Hundreds of redeemed heathen, rhythmically jumping for joy . . . There was no mingling of men and women—the men kept to their side of the tabernacle, the women to theirs. (Ridgway 1976: 82, my emphasis)

Missionaries viewed the revival as a 'cleansing of unrighteousness', a casting out of Satan. Informants in Takuru were unsure of the reasons for their revival behaviour, and many people told humorous stories comparable with the madness narratives. Whilst madness displayed for contemplation the anti-social nature of Europeans—they were like malicious spirits, the men who 'acted' like them were wild—revivals were initiated by promises of a restoration of autonomy through access to the white man's cult, his source of power and knowledge, through possession by his (Holy) spirit. Stephen (1979: 4) captures this process when she writes that 'cult "hysteria" should be recognized as a positive phenomenon, an ecstatic validation of the new order and the means of breaking with the constraints of the old.' Amongst the Wiru, the revival appears to have had two phases: 'Pungent conviction seized sinners until they trembled and shook, unable to be still until God spoke peace to their souls. And their liberation was manifested in what might be thought to be extravagant joy [of jumping]' (Ridgway 1976: 82).

The first phase of 'conviction' was marked and brought on by emphatic singing and praying, and the disruption of normal patterns of behaviour, for example, of eating and sleeping. Robin (1981: 158) reports that revivals in the Southern Highlands were generally more emotionally intense and violent—in one case leading to a death from an exorcism beating—than revivals in other parts of the world. In Pangia people directed violence inwardly, as if they had conceived a hatred of their own bodies. Suffering in order to release cargo from the control of Europeans, or white spirits, often appears as a theme in 'cargo cult' ideology, and Wiru suffered through the hard work of road-building necessary to transform them into the equivalents of Europeans. Violence was also a feature of wildman behaviour, although it was usually directed at others. Stephen (1979: 20), in her explanation of Melanesian religious movements, suggests that when accepted norms are challenged and drastic change is introduced, the whole community may need to be possessed. This state validates and facilitates a transition to a new order through an innovative cult. The violence of Wiru 'conviction', the physical repudiation of bodies and the confession of sin, points to the urgency of denying the past/sin.

The second phase of the revival was 'liberation'. The trembling, crying, violence and disorder ceases and there is a controlled group response—a rhythmic swaying and jumping, men on one side of the church, women on another. Speech also occurs, recorded by the mission as cries of 'thank you, Jesus', as well as visions of heaven and the crucifixion (the Wiru etymology of 'thanks' almost certainly connects Europeans with spirits). The 'joy of jumping' may be the 'ecstatic validation of a new order' to which Stephen refers. The two phases of the revival appear analogous to the stages through which individuals establish themselves as shamans or curers; that is, by possession followed by trance (cf. Juillerat 1975).[13] Visions are associated with the trance state as well as with 'liberation' and are linked with divine revelations of power and knowledge (Stephen 1979: 13). There was a movement from possession by the past/*ipono* to possession by the future/Holy Spirit. During the second phase heaven and Jesus were seen, people thought they could fly and perform other supernatural feats, and one man claimed to have the real knowledge of God with which he could raise the dead. It was as if people had already achieved European power, which was the power of an immortal body promised by the missions. Transcending the body's limitations through trance was a way of empowering the body, a way of transcending its colonial confinement. While wildman behaviour reflected feelings of alienation from the control of one's own body, revival 'hysteria' was a deliberate alienation of people from their own sinful, heathen bodies—'I felt I had looked at bad things and said bad things, that is why I slapped myself' (man recorded in Harvey 1973: 189).

A mission account of one group's concern about its failure to demonstrate revival behaviour points to the connections made between indigenous bodies, the body of Jesus, revelation, and the power of cult sacrifice, the latter now aligned with Europeans:

The Lowiti tribe left Mele station on August 4th and went home to cry to God. In nearly one hundred per cent strength, they fasted and prayed for five days. They told God, 'We love you but we aren't demonstrating as others. Why?'

On Thursday noon, they saw heaven opened to their eyes. The entire tribe saw visions in the sky. Many saw Jesus on the Cross. Others saw inside heaven where Jesus was with little brown-skinned children. Nearly all of them saw pieces of a red something falling from the sky. It seemed to fall like light flakes from the foot of the Cross. It landed on them and on the ground. Some tried to grab them up from the ground and found they had only earth in their hands. They rubbed this on their bodies.

They danced and jumped and shouted and cried in their joy over these visions. (Harvey 1973: 200)

The meaning of the red flakes as the blood of Jesus is evoked by an evangelical cartoon (Fig. 2) which, like Fig. 1, first appeared in the 'Wordless Gospel' series, booklets published by International Gospel Literature based in Chino, California, and distributed by some fundamentalist missions in Pangia.

In Takuru, at least, there was a precedent for using a human body in sacrifice (see Clark 1995), and it seems that Wiru had no difficulty understanding the crucifixion of Jesus as a sacrifice, if not in the Christian sense as an act required for the perpetuation of a moral humankind (cf. Read 1952: 236). Pigs, marsupials, and eels were the usual sacrificial animals, with the blood and fat of pigs, as symbolic equivalents

---

[13] Strauss (1990: 123) describes the possession of a Melpa 'medicine man' in similar terms to revival behaviour: 'He falls to the ground, his whole body trembles and is wracked with convulsions, and he foams at the mouth . . . He becomes frenzied, goes out of his mind. He dances until he reaches the point of complete exhaustion . . . he has been "taken and transported into ecstasy".'

Fig. 2. The Blood of Jesus

to humans, rubbed into cult stones to promote growth, health, and fertility, and to ensure group continuity. With people rubbing the 'blood' of Jesus into their own skins—the 'male' locus of the body's personhood—there is clearly a transfer of the meaning of blood as symbol to create an indigenous version of the Christian communion and the sacrifice of a body (V. Turner 1974), appropriating the cult power of Christianity, its essential substance, to achieve a transformation of the body and the desired equivalence with Europeans through access to heaven—the millennial world promised by development. Rubbing the blood of Jesus into skins was a forerunner of the logic of baptism (see n. 6). Failure to achieve equivalence in 'maleness' was expressed through another embodied metaphor—the phenomenon of 'shrinking men'.

The Incredible Shrinking Men

The explanation for the use of 'shrinking' as an idiom for the male experience of colonialism has been hinted at above. The body has an outside/inside dimension, the skin demonstrating masculine achievement, the body signalling a female constitution. This outside/inside distinction—*akalo/ekolo*—is also referred to by Wiru in explaining the nature of their relationship to the Mbuna source, such that Europeans were associated with the outside and were more 'male' than Wiru (this takes us back to my discussion of cassowary stomach symbolism in Chapter 1). The colonial space created new relationships between sexuality and power. Europeans, through the 'gifts' of development, featured in the constitution of the 'new' labouring and Christian body—with Wiru participating in this constitution through the Kongono cult—creating Wiru as 'female' in opposition to whites, to whom they were indebted for their colonized bodies. The body, particularly through the extension of inside/outside meanings to space, became a site for what Harkin (1988: 125) refers to as spatial/temporal/cosmological interpenetration. Wiru, of course, wanted to be as 'male' on their skins as Europeans, but this post-colonial cult world did not turn out as desired, and anxieties about shrinking reflect the gendered nature of colonial power, and point again to the body as a locus of interpretation—as an idiom through which a recognition of dependence and perhaps inferiority was eventually 'felt'.

Shrinking is an idiom of emasculation, and men often stated that during the colonial era they had to act 'like women', the unspoken assumption being that these actions were in respect of European men. Within the colonial space new domains of control and authority were made manifest, and the relationship between Wiru and whites became gendered. Acting 'like women' referred to men becoming more trapped in the producer role associated with women (as in their intensive involvement in the hard work of road-building), to their non-aggressiveness, to their compliance with European directives, and to men's general loss of autonomy.[14] During the development era there was extensive out-migration of men on the Highlands Labour Scheme, and up to 50 per cent of men (and 60 per cent of the married male workforce) were absent. This absence put increasing pressure on the labour of remaining men and women, and the local political economy of exchange and cult performance was dramatically attenuated—either put on hold or discontinued. Local headmen

---

[14] Mission insistence on monogamy as a requirement for baptism also weakened men's control over production if only one wife was allowed, and made men's work harder.

did not have the opportunity to reinforce their positions through the efflorescence
of exchange and the control of new valuables such as money (cf. A. J. Strathern
1978), and competition instead was for colonial positions of status and authority
such as councillor, village constable, pastor, or 'bosboi'—all positions imbued with
the appeal of a connection to the line of power from the outside.

The expression used to refer to shrinking is *ali koloi toko* ('man, to not spread
out from one stem'). The botanical referent is specifically to the growth pattern of
cordyline plants, which develop from a single stem, rather than by sending out
shoots like sugar cane (the latter provides an idiom for agnatic group identity).
Informants relate their perceptions of men's diminution—they are 'like rats'—to
two factors:

1. The fertility of the ground has diminished and less food is produced; men eat
   less and are therefore shrinking; and
2. Missions made men put on clothes so that their skin and traditional dress could
   not be seen.

It is obvious that men conceive of a radical change in the nature of their being,
and other factors can be related to this change. Acting 'like women' in development
is one; another is that Christianity, as an ideology stressing obeisance and meek-
ness, equips 'new' men with some of the attributes of women. In-married women
also have a problematic relation to the husband's agnatic group, and the stress in
Christianity on a wider brotherhood renders a man's relationship to his own group
in terms that differ from those of the precolonial era. Shrinking is also related to
the ageing process, *indipoko*, and the debilitating effects of coition with women; the
longer a man is married, the older and less 'male' he becomes.

Perhaps one of the more important factors in leading men to rethink their
masculine identity was the introduction of money, associated with the colonial
authorities and, like pearl shells and steel, linked to the outside world (money was
thought to be made by Queen Elizabeth II in Port Moresby). Money affected the
autonomy and independence of Wiru men, especially as they were not afforded
the opportunity to incorporate it into an efflorescing ceremonial exchange
system—to make money their own like pearl shells. Money came to symbolize
colonial control, and reliance on money for successful participation in local and
regional economies brought home much more forcefully Wiru dependence on a
world that encapsulated them into a different cultural order—and dependency is
associated with femaleness. Fewer exchanges and ceremonial occasions limited
demonstrations of masculinity, and Christian men are restricted like women in the
extent to which they can participate in the public domain of exchange, particularly in fundamentalist settlements where important death exchanges were abandoned. Men realized that they were compromised by colonial alternatives to the
attainment of self, and to some extent used accounts of 'taming' to explain to
themselves the reasons for their rapid acquiescence to colonial directives, for
acting 'like women'.

The sexual implications of shrinking need to be examined in more detail, especially in the context of changes that required men to live with women in the interests of maintaining a Christian household; men were prohibited from polygyny,
adultery, and pre-marital sex by missions, while at the same time women were
given more autonomy by the administration (see Chapter 6). The white growing
tip of the cordyline plant, referent of the *koloi toko* verb, is known by the term for
penis, *andene*. Maleness is on the skin, it is external like the penis, and shrinking is
related to a metaphor that links the penis, the external, and growth. Penile stria-
tions are compared with the growth rings on bamboo and certain trees, although
shrinking refers to negative growth. An analysis of the following story, said to be
true but told to me in response to queries about the status of women, allows for
certain conclusions to be made:

There was a man who had a very large penis, which he named *keke yule* [*yule* is a secret term
for penis, *keke* is the name of this particular penis]. Women were scared to marry him and
many refused. At a 'singsing' his brother tied a pig rope to his penis and led him around like
a pig. He killed three wives by having intercourse with them, but his fourth wife survived
because he only inserted his penis a little way. She went back to her parents claiming victory
[as in warfare] and planted a cordyline to mark it. However, she returned to her husband and
he fully inserted his penis and killed her.

A brief discussion of cordyline plants is required. They refer to the penis, to
maleness, in that they are planted to celebrate male achievements and death, and
serve as boundary markers for gardens, graves, and cult enclosures. Cordylines are
also worn as rear coverings by men—a boundary marker of a sort—and are planted
to indicate that a taboo has been imposed on a certain activity. In a general sense
they provide messages in their role as boundary markers between different
domains, for example between life and death, or between men and spirits (A. J.
Strathern 1982c: 120; Wagner 1972: 125–9).

The husband in the story is an exaggerated man, certainly not shrinking, who
is not quite human, perhaps even part-wild given his propensity to kill wives and
his association with a pig. The moral of the story is that women may think they
win a few battles but men are always the victors in the ultimate confrontation
(Wiru women would describe men as their enemies). The penis is used as a
weapon in men's attempts to control women, and it is significant that there is also
a cordyline motif to the story. The woman plants a cordyline (= penis) for her
victory over the penis (= man), a penis that later kills her—perhaps in retaliation
for her use of a male symbol, that is, for her presumption of winning. Shrinking
plays with the same sorts of meanings, but in a different context of gendered
power. It is now Europeans who exercise control over Wiru, men in particular,
that makes men 'like women' and emasculates them. The boundary to which the
cordyline appears to be referring in idioms of *koloi toko* is the one between Wiru
and Europeans, between Pangia and the Mbuna source, and the message is
inequivalence in power and wealth, expressed through the graphic image of

bodily detumescence—Wiru men were polluted by development, in a sense 'screwed' by its colonial agents.

This conclusion is related to the first reason adduced by men for their shrink-ing, namely that soil fertility has decreased and people eat less. It is quite possible that, with population expansion, the replanting of old gardens while men were absent on the Highlands Labour Scheme, and the growing of coffee on the best mixed garden land, soil fertility has generally declined, especially as agronomists discovered that the high pH clay soils of Pangia were not the best for crops (there appeared to have been a marked rise in the number of local famines during the colonial era[15]). For Wiru, however, fertility has declined because whites stole the 'gris' (grease) out of the soil and took it back to Australia, and because the spirit cults prohibited by the missions actually did improve fertility in general, a project in which Christianity has been less successful. Men said that they could not perform the cults again because they were now Christians and did not want to return to a sinful past, even though they recognized cult efficacy. The notion of whites stealing 'gris' is a further twist on cargo cult ideology, in which Europeans are often seen to be depriving local people of access to the secrets of wealth and abundance. In Pangia, whites did not so much withhold 'secrets'/knowledge (as they were all too willing to share them with Wiru through development propa-ganda and evangelism), as take 'secrets' from Wiru. Some people wanted their local members to lobby the Australian government for the return of 'gris' to Pangia. Men experienced a loss of autonomy not only in their own lives but in their control over the cosmos as cult power and the source of fertility shifted to missions and the 'outside', as the reference to Australia being the new home of stolen 'gris' indicates.

The second reason given by men for bodily diminution is that the mission made them wear clothes; a concern with the body as a site for interpretation was clearly not limited to the Wiru. The fundamentalist missions in particular worked on the body to transform people into Christians: they forbade traditional dress and bodily decoration, and made haircuts a requisite of conversion, although they attributed the desire for clothes less to their strictures than to the results of revival:

Immediately after the awakening, the people as a whole seemed to become conscious of their nearly naked bodies. Money materialized from its hiding place and clothes were bought [from the mission] by many.

. . . the Widu [Wiru] men who wanted to follow the Lord, and that was nearly all of them who attended the Bible Mission, had long ago given up painting their faces and their bodies with grotesque and artistic designs. But they still retained their large head of hair done up inside a loosely crocheted cap.

After the awakening, many of these huge heads of hair disappeared. They cut their hair in a European style. It was a great improvement. (Harvey 1973: 206)

---

[15] The decline of ceremony and ritual during the labour-hungry development era meant that an incentive to surplus production was much submerged, and famines further encouraged.

People were not allowed on the mission station or into church if they attended any form of 'singsing', and were led to a sense of shame about their traditional dress, an association with the Satanic past continuing into the 1990s, although wearing European clothes was also related to the Wiru desire to be 'like whites'. The idiom of shrinking indicates once more the realization by men that a price was paid for their complicity with the missions, as clothing covered and compromised the outside part of the body where personhood was created to counter the claims of matrikin for debts in body:

It seems that to be a Christian at Pangia one must wear clothes. Several missions here insist on it, but, very sadly, do not insist on washing the clothes, so we have many people clothed in filthy rags all in the name of God . . . a man can be as good a Christian in the raw as he can be in some Mother Hubbard outfit—particularly if the outfit is filthy and stinks. (Pangia PR3/71–72)

Dirt and smell are attributes associated with women because of their care of small children and their menstruation. Men view their traditional dress as clean and allowing for the display of their healthy bodies, and the attribution of shrinking to the mission clothing requirements seems to be because clothes with strong connotations of femaleness covered up the outside 'male' parts of bodies. The erect male body, with its virile head of hair and traditional dress, was deflated by Christianity. Men's skins became feminized, and men became less than men, especially in a context where kiaps were encouraging a greater autonomy for women. Men's control over women was being threatened while they experienced a similar control over their bodies by kiaps pursuing long-term development schemes, and by missionaries pursuing souls.

There is a precedent for men acting 'like women' in a particularly hostile and sometimes lethal form of Wiru gifting called *poi mokora*. The purpose of the gift is ultimately to question, perhaps even destroy, the recipient's sense of masculinity. It usually involves heaping cooked pork sides at the feet of the recipient, or giving him a whole pig. The donor, by giving more of his 'maleness', which (external) pig sides represent in Wiru symbolism (Clark 1991), literally attacks the 'maleness' of the recipient. Takuru people recount one particular fight, *poi*, in which they broke the bows and arrows of their defeated enemies and hung them in the branches of a tree. *Poi mokora* is said to break the bows and arrows of the man who receives it because, due to the quantity of pork he receives, he has to put down his weapons and spoil his hair and decorations, in other words his skin, by acting like a woman in assisting his wife to carry the pork home. Such a gift has the potential to harm or kill the recipient or his children (groups may give *poi mokora* to other groups through gifts of extremely valuable *yombo* pearl shells (Clark 1991)).

People are in debt over their lifetimes to matrikin for the body that they have created. Just as women do all the 'hard work' in childbearing, men believe that they did all the 'hard work' in creating the Christian labouring body under the development regime. The difference is that men are indebted to God and the colonial authorities for their 'new' bodies. Missions are sometimes referred to as 'mother' for the nurture they provided in transforming bodies from 'wild pigs' to Christians, and the colonial administration was called 'father' for the discipline and education it provided in the productive acts of labour so necessary to achieving the rewards of Christianity. The 'gifts' of development that created colonized bodies are debts that Wiru men cannot repay, imparting a cultural sense to the dependence that men felt towards Europeans. In effect, Europeans from the outside Mbuna source gave the colonial equivalent of *poi mokora* to Wiru men, making them, relatively, less 'male' through metaphorically breaking their bows and arrows in pacification, and coercing them into acting like women in respect of white control. The ritual–exchange model, in terms of which Wiru responded to development and Christianity, underpinned and constructed the colonized culture of Pangia.

Pacify and Convert

For Foucault, the discourses and practices of disciplinary regimes which led to the confinement of the body not only constituted the complicit or 'docile' subject but also created it as an object capable of being used productively in factories, schools, and so on. Just as feminists have criticized Foucault for his neglect of the sexed body (Grosz 1990), an anatomy of colonial power in Pangia needs to take into account the fact that the Wiru body was pre-constrained in its use in colonial discourses and practices. This body was not only racialized, it was subject to its own indigenous meanings which affected the emergent colonized culture. The Wiru body suffered the discipline of colonial representatives but not quite in the sense Foucault would suggest—as demonstrated in the creation of new subjectivities through people's own agency, such as suffering in revivals. The person was not simply a complicit subject produced by discourse, which is often the kind of subject posited by Foucault, who nonetheless remains useful for a discussion of how discourse and praxis operate in the process of colonial subjectification, creating bodies and souls.

Just as Foucault critically unpacks the terminology of Western technologies of power/knowledge, and demonstrates how particular concepts of 'madness' and 'perversion' serve these technologies, it can be seen that 'primitive' and 'heathen' were essential concepts in colonial discourses. The Pangia administration viewed Wiru as undeveloped and backward, while missions saw them as heathen and sinful. Particular forms of discourse, essential to the colonization of savage bodies, produced deviant subjects. Administration and missions co-operated with each other, if sometimes grudgingly, because both arms of the technologies of development viewed their work as interrelated and part of the same process, which was to transform the savage into a modern Christian, without pigs or idols. The past, with its warfare, tribalism, cults, and pig kills, all wasteful of labour and resources, was a hindrance to the creation of a Christian ethic and a spirit of development. Captured within the colonial space, with its imposed regime of power and knowledge, Wiru were to become law-abiding and hard-working Christian peasants, citizens of a colonial state.

Threats of hell or imprisonment conspired to legitimate the colonial technologies; progress was 'for their own good' and designed to rescue Wiru from the life of the savage. Coercion and intimidation served to support the colonial regime and to further its 'normalizing' agenda, while at the same time Wiru came to desire the perceived benefits of development, and co-operated in such things as road-building and conversion. They wanted to be powerful and wealthy, 'like whites', to experience a new subjectivity by accessing colonial power–knowledge. Both administration and mission treated the Wiru body as an object; they wanted to control its soul and labour, to make it respectful of and compliant with the colonial order: 'Discourse, therefore, has to trace the meeting line of the body and the soul, following all its meanderings: beneath the surface of the sins, it would lay bare the unbroken nervure of the flesh' (Foucault 1980: 20).

The mission realized that 'agony of soul' (Harvey 1973: 190) had to be manifested before conversion could take place. But as Foucault (1979: 30) indicates, the 'soul is the effect and instrument of political anatomy; [it] is the prison of the body.' The administration, conspiring with missions to produce fear, stress and anxiety, believed that 'hard work' and labour schedules would teach Wiru to appreciate the virtues of development and peace. Indigenous understandings of 'work' were revalued, and its social basis undermined and partially commoditized. Missions sought to control sexuality through clothing and new marriage regulations and taboos. Sexual intercourse, indigenously equated with notions of 'dirt', became part of the colonial discourse on medical hygiene—such as the equation of latrines and keeping pigs out of houses with development—and sin. Changing notions of sexuality and sanity (all Wiru were mad/wild before they became Christians) transformed Wiru subjectivity.

The Wiru experience of Europeans was similar to what some commentators on the postmodern condition and the relationship of people to machines call 'species anxiety'. Europeans, as another type of human, were known through their superior technology and morality, like the pure extraterrestrials of *Close Encounters* described in Chapter 2. It was certainly not the case in Pangia, as McCarthy (1963: 79) asserts for parts of New Ireland, that 'European civilization had met the natives and then proceeded to crush the lives out of them.' Kongono and other responses to development were motivated by the desire to overcome the Wiru version of 'species anxiety', to make the 'species' equal, and the reasons for their failure lie as much with the administration and missions as with themselves. What the twin arms of the colonial technologies failed to recognize, and what Foucault could perhaps not consider, was that Wiru operated in the colonial space in terms of their own understandings of the body and its relation to the construction of power and knowledge.

The body is gendered and racialized, and supplies a trope not only for cultural innovation (cf. Wagner 1986), but for the interpretation of experience. Wiru created a body which was *not* that of the Christian peasant desired by missions and administration, although it was the product of a colonial age of reason. The body was a surface and a depth upon which Wiru inscribed their own history and read off their own understanding of events. Madness, revival 'hysteria', and shrinking were embodied expressions of a particular Wiru experience of colonialism. Madmen used their bodies, if only in tales, to deconstruct the nature of administration control and present to their audience, for reflection and assimilation, the effects of new relations of power on a society undergoing an uncertain and disordered transition. Revivalists, like those people involved in *ka kongono*, attempted to use their bodies as an actual vehicle for transformation. Shrinking came into play as an interpretive trope when experience proved that the new age through development was not forthcoming, and that male subjectivity was feminized. 'Madness' was resistance to a truth produced by guns and jail; revival 'hysteria' was submission to a truth produced by confession and hard work; and shrinking was a recognition of the truth about where power lies in colonialism. An ethnohistory of the body reveals that there was an epistemic mutation in Wiru systems of thought, leading to a new relationship between body and soul in the creation of a colonized culture. Madness, 'hysteria', and shrinking comprised moments in the genealogy of colonialism and the colonized subject in Pangia. Events mediated the relationship between the body and historical praxis, in the process transforming the body itself.

6

Renouncing the Stone

Many Highlands anthropologists have pointed to the ways in which 'valuables are used to articulate social relationships' (Merlan and Rumsey 1991: 228), acknowledging that 'things' can have revelatory qualities (ibid.; M. Strathern 1990). But apart from the 'first contact' period, little attention has been paid to the ways in which Highlanders conceived of relationships to Europeans through valuables, or to what such things as money revealed about the colonial situation (cf. Merlan and Rumsey 1991: 229). Lederman (1986: 13) states that, for the Mendi, 'social relationships are made through the dispersal of wealth, not its accumulation', and that valuables only occasionally have a 'transcendent social meaning' (ibid.: 84). This 'meaning', in Annette Weiner's recent argument (1992), comes from an object's inalienability, and she would argue that social relationships are created and underpinned by retaining valuables such as heirloom shells while using other shells in exchange (see Clark 1995 for a discussion of inalienability and *yombo* pearl shells in Pangia).[1] Weiner's insights can be used to ask a series of questions about colonialism in Pangia. What sorts of relationships were constructed with Europeans through the dispersal and retention of wealth, and is keeping rather than giving more determinate of the relationships which emerged? Can colonialism be considered as a form of exchange, and if so what were the gifts or exchange 'objects' involved in transactions?

With respect to the notion of inalienability, Gregory (1982a: 345) writes that: 'The link between a thing and its producer is not, as Mauss would have us believe, a spiritual relation created by giving away a part of one's "spiritual essence", but rather a link that derives its strength from the politics of power relations between groups.' Annette Weiner provides much in the way of ethnographic support for this statement in her book of a decade later, and I will consider the politics of giving where the 'groups' involved in exchange were Highlanders and Europeans. It has to be stressed that exchange is never meant in a merely economic sense. Weiner restricts her argument about keeping-while-giving (or KWG) to forms of exchange within particular societies. I want to extend her analysis to consider the colonial and postcolonial interface, more specifically the object-mediated encounter between Highlanders and Europeans, and later between Highlanders

---

[1] Lederman (1986: 86) suggests that Mendi heirloom shells are held out of circulation mainly because of pacification, preventing the primary use of these valuables in warfare compensation payments. While not denying that colonization has contributed to the non-circulation of heirloom pearl shells in Southern Highlands societies, it seems clear from informants and the literature that people still desired to keep these valuables back from exchange (Clark 1995).

and the independent state.[2] For Weiner (1992: 56), the *mana* and serial ownership of Polynesian inalienable possessions (or IP) encode and represent a 'cultural history', but how would a colonial history of valuable objects, including money, read for the Highlands (cf. Thomas 1991)?

A Colonial 'Cultural History'

Ceremonial exchange systems in the Highlands have often been considered for their role in linking dispersed communities within and across geographic and cultural boundaries, temporarily creating wider unities as valuables are produced, promised, and transacted. Yet, despite disclaimers made by many of their ethnographers (A. J. Strathern 1982a), the language of economics often pervades and problematizes much of their analyses—there is discussion of 'profit/interest', 'finance', 'debt', and even 'alienation' (see Damon 1982; Feil 1982; Gregory 1982b; Lederman 1986: 84). The Huli region created temporary unity amongst its parishes and, to a lesser extent, its neighbouring cultures, through rituals of sacrifice along 'roads' connecting key ritual sites. Despite many parallels with ceremonial exchange, such as the notion of roads creating wider regional interconnections (Modjeska 1991), ritual has been more clearly marked as 'religious' than 'economic', and few would write of sacrifice in terms of creating gift-credit with the spirits. The 'political economy' of exchange is more amenable and accessible to Western cultural categories. Andrew Strathern (1982a: 551) comments that 'there is no doubt that the Highlands systems of prestige gift-giving do map themselves on to an introduced capitalist system in a remarkable fashion.' While Strathern (1979) does pay attention to such things as the cultural meanings which money takes on among the Melpa, it seems that his use of 'capitalist' refers more to an economic system of the West, so that exchange maps on to what became 'bisnis'. If capitalism was discussed as a cultural system in which concepts of self, personhood, and the group are ontologically grounded, then Strathern's Janus-like configuration of exchange/capitalism could develop real analytical value.

The impact of money, the (temporary) cessation of warfare, changes in gender roles, and so on, have admittedly been considered in accounts of exchange, but often to demonstrate the resilience and flexibility of exchange systems in the 'big man in history' style, and less for the way such sytems became embedded within the colonial system of power itself. It may be more profitable to view the persistence, or what in the introduction I called the discontinuity of exchange—in the context of a colonial mandate which viewed it as antithetical to development—not as mere resilience, nor even only as attempted resistance to the colonial state, in a similar way to some analyses of cargo cults (Lattas (ed.) 1992), but as a mode of incorporating the state into Highlands communities and creating a new cosmology

---

[2] A comparison can be made with Pannell (1994), on the consubstantial relationship of Aborigines to land and sacred *tjurunga* held in state museums.

of power. In his later ethnography, Andrew Strathern seems to hint at the potential for resistance when discussing *moka* as an indigenous production of history: it 'is "anticapitalist" history, stressing the paramountcy of exchange as *against* the significance of units of production and the creation of inequality through differential access to these' (1991: 227, my emphasis). Interestingly, given his earlier alignment of exchange and capitalism, Strathern is here concerned to stress their differences, while persisting in his view of capitalism as more a mode of production than a cultural system. He also suggests that there are two sides to Melpa reciprocity—competition and friendship (ibid.). While the interpretation of motivation and agency remains primarily 'economic', could this model be extended to Melpa interaction with Europeans and later with the independent state? Is it the lack of an equitable arena for competition or even friendship that leads to 'raskolism' and resurgent 'tribal' warfare?

The Melpa dyad of competition/friendship has to be reconsidered if we subscribe to Annette Weiner's thesis that it is KWG which underpins exchange, creating differences for which 'friendship' becomes a mystification for 'groups "coming to terms" with one another' (A. J. Strathern 1991: 227). Melpa, according to Weiner (1992: 118), lacked the conditions for 'true' IP to emerge, so that KWG is less pronounced among Melpa than it is among, say, Samoans. The differences that emerge out of Highlands exchange would be less hierarchical and permanent than in Polynesia, at least until class inequalities began to emerge with colonialism. Nevertheless, it is the logic of KWG, even if it cannot be fully expressed through IP, which underlies exchange. Some support for Weiner can be found in the literature on the millennial cults which preceded or accompanied European arrival in the Highlands (Feil 1983; Biersack 1991), as well as that dealing with later Christian revival movements (Robin 1982). It seems that one aim of cult activity was for a 'world without exchange', that is, an end to difference (even gender differences as taboos on sexual separation were often suspended) and, more clearly stated in revivals, an equivalence in power and possessions with Europeans, as Chapter 5 indicates. It is only when exchange 'finishes' that true equivalence, an absence of difference (friendship), is possible. Such desires do not just find expression in cult or revival settings: some Tolai fervently wish for the end of *tambu* (exchange), which is seen as a barrier to political independence and the proper operation of business (Epstein 1979: 197); and Neumann (1992: 276) points to the strong emphasis on Revelations in Tolai prayers for the dead, accompanying the distribution of coils of *tambu* shell-money.

Exchange is what people engage in while waiting for the millennial promise of its demise. If exchange creates difference, how was it that many Highlanders eventually perceived Europeans to be human because they engaged in exchange with Highlanders, despite their strange behaviour and appearance? Another, almost legendary story recounts that this identification was made after Highlanders observed that the Leahys' faeces smelled the same as theirs (Connolly and Anderson 1987: 44). This last account is too easily interpreted as another example of the pragmatic empiricism attributed to Highlanders. But this is a misinterpretation, reflecting more upon a constraining European empiricism than it does upon Highlands definitions of what constitutes humanity, namely a minimum capacity for exchange (and some Highlanders believed that explorers pulled wealth out of their backsides, see Clark 1995). In these terms, the two Highlands 'explanations' for European humanity, exchanging and defecating, are remarkably similar (cf. Mimica 1988: 159). Exchange may have confirmed Europeans as generically human but it was certainly a different kind of human from Highlanders. The Leahy brothers did not become Melpa, rather exchange confirmed they were not malicious spirits (A. J. Strathern 1971b: xii), setting up a series of other differences, such as European–Melpa. At a later time in colonial history, when Europeans were more familiarly human, Highlanders continued to differentiate themselves from Europeans because the latter would not exchange on the same terms with them but would rather *sell*, an exchange of money for goods in the 'commodity' not 'gift' economy, creating further inequalities in power and ranked differences.[3]

Annette Weiner (1992: 2) correctly disputes the distinction made between 'us' and the 'savage' in terms of the 'savage' having reciprocity, yet paradoxically Europeans are often admired by Highlanders for their apparent lack of the gift, such as bridewealth, in their own societies; that is, they are admired for their creation of a world without exchange. This admiration is often tempered by a recognition that the latter implies a different form of sociality; I have heard Huli say of Europeans that brother sells to brother, a characterization which makes them not less than human, but not the same. If development had fulfilled its promise in Pangia, if 'cargo' had come, then exchange would no longer be necessary and everybody could live in a state of equality, as is the case in heaven (Wiru heaven is *ta koniyo*, a beautiful place). Just as Europeans were often accused by Seaboard cultists of holding back the secret of cargo, then what the former are keeping-while-giving to Highlanders is access to the European world by 'holding back' the knowledge for an equitable engagement through exchange. Exchange is necessary to ensure the end of exchange, and millennial cults have in the past attempted to hasten this process, requiring faith to be demonstrated by killing all pigs, not planting gardens, or giving up cults to embrace the Christian church. There is, however, a certain 'evil' to holding back on knowledge.

Karavar people of the Duke of York group created the word 'Kaun' (probably derived from 'account') for their cargo cult activities because English terms to do

---

[3] I am aware of the debate surrounding the distinction between gifts and commodities (e.g., Appadurai 1986; Thomas 1991; M. Strathern 1988), but prefer to maintain it both as a heuristic device and because Wiru seem to make a distinction between exchange and selling. Interestingly, the initial and perhaps still current Tangu definition of Europeans as *imbatekas* constructs them as non-reciprocal and uncontrollable beings, part of what Burridge (1965: 230) calls the 'divine', beyond the moral order. In the Highlands, reciprocity with Europeans constructs a new moral order, as did later selling.

with business 'are uttered with a kind of awe and are thought to refer to secret and powerful procedures which the Kaun is attempting to master' (Errington 1974: 258).

There is an expression which continues to elicit awe in Takuru Wiru, and which is connected to notions of money, development, and the millennium. When I asked people what the attraction was for them engaging in Christianity and labour-intensive schemes, at the expense of spirit cults and numerous exchange activities, a frequent response was that 'this was when we obtained the power of 666'. 666, the number of the beast (Revelations 13: 18), is a complex concept in Pangia, multivocal in its meanings. 666 is linked to the impending end of the world, and perhaps to the potential for a 'new heaven'. It has a power like magic or taboo to control or enforce behaviour; people say that if, for instance, you lie or commit adultery because of 666, you will go to hell.

For my purposes what is interesting is that 666 is associated with the power of Europeans as the source of money. The most recent manifestation of this was a belief common in Takuru in 1981, that if 666 was found on the serial number of a banknote, its owner could go into a store and purchase as much as he wanted with that banknote. Alternatively, if in making a withdrawal a person received a piece of paper with 666 on it he would be able to do the same things (some people told me that these beliefs originated in the Hagen area, which may or may not be true, but Hagen is known as a key centre for Europeans and business). Being able to obtain luxury goods without money is a characteristic of Wiru perceptions of heaven (cf. Robin 1982: 337), a place with strong European overtones. There was a degree of scepticism about these claims, I might add, but they do indicate the link between 666 and money. What initially puzzled me was why people who were nominally Christians placed so much emphasis on numbers which the mission presented as intrinsically evil (sermons are given on money as the root of all evil). I have already suggested some reasons for this ambiguous view of money in Chapter 3 and above, and they are complemented by the fact that Takuru Wiru also view 666 as a puzzling and mysterious concept.

Just as Karavar people saw Europeans as holding the secrets of 'business', Wiru view 666 as one of the secrets of the power of Europeans. During the development era, and to some extent today, it was believed that the Ten Commandments were a code for behaviour—or rather for how moral Europeans behaved—which, if followed in conjunction with church attendance and 'hard work', would help transform Pangia and make Wiru 'like whites'. In the early days of the missions in Pangia, the patrol reports complain of the unusually large amounts of money given in donations at church services, to the detriment of money remaining in the district to encourage the local economy ($26/adult male p.a. in donations as compared to $2 p.a. in head tax; Pangia PR8/70–71). It is not too far-fetched to suggest that this was an attempt to obtain the secrets of 666—or at least to thank God to ensure his continued benevolence by giving what he symbolized, money—

just as Karavarans attempted to purchase the secrets of 'business' from Europeans (Errington 1974: 264).[4]

Development was not a total failure in Pangia, at least from the European perspective. Until the discoveries elsewhere in the province of gold, oil, and gas in the 1980s Pangia was one of the wealthiest of the Southern Highlands districts, as nutritional indicators for children collected by the Southern Highlands Rural Development Project indicated. Pangia is the 'home of peace, place of love', and Wiru have been 'tamed' or rendered closer to the ideal of domesticated European order. The arrival of a new cult recreates society (Sahlins 1985), but for Wiru the expectations of the colonial era were not fulfilled. They are not the equivalent of *kianango* (red men/Europeans), and the disappointment and anomie that followed the decline of development hopes were little different from that experienced by followers of failed cargo cults (A. J. Strathern 1982b).

Robin (1982: 341), a psychologist who studied revivals in the Southern Highlands, states that, 'Eventually, these activities will probably take the form of a cargo movement, in a syncretic relationship with fundamentalist Christianity and traditional indigenous beliefs and practices.' This appears odd in the face of his earlier opinion (ibid.: 337) that in the Southern Highlands Province 'revival movements, material goods and calls for cargo do not seem to have played a significant role'. The conditions under which cargo will become a feature of future revivals are not explicated by Robin, and his use of 'cargo' seems overly materialistic. It is interesting to speculate, though, why so-called materialistic Highlanders have not made 'cargo' more of a theme of revival movements. In Pangia, revivals are not really concerned with material 'cargo', but if this concept is widened to include millennial notions, such as a moral and monetary equivalence with Europeans in an afterlife, then revivals do have a 'cargo' aspect (cf. Feil 1983: 103). There is no reason that cargo has to be material or temporal. Most revivals are initiated by fears of an impending apocalypse, so it is not surprising that 'cargo', in this sense, is concerned with life hereafter and not in the present.

I argued in the previous chapter that the earliest revivals in Pangia, occurring at a time when Wiru were first coming under the combined pressures of development and the need to abandon tradition, were concerned with replacing the old pagan 'body', through acts of self-directed violence, with a new Christian one. This was related to the necessity for people to become Christians in order to engage in a money-based moral community. The fundamentalist emphasis laid bare the hopes for a Christian development, the creation of a 'new man' with the potential of being the moral counterpart of Europeans. Cult activity in precolonial Wiru culture was characterized by exchanges between people and spirits, and concerned with fertility and wealth, each term implying the other. In terms of the logic of cult

---

[4] The situation was complicated in Pangia, as discussed in Chapter 4, by the fact that missionaries gave presents to ensure Wiru adherence to their denominations, and that Wiru never really adopted the concept of 'buying' European knowledge; rather it had to be discovered by thinking through concepts like 666.

as ontology, the response to Christianity and development was the attempted creation of a new world, in which access to wealth (money) was a diacritic of European power and identity. Christianity supplied the logic for a transformed ritual exchange system—changed relationships between people and spirits—and for the type of work deemed appropriate in ritual, in this case labour and prayer for development.

I talked to many missionaries who had experience working in diverse areas of the Southern Highlands, and many were of the opinion that Wiru were by far the most mercenary inhabitants of the province. Their desire for—and rapid conversion to—Christianity was explained in similar terms, that is, avarice. This explanation was refuted in Chapter 4, in which I argued that it was not simply greed on the part of Wiru, as they found themselves in a situation in which money was the measure of man (Burridge 1969: 42–4); rather it was through money that Wiru hoped to measure up to the white man. A few Wiru did manage to realign themselves with the European power, especially those who, not surprisingly, operate as Christian businessmen. The District Supervisor of the Wesleyan Church in Pangia has extensive business interests including coffee-buying, owns a four-wheel-drive Toyota, lives in a European house, and is called the 'black white man' (*lianea kianango*). Such a description does not remove him from the constraints of the system, and I never met a man more afraid of poisoning or sorcery.

Colonialism, then, could be viewed as a form of exchange in which Europeans—patrol officers, missionaries, plantation managers—were keeping-while-giving the 'secrets' of development, including the key to the ability to live without the necessity for exchange. For Annette Weiner (1992: 62–3, 104), it is KWG, particularly through the group control of IP, that leads to the development of rank and political hierarchy, raising the question of whether colonialism has created a political hierarchy of the state and its Highlands citizens. The state possesses and controls wealth, power, and knowledge, and many Highlanders complain that they cannot access these resources, that they are not distributed equitably by the state. Yet KWG has not, for the moment at least, created a political hierarchy in people's perceptions. The reality, of course, is different, but people do not 'see' the operation of institutions in a purely political economic sense. The state, in Pangia and Tari at least, is viewed not in hierarchical but egalitarian terms, in fact it is perceived as operating like a big man (Clark n.d.). Any tendencies towards hierarchy are defeated because people often see the state as acting like a failed or destructive big man, not as a totalitarian or efficient regime of power that exists 'above' them.

This is not necessarily a criticism of Annette Weiner because it is more the KWG of inalienable possessions which creates hierarchy. For example, she argues (1992: 128) that for the Melpa, at least, colonialism inhibited the control of pearl shells by big men—pearl shells were replaced by money, which is all too alienable (A. J. Strathern 1982a)—that could have led to the development of a chiefly system. This was only if another requirement of hierarchy was fulfilled, namely a group association with IP, otherwise KWG leads to differences between individuals as opposed to groups, too idiosyncratic an outcome if ranked groups are to emerge (A. B. Weiner 1992: 129). The supposedly democratic state has no IP, as everything is the property of the people and not of specific groups; what the state has is perhaps meant to be alienable (some Tolai actively renounce their IP of coils of *tambu* wealth, once referred to as their 'god', to embrace money, the icon of the state; ironically the two-kina note has representations of *tambu* on it). Yet the basis for many Highlanders' complaints about the state is its lack of reciprocity—they vote, but what does the state give? This creates less hierarchy than it does resentment, defeating and fragmenting any tendencies to 'seeing' hierarchy, such as in the private ownership of land, while at the same time mystifying the basis for the emergence of class relations in the Highlands.

To the extent that Highlanders conceive of their relationships with Europeans and later the state through exchange and its guise as 'bisnis', Annette Weiner's model, which deals with exchange within societies, would have to be modified to account for transactions between the 'tribe' and the state, basically to allow for more sophisticated explanations than that of 'false consciousness' in accounting for the development of state forms. Her model was not meant to be pushed this far, but it can still be used to understand earlier phases in colonial interactions, particularly with respect to the gender basis of KWG. For Weiner, politics has to override gender for hierarchy to emerge, and perhaps it is because gender provides a model for the experience of history and agency that people do not 'see' hierarchy in the Highlands (Biersack 1995), stressing instead horizontal connections. Shrinking men as embodied history is one example—Wiru men were 'women' to the male patrol officers, their weapons of war destroyed, just as in the practice of *poi mokora*, a lethal gift which makes men put down their bows and arrows to carry away heaped sides of pork, like women. Colonialism was a lethal gift, one which men could not repay because of the resources and knowledge kept back by Europeans; this KWG constructed inequalities based upon a permanent difference, a difference which millennial cults in other parts of the Highlands desired to abolish through the creation of a (European) world without exchange.

A devout Wesleyan pastor once told me that money, not God, was the most important thing in the world. Prayers often start with thanks to God for money. This is not another example of Highlands materialism as it is possible that money is to some extent sacred, cosmologically authenticated by its association with Europeans and their God, and by the attempts of Christian missions to generate local 'bisnis', reinforcing the link between cult activity and wealth creation.[5] The problem with money is, of course, its alienability; it does not lend itself to the construction of cultural histories through its rarity or singularity, and it is only

---

[5] This observation makes for an interesting comparison with Tolai attitudes to *tambu* shell-money: 'The Tolai "love for money" to which early observers attested . . . has never been an end in itself but a consequence of Tolai beliefs as well as an expression of a Tolai way of regenerating society' (Neumann 1992: 189).

through amassing and displaying money for an exchange event that its abstract properties can be converted into cultural capital (cf. A. B. Weiner 1992: 120). To validate money is not to demote God to a place-getter, rather it asserts their fundamental co-identity; *yombo* pearl shells in Pangia were said to have been worshipped as God before he was known, and now it is the turn of money. The quest for money, the pursuit of God, are attempts, through accessing the not purely monetary power of Europeans, to become independent of the state, or at least to incorporate it into local cosmologies and redirect its power to Wiru themselves.

The ultimate IP of colonialism in Pangia, for which money was the most potent manifestation, was being European, in whom the powers of regeneration and the meanings of being human were now located. The development era in Pangia was one in which Wiru desired to become like Europeans. The control of IP creates differences at the ontological level of culture and personhood as well as in the political sense implied by Annette Weiner. Granted that Europeanness is embedded within the state, the latter is to some extent sacred, like big men, and for Weiner (1992: 43) this quality was 'the source of political power because it retained rather than mediated difference, using violence, sacrifice, and expenditure as resources for the construction of a hierarchical order.'

Some of the problems with law and order that the independent state currently faces in the Highlands refer precisely to a problem of alienation, not in an economic, or even psychological sense but in the way that violence lies at the heart of colonialism. It could be that many rural Highlanders, unable to create a world without exchange like the beautiful Wiru heaven where everyone is guaranteed wealth and immortality, cannot alienate to themselves the means to eliminate difference.

Difference is to be explained as a product of cosmology as much as by the politics of gifting—not that the two are inseparable. Wiru bodies are created by maternal kin, and individuals are indebted over a lifetime for the health and growth of their bodies, mirroring cult concerns with ensuring a continuing creation of the world. God, part of the 'absolute value' of Europeanness, creates bodies as well as worlds, and indebtedness and new forms of difference become part of the cosmology of colonialism.[6] The nature of the gift, in the context of the dangerous power of the state, influences the way in which this cosmology is revealed (Clark 1993),[7] and the rest of this chapter will attempt to unravel some of the meanings of money and sacrifice in the making of this revelation. It will focus on the relationship created by sacrifice between people and spirits, and elaborate on its characteristics and 'functions' by contrasting pagan and Christian sacrificial acts, and indigenous

---

[6] In my article about Huli experiences of the Mt Kare goldfields (1993), it is indicated that Europeans and the state control wealth and regeneration in a new cosmology of power, which can pollute Huli men.

[7] Epstein (1979: 192) writes of how Tolai attitudes to *tambu* influenced attitudes to money and the future. In so far as *tambu* reveals the presence of the sacred, perhaps money reveals the power of Europeans.

understandings of them. This contrast will display the discontinuities in a particular logic of sacrifice as it works itself out against the conflict between gifts and commodities.

I have already written of the importance of the inside/outside contrast in understanding Wiru reactions to colonialism, and of how this contrast itself shifted once the outside encompassed the world order, when the valuables that flowed along watercourses were replaced by commodities driven along roads. The trade road from Ialibu to Pangia was known as *olimari karapepine* ('man-child *karape* tree-base'). Trees are markers of community, so the gloss 'people community' can be proposed for this term for the road-link into the Highlands. The location where the Pangia road met the Ialibu road was described as a junction or *paru*; Kerr (1987: 112) acknowledges *paru* as one of the key linguistic terms in Wiru, translating its meaning as 'a trinary unit, the product of a single stem normally branching into two independent arms; a static association; [the] branching process is potentially open-ended, proceeding serially at random points along the length of the branch, river, or track; focus is at the point of disjunction.' In Kerr's theory of linguistic-cultural connectivity, *paru* is related to *ka*, the term for a track linking areas of settlement and work, and also for the 'life principle of people and plants' (ibid.: 113). The track to the Highlands is associated with life, regeneration (man-child), the source of culture and community, and disjunction. Europeans, with their promises of wealth, heaven, and development fitted into the cosmological scenario of connectedness to the outside, influencing Wiru receptivity to their messages and transforming the meaning of this connection as valuables took on commodity forms and created new kinds of difference.

Terence Turner (1991: 298) makes a useful observation about the Kayapo of Brazil that relates to the Pangia situation:

The relation between native and Brazilian society which constitutes the structure of this new social totality [the incorporation of Brazil into Kayapo cosmology] is replicated at all levels of social organization, including the household and the individual person. Just as the new social totality is now seen as made up of a native side and a Brazilian side, with the boundary between them defined by the movement of commodities and by the struggle to assert autonomy against the source of those commodities, so the household and the individual have likewise become double beings, diametrically divided between an internal, indigenous Kayapo core and an external facade composed wholly or in part of Brazilian goods and forms. The prototypical commodities involved are clothes, in the case of the person, and in the case of the domestic group, the Brazilian-style house and other items of personal property such as cooking pots and suitcases for storing possessions.
... The new view, moreover, is not formulated in the same terms of ritual and myth, nor as clearly articulated with the structure of village space, as the traditional cosmology; rather it is implicit in new social forms, attitudes and rhetoric relating to interaction with Brazilian society, in particular the usage of Brazilian commodities.

It is possible that Wiru could also be characterized as 'double beings', with a Wiru core and an external façade of Europeanness. Their invocation of clothes

covering the skin, in explanations of a diminution in the core of their being,
supports such a view, although I am not satisfied with accounts that reduce explanation to a simple opposition of core and externality. The commodity is certainly
crucial in the construction of social beings, but these are perhaps 'new' ontic entities rather than divided beings comprised of a bricolage of Wiru and European
elements. Wiru now have a different body as well as skin, even if they are not the
ones they wanted, and to elaborate on this claim an account of ritual is necessary.

A Brief History of Cults and Sacrifice

The crucial features of pagan cults were that they involved offerings of pigs,
marsupials, and eels, and that certain stones were of central importance as trans-
ducers of the cosmological. The Wiru symbolic and ritual system makes much use
of the oppositions between male and female, and it is within the category 'female'
that the cosmological locus of fertility, health, and reproduction is lodged (Clark
1991). Men control cults but, because of women's life-giving and supporting role
(cf. Kerr 1984), the regenerative power of the cosmos is 'female'; as the single
wealth valuable capable of regeneration, pigs too, as a category, are 'female'.[8] The
cult stone, *tomonuia kue*, of the *Tapa yapu* patrilineal spirit cult is terminologically
associated with the egg, *mu*, in the region where a foetus develops inside a woman,
tomonu. *Mu* is also testicle, and the cult stone itself is comprised of two separate
stones, a round one often with a hole, and a smaller elongated stone that fits into
the hole. Not surprisingly, given the overt sexual content of Wiru symbolism, the
larger and smaller stones are referred to as vagina and penis respectively, or as
mother and child, and in the Tapa ritual men would attach themselves to each
other and to the stones, known also as *tapa mu* (ancestors' testicles), by vines tied
to their scrota.

Despite the outwardly 'male' emphasis in Tapa, female themes of fertility and
reproduction continually creep into the meanings deployed in ritual performances.
The thick fat of pigs, also called *tomonu*, was rubbed into these stones together
with blood, ensuring the growth and health of people and pig herds; the bones of
pigs and marsupials were also ground up and burnt to appease angered spirits, and
pig fat was rubbed into the body to make people look healthy and attractive. Tapa
ritual was most often performed for the propitiation of ancestral spirits divined to
be responsible for individual illness or misfortune, but the spirits could be collec-
tively appealed to for the health and well-being of the settlement they represented
through the skulls of important men stored in the cult house (and appealed to for
success and protection in warfare, to which end stones were sometimes taken on
raids). The belief that pig herds are smaller today is related by men to the fact that
the Tapa and, more particularly, the Timbu cults, are no longer performed. The

---

[8] All the pigs of a settlement are called *x aroa* (*x* female), *x* being the name of the stream from which
people of that settlement draw their water, equating femaleness with flow, wealth, and life.

cult stones of Tapa were stored in gourds in a hole under the floor of the cult house, and they needed to be kept moist with tree oil during storage, or the blood and fat of pigs on ritual occasions. Sacrifice was the method used to ensure the stones did not become too dry, thus angering the spirits, who would send sickness to humans and, in the case of Timbu, also to pigs, as well as causing droughts or crop failure in gardens—problems again rectified through sacrifice.

Timbu was a later arrival into Pangia, perhaps in the early to mid-nineteenth century, and stones did not play a role in its performance, reflecting perhaps the importation of this cult from the Papuan coast rather than from the Highlands. This cult involved Wiru in more elaborate, collective, and complex ceremonial than did Tapa, and its themes were more centrally those of fertility and growth in people and porcine populations. Timbu was part of a ceremonial cycle involving pig-kills of several hundred animals every four to six years; the sacrifice of animals and the filling up of the *lowalia* pole of the cult house with bones; and the weaving of fertility emblems, *timbu mara*, for each group involved (the attachment of these emblems to the red 'top hat' *alipo* wigs of decorated male dancers also invoked female/male, vagina/penis associations—as did their later attachment to the sacrificial bones of the *lowalia* pole). Timbu was an amorphous spirit entity about whom people seemed to have no clear idea, distinct from ancestral spirits but in some way 'female'. An integral part of Timbu ritual occurred when decorated, dancing women had released into them, through tightly woven and decorated bags suspended from the forehead and worn on the back of the neck, the power of Timbu to regenerate the cosmos—these women may have momentarily represented the Timbu spirit. Allusions to the symbolic importance of women's ordinary netbags, carriers of food, children, and wealth, were clearly made.

The culmination of the Timbu cycle was a political as well as cult occasion, and it brought settlements from within an encompassing district together. Allies and sometimes even enemies were invited to receive gifts of pork as death compensation or for assistance in warfare. Although it was never cited to me as a major feature of Timbu, there is some evidence to suggest that allied districts attempted to stage the concluding pig-kills at about the same time, creating a wider unity through ritual and exchange. Life-cycle payments to matrilateral and affinal relatives were another important feature of these culminating pig-kills. The *lowalia* poles, upon which the bones of pigs, eels, and marsupials sacrificed to Timbu were lashed in specially woven frames, were extracted from the cult house and relocated on to the major ceremonial green of the district at the time of pig-killing. These poles were often planted next to the skull shrines of important men, who may have been those who first brought Timbu into the district (Kerr 1984).

The Female Spirit cult, *Aroa Ipono yapu*, was the most recent cult to arrive in Pangia, perhaps in the early 1900s. Like Tapa, it involved the manipulation of stones (*kue*), although in this instance the stones were gendered according to whether they belonged to the 'male' or 'female' sections of the cult house. This cult was concerned with ensuring health and fertility through its performance, together with the observation of taboos relating to menstruation and sexual intercourse, including the confinement of women to menstrual huts. The Female Spirit was strict and would punish those who broke taboos by sending sickness to the community at large, and by causing accidents in which bones were broken. There was no linking of the Female Spirit to menstrual, lactation or pregnancy problems experienced by women, which were caused instead by their maternal spirits. *Aroa Ipono yapu* was a Highlands cult and, although it celebrated a 'female' principle, women were exluded from participation and denied the public recognition of their importance allowed in Timbu. Gender relations altered with cults as they arrived over time, not necessarily in a way beneficial to women; Christianity signalled another transformation and, from the perspectives of women, an improvement.

When the stones themselves were not propitiated as the conduits of spiritual power, or did not exist, as in Timbu, certain parts of pigs were burnt to appease the spirits or to complement the stone rubbing. Internal organs were used, especially the kidneys (*lawene*), liver (*kolorini*), as well as the tail meat (*andapini*). These organs are not, in a cultural sense, offal.[9] They are the analogues of human organs which are the centre of affectivity and action within people, and which influence the capacity for thought (*wene*) usually located behind the forehead, and believed to be stronger in men (the weight of women's netbags, suspended from the forehead, is said to push women's *wene* to the back of their heads, thereby weakening it). The *andapini*, associated with pig scrota, means literally 'old man base'.[10] This part of porcine anatomy is where, according to Wiru, ancestral male spirits 'live'. That is, a line of male ancestors is somehow immanent in that part of a pig associated with scrota which enables (*pini*) reproduction. This relates to ideas connecting ancestral power with Tapa stones and men's testicles. The sacrifice of *andapini* maintains the link between living men and their ancestors, ensuring the continuation of male strength and prowess. This is an idea compatible with the link made between *mu*—cult stones, testicles, and eggs—and sexual, cultural, and cosmological reproduction. Although pigs are part of the generic category 'female', offerings made to spirits are symbolic of the 'male' (*andapini*, certain organs and bones). This is related to cult attempts by men to control the 'female' forces of fertility and reproduction, and to mystify their 'female' locus.

Expressions relating to 'sacrifice' employ the verb *yoroko*; 'to burn or cook'. *Londo yoroko* ('smoke burns'), or *pine yoroko* ('base burns'), are the usual expressions—'base' in the latter usage refers to the 'cause' of things, be it sickness or the conditions necessary for existence. That fire is used to burn offerings is important. Fire (*toe*) has a 'mouth' and 'eats' (*nako*) what is burnt. The word for 'flame'

---

[9] The intestines, *tepe*, are associated with excrement and are given to women after butchering to acknowledge their efforts in pig-raising.

[10] Large pigs were preferred for sacrifice and were thus usually male (H. B. Kerr, pers.comm.). I do not know if male pigs were chosen for sacrifice because of their size or their maleness. In Wiru belief, testicles function in penile erection by turning flaccid into hard. *Andapini* are related to concepts of male strength (hardness), which relates to their association with the scrotum.

translates as 'the spirit of the wood speaks' (Kerr 1975: 290), and special trees associated with group identity and male continuity—usually casuarina—are selected for use as firewood for cult houses. There is a sense, then, in which fire is the 'mouth of the spirits', a notion similar to one expressed in Hindu cosmology (Gray 1987). *Toe* also refers to skin peeling off with respect to the growth or decline of the body, and is used in reference to snakes shedding their skin and creating new bodies (cf. Kerr 1987: 117). Even if these two examples of *toe* are homonyms, there is still a semantic field in which both meanings of *toe* resonate (see Chapter 1). Fire, through 'eating' an offering, is linked into concepts of life, death, and continuity.

According to informants, the meaning of *yoroko* in ceremonial contexts is that the relationship of those involved in 'cooking' is changed, just as the form of meat which is 'cooked' is changed. *Yoroko* implies transformation, and Kerr (1987: 105) defines one of its meanings as, 'to change from one state to another in a cyclical process [of land use, of life and death]'. The Maring ritual cycle, culminating in the sacrifice of hundreds of pigs, is concerned 'with the mediation and amelerioration of those oppositions [between spirits and various qualities] and the *transformation* of those relations [between people, spirits and qualities] through the dynamic of the cycle' (Rappaport 1968: 84, my emphasis).

Most, if not all rituals are concerned with effecting transformations. In Wiru sacrifice, at least, this is made explicit, and I gloss 'sacrifice' as a particular type of transformative ritual, perhaps the most fundamental, but not analytically separate from the category of 'ritual'.

The verb *yoroko* has important cultural connotations, and is used in other contexts, for example *aroa yoroko*, 'cooking the woman'—the exchange of wealth for a bride's reproductive potential. 'Cooking the woman' has elements in common with sacrifice: '. . . through their marriage women are taken out of circulation, "consumed" and used until their reproductive capacity is exhausted' (Meillassoux 1981: 68). Destruction, in some sense, may be a motif of occasions described by *yoroko*. Transformation remains, however, the dominant motif of this exchange—the transformation of a relationship between groups into one of affinity, and of a woman's status from daughter to wife. The use of *yoroko* as a verb for sacrifice suggests that these acts attempt an alteration in the relationship between people and spirits, into a relationship more favourable to people. In other words, a ritual realignment with the source of power for the improved health and fertility of people and pigs, just as a similar realignment was later attempted with Europeans. Pigs are a major wealth item, and wealth was an obvious concern of cult activity, as well as an indicator of the state of the relationship between people and spirits. The importance of wealth also suggests the possibility of a relationship with Akolali, a benevolent sky being later identified with God, who was responsible for dreams announcing wealth. Possession of Akolali's healing bones also meant that wealth would be multiplied (Kerr 1984: 7).

Cults, Christianity, and Colonialism

Christianity was an 'alternative' which Wiru embraced readily and with enthusiasm. This heralded the end of cults and of all sacrifices to 'traditional' spirits, who became glossed generically as 'Satan'. As previous chapters have demonstrated, Christianity is largely comprehended and performed in terms of a persisting cult orientation to the continuing problems of health and fertility. Christianity does, however, address the problem of wealth (money) in a more direct way than did pagan cults, partly because access to money has become a dominant concern, subsuming health and fertility, in the postcolonial context, and partly because the cult of Christianity is now directed towards Akolali/God, who was never the focus of ritual performance. Money is a valuable which relates to, and demands some participation in an intrusive and encompassing cultural system. Money is the link between Christianity and capitalism, and is the anvil upon which different constructs of the person are made.

In Takuru, my fieldwork settlement, Wesleyanism is the dominant Christian cult. The fundamentalist evangelism of its missionary promoters lends a distinct flavour to the beliefs and practices of the Wesleyan cult, which tempers generalizations about the existence of a regional Christian cult in all settlements of Pangia. Observations based on brief experiences in non-Wesleyan settlements tend to support the notion that there is a conglomeration of separate Christian cults; people strongly differentiate settlements along denominational lines, and make value judgements about the efficacy and 'truth' of other churches. As the Lutheran people of Tunda say of the Wesleyans in Takuru:

> They are good Christians over there, they have turned their stomachs and they cry a lot over their sins, and their legs shake, but one thing is that they are always saying Jesus is coming . . . Really those people are acting like God, predicting things, whereas only God himself knows his own intentions (A. J. Strathern, pers.comm.).

Traditionally, cult performance and membership demarcated district groups. Church attendance and denomination continue this demarcation, so I suggest that Pangia evinces a series of Christian cults rather than a single and encompassing one. Although there does seem to be a generic term for the Christian cult, 'Lotu' *yapu*, this was also the case for cults such as Timbu, in which there were 'denominational' differences between districts (H. B. Kerr, pers.comm.), with some places performing ritual embellishments unknown in other areas. Traditional cults were mutually exclusive between districts, Christian cults are mutually exclusive between districts or settlements of different denominations.

Today, pigs continue to be killed when people are sick but, like the neighbouring Kewa (Josephides 1985: 79), the appeasement of spirits is not overtly the aim of these acts. Ancestral spirits have not ceased to exist with the acceptance of Christianity, having been confined instead to the category of 'Satan'. If one has 'Satan sickness', regardless of whether matrilineal or patrilineal spirits are suspected, it is expected that one will probably die. The understanding of Christianity is such that Takuru people recognize that any attempts at appeasing 'Satan', whether by sacrifice or by making payments to matrilateral kin, is sinful. Why then are pigs killed? Are people still covertly sacrificing to pagan spirits? To the latter question I would, for the most part, answer no, and in response to the former, there is still an element of sacrifice in present-day pig killing. Informants told me that before they killed pigs if they were sick, but today they pray. The locus of punishment and relief has shifted from spirits to God, and pigs are killed to 'thank' God in the hope he will intervene in 'Satan sickness'. There still seems to be some hope that the smell from the cooking pig will also influence 'Satan' in the form of spirits of the recently deceased; people know this is sinful and would never openly admit to it, but as an alternative this course of action is often believed to be effective.

When pigs are killed at times of sickness, instead of offering *andapini* to spirits they are presented to pastors, as the ritual specialists of God. These gifts, like church donations, are spoken of as being given directly to God, through the mediation of pastors, for his continued benevolence. During ceremonial pig-kills some of the *andapini* tail meat from pigs is often collected in a netbag and presented to pastors of the church, as the focal point for the unity and identity of the pig-killing settlement. The Christian church incorporates elements of the major Wiru cults. The church, like Tapa, conflates the denominational membership of the congregation with the major descent group(s) of the settlement. Adam and Eve are the ultimate Tapa ancestors, from whom all people are descended, even if this descent is still conceived of in group/denomination terms, rather than in terms of a universal Christian brotherhood. The church does not pursue the concern of Tapa with male health and prowess, except in the general sense of God being responsible for the health of all people.

Timbu was also concerned with demonstrating group membership, and the major chant of this cult recited the names of 'every significant male ancestor' (Kerr 1987: 121); it seems that Timbu took on some aspects of Tapa, just as Christianity assumed aspects of previous cults. Timbu, with its concluding pig-kill and pork distributions to allies and affinal-maternal kin, seems to have been an occasion for the presentation of district unity to other districts, Tapa having more intra-district connotations. Timbu can be equated with a more encompassing idiom of membership paralleled, for example, by all the people from different districts who belong to the Wesleyan denomination, and who may come together to celebrate Christian occasions such as Easter. More importantly though, the church, through prayer, donations, and offerings, has taken over the Timbu concerns for the health and fertility of people and pig populations, upon which the continuity of society depends. Pigs are also killed to 'thank' God if death or injury is believed to have been avoided through His intervention. He is also responsible for pigs, as was Timbu; as remarked in an earlier chapter, holy water was stolen in Catholic settlements for rubbing into the skin of pigs to make them grow and behave.

The Female Spirit cult, being a later arrival, has in some ways been more strongly associated with the most recent cult, Christianity. The notion of a singular and personified deity facilitated the acceptance of a concept of one cult for a singular and supreme deity. Christianity continued to stress the importance of the male–female distinction which is such a prominent feature of Wiru cosmology. The sexual, dietary, and behavioural taboos of *Aroa Ipono* have been replaced by those of Christianity, and taboo breaking in both cults leads to punishment from the deity. For most Wiru, Akolali is now God, and the perception of Akolali as God has a 'Female Spirit' dimension. As Chapter 2 indicates, many Wiru first encountering Europeans believed them to be 'sons of the Female Spirit', and when these 'sons' were missionaries some conflation between God and the Female Spirit was unavoidable. Some older men are confused as to the gender of God, surprising in fundamentalist settlements where a male chauvinist view of God is often promulgated. This is also related to the importance of the 'female' in cosmological beliefs; even Akolali has a female counterpart, called Akolaroa. Both were associated with dreams of wealth, and today people dream of a heaven which is associated with God, valuables, and the end of exchange. As one Wiru author observed: 'Religion is the most important aspect that unites the various [Wiru] tribal groups together. People strongly believe that people who don't give their hearts to the Lord won't be a prosperous person here on earth nor in the spirit world' (Paia 1977: 55).

The crucifixion of Jesus and the practice of communion provide a background against which the impact of Christianity on notions of sacrifice can be assessed. When missionaries and native evangelists presented the crucifixion to Wiru, they had no difficulty in recognizing it as a sacrifice, if not, as Chapter 5 indicates, in the biblical sense. The rubbing of the blood of Jesus into the skin was informed by the logic of sacrifice but was a peculiar transformation of former practice. Instead of rubbing substance into cult stones, as an offering to spirits, people rubbed the substance of a deity, a European sky being, into their own skins. The system of cult practice had by this time been totally undermined, being perceived as the sinful opposite of Christianity. That is, cults were an inversion of Christianity and, as an alternative to cults, Christianity in its practice initiated a transformation in sacrificial logic. Wiru, in a sense, made offerings to themselves, not as spirits, but so as to incorporate the essence of the European deity, and to make themselves 'like whites'.

Christian communion deals with the same transformation, and highlights the fact that change was neither systemic nor a purely 'logical' transformation of cultural themes. People are confused to some extent about communion and what it is supposed to achieve. Communicants consume the 'blood' and 'skin' of Jesus, and believe that failure to engage regularly in communion prohibits entry into heaven.[11]

---

[11] Wesleyanism does not accept transubstantiation in the communion, but Wiru tend to believe this concept literally. Wiru did not practise cannibalism in any ritual or widespread fashion, although the occasional consumption of uncooked fingers or ears was not unknown. People would drink the blood of the dead to prove their innocence of complicity in their death. Unlike Huli, Wiru do not see themselves as responsible for the death of Jesus (Robin 1980: 350).

This is related to the fact that the communion wafers and grape juice are believed to be *yomborono*, curative substances belonging to ritual specialists who obtained their power from spirit possession.[12] They are also known as *ne*, or 'food'. In Wesleyanism the ritual specialists are pastors, men who have been strongly influenced if not possessed by the Holy Spirit. Communion *yomborono*, like its traditional counterpart, wards off the attacks of spirits, that is, Satan. It also 'cures' people of sinful behaviour and strengthens their Christian being.

I initially assumed that the interpretation of communion offerings as 'food' was a pragmatic one, yet communion offerings are 'food' composed of the body of Christ, just as food was offered to spirits through sacrifice or rubbing blood into stones. It is Christ who is eaten to aid the construction of the consumer as a Christian. People are confused, however, because although the practice of sacrifice is inverted in communion, its aims, in the context of the more powerful Christian cult, are not achieved.[13] Informants claim that they are still hungry after communion; if spirits are satisfied with what they are offered, why then does communion not fill their bellies? These statements are literal and metaphorical and refer to the fact that communion is not seen to work. Through communion people hoped to become 'like whites'. It is supposed, like sacrifice, to effect a transformation, to turn people into good Christians and change the relationship of Wiru to God. These metamorphoses have begun but they are by no means complete and many Wiru remain pessimistic as to the final outcome.

Jesus relates to notions of sacrifice in other contexts. It is his sacrifice which perpetuates health and fertility, rather than a sacrifice to him for this perpetuation. Jesus on the wooden cross bears similarities to the bones on the *lowalia* pole which, as symbols of male procreative power—themselves contained within a 'female' frame woven around a pig scapula—influence the release of forces which ensure cosmological regeneration when *timbu wara* fertility emblems are attached to them. This may appear fanciful, but consider the following. Crosses are often planted in gardens by Catholics and Lutherans to ensure their fertility and the growth of crops. The cross is a symbol of sacrifice, and it is the blood or substance of Jesus which infuses the soil with fertility. There are also some resonances with the concept of *kengou*, the decomposing substance from the dead bodies of men, which replenishes the 'gris' (grease) of the soil. It is no longer necessary for sacrifice to be a repeated act of immolation, the power released through sacrifice today is real but symbolically embodied in the cross. The crucifixion of Jesus was required only once, operating as a symbolic guarantee of God's benevolent control over health

---

[12] In one *yomborono* bundle I saw a picture of a popular missionary and his family, as well as a strange piece of red plastic which the missionary was said to have given the bundle owner. The picture and the plastic were believed to have protective power, illustrating the connection made between *yomborono* and Christianity.

[13] In pagan cults men would eat, in communion, the flesh of animals sacrificed to spirits. In Christian communion that which is sacrificed is also eaten, but in this case the sacrifice is on the part of the 'spirits' not men. This is part of the inversion referred to in the text.

and fertility. Control over these qualities is achieved through mediating acts such as the planting of crosses in the ground, accompanied by appropriate prayers. Prayer is a means of making a 'spirit' request without sacrifice, *kowiriko*, although many Wiru also use the expression *kulio piko*, which refers to twisting the ear of a sacrificial pig in supplication (H. B. Kerr, pers.comm.).

There is another manifestation of the interplay between Christian and pagan beliefs about sacrifice. A *kendo* is a casuarina tree with a raised, buttressed base. It is made on the ceremonial green of settlements. In the soil at the base of the tree were sometimes planted the skulls of important men, mixed with the ashes from sacrificial fires. Trees are important symbols of male continuity and group unity, and traditional *kendo* were the focus of sacrifice to ancestors and of ritual activities, including exchange. Today, crosses are often planted in *kendo*, reaffirming sacrifice as a symbol rather than an action.[14] They may also be planted on the ceremonial green for the duration of Christian events such as baptism, as were the *lowalia* poles at the endpoint of the ritual cycle. Ideas such as descent from Adam and Eve, God the Father, and denominational membership are also confirmed by the 'new' *kendo*, called 'Kris mak' *kendo* ('Christ sign *kendo*'). Both types of *kendo*, usually the 'new' kind, continue to be the focus of ritual activity in Christian ceremonies, and they are where church 'komiti' men gather during food distributions which celebrate such events. The 'bones' of Christ are analogous to the bones of men planted in the *kendo*, related to Tapa concerns, complementing the descent-group membership of the church (Clark 1989), but are also reminiscent of the Timbu aspects of Christianity with respect to God's control over health and fertility. It is the various resonances between Christ, bones, *kendo*, and *lowalia* poles which make the cross a powerful multivocal symbol of the Christian cult, yet Akolali's (God's) bones are an omen of wealth, such that money also resonates with the meanings of Christianity. And it is money, most of all, that helped to create and perpetuate a colonized culture.

Fish Cooking, a New Exchange

These two examples of the Wiru deployment of the Christian cross support the argument so far, and now exchanges inaugurated by Christian occasions will be discussed to discover if sacrifices are still made. While the Timbu cult and its rituals have been discontinued, the pig-killing cycle and its associated exchanges still take place, even if their meanings have not persisted unchanged. Pig-kills appear to be mostly secular affairs but gifts of *andapini* to pastors do occur, and prayers may be recited to ask for God's blessing upon the occasion. The cult context of exchange has been replaced by a new cycle of exchanges with a Christian impetus

---

[14] Unlike Wiru, the Huli may directly sacrifice pigs, known as 'church pigs', to God near a Christian cross (Frankel 1986: 166). In the early days of colonialism in Pangia, crosses were often planted on the site of dismantled and burned Tapa cult houses.

called *mou yoroko*, fish cooking (cf. A. J. Strathern 1984: 102). Pigs are killed and distributed but it is store-bought tins of fish, cooked in earth ovens in their hundreds, which are the ideal exchange item.

A *mou yoroko* is held for deaths, baptisms, church openings, and other Christian events. They are also given to reciprocate previous *mou yoroko*, so while their religious origin may not be overt they are always Christian occasions. The ceremonial pig-kill, shorn of Timbu may, in some fundamentalist settlements, be succumbing to attempts to turn them into *mou yoroko* (see A. J. Strathern 1984: 101). Both are concerned with the status of groups and individuals, and both make political statements through exchange. The same recipient settlements often attend the two ceremonial occasions. Shared church denomination may create new exchange links, but does not prevent *mou yoroko* between settlements or districts of different denominations, especially if they were once allied. These new exchanges vary in the size and quantity of goods distributed according to the occasion and the type of political statement being made. At one *mou yoroko* I attended, eighty pigs were killed, and 400 kina of pork, 5,400 kina of freezer meat, and 3,000 kina of tinned fish were bought to give away.

What interests me is the emphasis on fish and the use of the verb *yoroko* in these exchanges. This use for an important politico-religious event never means merely 'cooking'. It signifies that through what is given, in this instance fish, there are changes in the relationship between groups in terms of a cyclical process of life and death. According to the linguist Kerr, the generic underlying form of *yoroko* is *yoro* ('log'), and the use of the term in linguistic constructions signifies a bridging function and unitariness, unlike other key words that signify a bend, fork, or sphere (1987: 112–13). *Yoroko* can be glossed by many English expressions, such as cooking, reciprocating, and burning, but when informants translated expressions such as *londo yoroko*, *aroa yoroko*, they invariably used the pidgin expression 'kukim' (Melanesia Pidgin, cook), emphasizing a change from one state to another. The meaning of *yoroko* in sacrifice refers to transformation, unitariness, and bridging—the act constructs a 'bridge' between people and spirits and temporarily transforms their relationship into one of equivalence, or at least a movement towards it, and a release of power from one domain into another (the bride is a bridge between groups whose marriage, it is hoped, brings unity).

Mou yoroko are cult occasions—prompted by such events as death and baptisms—and as such are vitally concerned with a cyclical process of death and regeneration. Yet the cycle is also dependent on God's continued benevolence, and these events 'thank' God for pigs, health, and so on, and acknowledge Akolali's control in a similar fashion to the gifts of *andapini* made to missionaries and pastors, and also to the anthropologist (gifts which are alienated).[15] These gifts are

---

[15] This notion of 'thanking' God bears interesting similarities to aspects of Maring sacrifice: 'In the address preceding the sacrifice for the spirits of the high ground, in addition to being thanked for their help in warfare, the spirits are thanked for the *ma* [marsupials] they have provided and are told that they will now be given pigs in exchange for them' (Rappaport 1968: 176).

frequently given in the *mou yoroko* context and, although there is no explicit animal sacrifice, there is a sense in which these events please God through their performance and the smell of fish cooking. *Mou yoroko*, a new cycle of exchanges celebrating people's relationship with the 'spirit' world, complement the rather more secular ceremonial pig-kill which previously had this function, and which continues because of its important role in life-cycle and intergroup exchanges. This new cycle has to be separate because the cult aspects of the pig-kill are now considered sinful and no longer appropriate to the 'new world' created by Christianity. *Mou yoroko* also indicate a relationship with the outside world, as did other cults: 'Wiru society cannot be accepted as a system in isolation on the ground. It must be tied to the still larger system of an outside world from which the religious ceremonial came' (Kerr 1987: 121).

The use of tinned fish is a recognition of a link into another world, and a commentary on the nature of the changing relationship to this world with colonialism. Tinned fish (MP, 'tinpis') is an important luxury food that people desire to eat as a staple, replacing the devalued 'kanaka' food that they must eat to survive, but it is not in the same league as valuables such as pigs, shells, and money.[16] Part of the reason for the symbolic power of 'tinpis', as a product of the Christian world, is its emblematic association with Europeans. It has to be bought with money, the ultimate icon of Europeanness, and is beyond the capacity of the domestic economy to produce except through the intervention of an external world, primarily through the sale of coffee or labour. Fish-cooking has replaced pig-killing as the context for cult practice.

I suggest that the impetus for the *mou yoroko* terminology comes from the fact that the perceived power of whites derives in part from their connection with the domain of *uali*, or water spirits. Watercourses are associated with the flow of wealth and the travels of the dead, both of which are to some extent under the control of God. Fish are associated with the domain of *uali* and, as living creatures are held to be the most antithetical to human beings because they live under water and do not speak (as far as I could determine Wiru made no association between Jesus and the fish symbol, as is done in the West). There is no communication or exchange between people and fish, so that the tinned fish of Europeans becomes a very appropriate symbol not just for the cyclical exchanges which celebrate Christianity, but for the nature of the relationship between Wiru and Europeans, the latter keeping-while-giving—that is, not engaging in a true communication with Wiru. One of the more popular brands of 'tinpis' in Pangia is '777', and I was told that this brand name was a sign that 666 was coming soon, the association of 666 with Europeans, evil, the millennium, and true power through wealth having already been commented upon.

---

[16] Mendi people believe that store-bought food has 'special nutritive value' through its association with a 'strong' Western society (Lederman 1981: 23). Consumption of items like tinned fish may be related to the desire to become like Europeans. A Huli friend once told me that gold stolen from the Porgera mine in Enga Province is turned into ingots using an empty fish tin as the mould.

Sacrifice and Selling

In order to tie up the various arguments into a more or less coherent whole, it is necessary to examine Wiru perceptions of money and selling. At an early stage in Pangia's colonial history the deviant power and symbol of Europeans was identified as, and located in steel. Today the role of steel has been assumed by money, known in the vernacular as *kue* (stone).[17] The use of the term 'stone' for money is not merely descriptive of the hardness of coins, otherwise one might expect the extant term for 'steel'—*kapona*—to have been adopted instead. In the Highlands money quickly became part of the category of valuables, hidden away from prying eyes, as opposed to luxury goods, with the later introduction of paper money turning coins into luxury items (Salisbury 1962: 125), and finally into a form of money associated with women. What has not been considered is the possibility of a connection between the qualities of money as 'stone' and the stones of cults. 'Stone' conveys notions of strength, solidity, and power and, while never explicitly expressed, money operates in a similar fashion as cult stones; when older men were asked why money was originally known as *kue*, they referred to its power rather than its hardness. *Mu* as *tapa* stone and as testicle is what made men strong, and now it is money that makes men strong. Introduced cults like the Female Spirit brought a new stone, and Christianity brought money, itself the object of the Kongono work cult in which Wiru attempted to create a moral equivalence with Europeans.[18]

There is, of course, a difference between pre- and postcolonial cults. The former operated through the manipulation and control of cult stones, while Christianity is based on obtaining control of money, *kue*, which is in European hands. Money is like cult stones because it provides a way of breaking into and releasing the power of the spirit domain. Selling is like sacrifice in this respect in that it is transformative of the relationship between different or opposed

---

[17] The word for money in other Highlands-societies is also the word for 'stone', for example, Melpa *ku* (A. J. Strathern 1982a: 550); Siane *kifana* (but only for coins; Salisbury 1962: 125); Maring *ku* (Healey 1985b: 138); Kuma *ku* (M. Reay, pers.comm.). In other areas the word for money is the same as that for shell valuables, for example, the cowry for the Baruya (Godelier 1977: 235), the pearlshell for Chimbu (Brown 1970: 255).

[18] It was mainly in the Female Spirit cult that the stones used were referred to as 'stone'—*kue*—and in Tapa the stone was usually known as *mu* rather than as *tomonuia kue*. Paper money is known as *kue tara* ('leaf money'), coins as *kue lene* ('eye/seed money'), and are associated with men and women respectively, just as the Female Spirit had male and female cult stones.

It would be interesting to correlate the use and persistence of 'stone' for money with areas which had stone cults. I suspect there are other factors involved, historical and structural, in any explanation of 'stone' money. The Kewa of the Southern Highlands, for instance, had stone cults but money is apparently known only as *mane* (Franklin and Franklin 1978). Whether my interpretation of the stone–money connection in Pangia is in any way applicable to other areas is not clear from existing ethnographies, although there are indications that this interpretation could be pursued: '[Melpa] churches were cult-sites, and to this day the idea that money is to be found in Christian cemeteries is very persistent' (A. J. Strathern 1984: 43).

categories.[19] Money can be used as an offering to thank God, *kue Gote mereko* ('money God to give'), and mediates, like cult stones, the relationship between people and 'spirits' (church donations are not a sacrifice). A wealthy man has more successful relations with God, an idea not totally alien to the beliefs of some Western churches. The power of Christianity, God's benevolence, is released through the control of money, and it is money which allows Wiru a measure of equivalence with whites. Money, like cult stones, is related to notions of success and protection through spirit intervention, and both symbolize the locus and conduit of cosmological power, whether of cult spirits or God. Christian work can be described as *kue kongono*—the same term for fortnightly pay—for which the reward lies in heaven (*poanea kue*, 'bad stone', is work done by sinners).

It hardly needs to be emphasized that money is only *like* cult stones, and as memories of cults fade only traces of its earlier association as a transducer of power remain. Cult stones, unlike money, never entered into the exchange system. They remained the inalienable property of the groups which performed cults (although they could be stolen in raiding and repatriated through *kioli* exchange). Money is not sacred, it can be used by women and children, although attempts are made to keep paper money under male control. This is the problem of money for men: it is an exchange valuable obtained largely through the household production of coffee for sale (cf. A. J. Strathern 1984: 94). It 'leaks' out of men's control and is also the mediator with an external economic system which constrains men to act 'like women' (cf. Godelier 1986: 195). Money is perhaps not totally secular, for it is what relates people to God and Europeans, just as stones related people to spirits (cf. Gregory 1980). Its ambiguous status as a valuable and a commodity compounds this problem but complements, in the context of Christianity and development, the transformation of precolonial notions about the power of 'stone', making it into a medium of exchange as well as the concrete instantiation of spirit—just as the sacrifice *of* a deity instead of *to* a deity altered through praxis a logic that linked people to cosmological beliefs. Sahlins (1981: 53) describes a similar situation in Hawai'i when 'sacrifice turned into trade', turning Europeans into men. The following indicates that, in Pangia, sacrifice turned into selling and money became the sign of God, much as it did for Weber's Protestant businessmen—though, for Wiru, not as a sign of one's presence among the elect but of one's potential to become European.

There is an attribute of money that provides some support for its connection to the cosmological domain. The verb for 'to sell' is *yoroko*. I am not suggesting that to sell anything for money is directly akin to sacrifice in the sense so far discussed, but rather that money has come to be linked into the cyclical process which reproduces

---

[19] For the Onabasulu of the Great Papuan Plateau, money is so transformative of categories that it is compared to magic because of its potential to dissolve different spheres within which goods must be exchanged (T. Ernst, pers.comm.). Onabasulu and Wiru do not equate money with pearl shells, unlike Anganen who compare the latter with 20-kina notes (Nihill 1989), because money is totally unlike other valuables.

culture. To sell in a general sense refers to the relationship between Wiru and the outside world, the origin place of money, valuables, and cults, upon which this reproduction depends. Selling is a movement in the direction of altering this relationship, preferably a transformation towards equality. In an economic sense, *yoroko* as selling contains the notion of alienation implicit in sacrifice (Gregory 1980). The selling relationship is often impersonal; one gets something back, usually money, but what is sold is alienated from the producer. The animals which are sacrificed all come from the realm of production. Although pigs are the most important sacrificial animals, in that they are the closest approximation to people, marsupials and eels are the 'pigs' of bush and water spirits respectively. In an economic sense, the use value of these animals is destroyed, or alienated; this explanation is supported by the vernacular term for buying, *oro toko*, which can be glossed as 'to redeem' (H. B. Kerr, pers.comm.), i.e. bring back into the system of use value. *Yoroko* suggests a transformation of use value, but into what? Perhaps into 'food' which appeases spirits and encourages them to make returns of those things necessary for the reproduction of society. Sacrifice is an exchange involving a transformation of the universe of alternatives which people inhabit. This may be why selling, rather than church donations, resonates with meanings of sacrifice.

The economic explanation is not satisfactory as the 'returns' made by spirits are never merely economic, and the transformation that was desired through money and selling, whether of coffee or labour, is emblematic of the colonial process, namely the conversion of Wiru into Europeans. The use of *yoroko* in selling perhaps comments on the transformation from production of use value to production of exchange value, in which use value is destroyed, but it also provides a metacommentary on Wiru perceptions of the encompassing capitalist system (cf. Taussig 1980). The latter has become part of the 'cyclical process' and Wiru are as dependent on this system as they were on the goodwill of spirits. This is not to suggest a separation between economic and ritual activity. Money is what God represents, and selling and Christian performances are part of an attempted ritual realignment with the true source of power, health, and fertility in the cosmos of Christianity and capitalism.

The seller obtains access to an important valuable—money—but loses control of the exchange relationship and is unable to assert or reinforce individuality or group strength. That Wiru believe themselves to be disadvantaged in these 'power relations' is evidenced by equations made between money and 666, and the fact that men believe themselves to have been 'shrinking' since pacification. Money has a dual function, like Baruya salt which is produced for export and operates internally as a valuable (Godelier 1977: 128–9). Baruya themselves compare salt with the 'big money'—paper notes—of Europeans (ibid.: 235). The point at which money changes its function, when *kue* becomes a commodity with exchange value, is when the social nature of people is denied. This never occurred in the transformations glossed as 'sacrifice', in a past when the cosmos was not as capricious and uncontrollable as the market. The transformations that this chapter discusses can be diagrammatically, and somewhat mechanistically, represented as shown in Fig. 3:

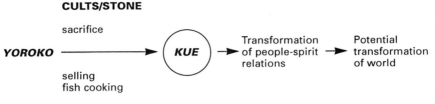

FIG. 3. Stone-mediated Transformations

A final point about sacrifice remains to be made. These acts are aimed at more than transforming people–spirit relations. There is a sense in which there is a potential for changing the world. The endpoint of the Timbu ritual cycle is a 'time of peace', and there was a sense in which Timbu was a celebration of life and health, not just a ritual of propitiation and request (cf. A. J. Strathern 1968: 549). The desires associated with the culmination of the Timbu cycle compare with the way in which 'lotu' made Pangia a 'place of love'—the promise inherent in 666 of a world without exchange. Sacrifice is related to a concept of a new order in which the possibilities of a world without war and sickness, with easy access to wealth and food, may be realized through ritual performance. It may be that this concept is immanent in sacrifice, which is concerned with what Murphy calls 'the restless push towards new forms' (1972: 97), as well as with ensuring cyclical continuity at another level.

In a way, Christianity and development were what Wiru were sacrificing and performing Timbu for, and once they arrived these cult practices were no longer necessary. The shift from a sacrifice to the 'gods' to a sacrifice of the God necessarily invalidated and transformed these practices. A new order had been inaugurated, a new cult had arrived with its own meanings of sacrifice, constructed by Wiru not Europeans. Signs of the ultimate transformation of Wiru into whites were present. An enduring 'time of peace', achieved through Christianity and money, was believed to have arrived. *Yoroko*, in the context of selling, refers perhaps to the construction of a bridge into the power of 'stone' (cf. Lévi-Strauss 1966: 225), letting loose the linear and alienating logic of capitalism. Wiru may have wished for cyclical continuity, and laboured mightily for it through Kongono, but chaos sometimes disengages meaning from praxis and discontinuity is instead achieved.

Money threatens social relations and is often referred to in church sermons as the root of all evil, a reference obviously influenced by European missionary proselytization, although this interpretation of money's effect on sociality remains particularly Wiru (even as Wiru share European notions that money causes friction, envy, crime, and so on). Wiru make a strong connection between evil and Satan, and between 666, the power of money, and Europeans, yet money is the most desired wealth item. This is the fundamental contradiction of postcolonial Wiru culture, and attempts to reach a resolution will shape its form in the years to come. While an analysis in terms of structural transformation helps us to understand the direction of cultural change proceeding from the event of development, as an explanation it privileges a symbolic system over ontology, and reifies its explanatory importance. The attribution of meaning to action may help to construct the relations between categories, themselves setting the limits for this attribution. Yet it may be that almost anything is possible within these limits, including the subversion of the symbolic system (cf. A. B. Weiner 1987: 157).

Radical change was eagerly embraced by many Wiru, indicating that it is not the symbolic system which submits categories to worldly risks but the people who act in reference to this system (Sahlins 1985: xiii). It was Wiru who created the Kongono cult, and who gave a particular meaning to the sacrifice of Jesus but, while not denying their autonomy, the incorporation of Wiru into the hegemonic discourses and praxis of colonial agents led to epistemic ruptures that produced confusion, anxiety, and discontinuity. The contradictions produced by colonialisms are not to be understood solely from a Marxist perspective, as conflict between modes of production, control over labour and products, and so on, or from a structuralist viewpoint that emphasizes a transformation in logical principles. I would not deny Marx's point that production affects consciousness, neither would I deny the existence of a symbolic logic. Rather what these chapters have emphasized is the importance of accounting for fundamental discontinuities produced by colonialisms. A major discontinuity, indicated by the analysis of contemporary usages of *yoroko*, is that Wiru interaction with Europeans and the state became defined less by keeping-while-giving and more by keeping-while-selling.[20] Valuables such as money revealed to Wiru the nature of a colonial power that they could interpret but not completely understand.

---

[20] It could be suggested that the inalienability of cult stones in A. B. Weiner's sense was replaced by the alienability of products and labour in a Marxist sense.

EPILOGUE

The Present in the Past

When I returned to Pangia in 1989 I brought with me a pair of small but powerful binoculars whose purchase I could not resist in the duty-free shop. Much of my time was spent in walking between settlements, as much for pleasure as for any incidental data collection, usually in the presence of young men with varying degrees of education and experience of the world. It was enjoyable to use the binoculars to view the bird life and the shifting colours of the rolling garden and bush landscape as the clouds obscured and revealed the sun. My indulgence proved to be a big hit with the men accompanying me, who could not get enough of this transformed vision of a familiar landscape. One of my more educated companions surprised me by asking if it was possible to see *ipono*, spirits, through the binoculars, and I was forced to once again confront the difference between their worldview and my own. Fifteen years after the end of colonialism there still existed a magical view of Europeans and their technology, despite the education and labour migration that these men had experienced—none of whom was old enough to have witnessed spirit cult ceremonies or to have worked on the roads under kiap supervision. In an earlier chapter I wrote of beliefs that my presence in Takuru kept Satan away from the settlement, and that Europeans lived in a world without exchange. These beliefs connect to my binocular anecdote to suggest that one of the legacies of colonialism in Pangia is a particular attitude to Europeans and the outside world of power and wealth that they inhabit. The postcolonial state, despite its national constitution, continues to resonate with the meaning of Europeanness (Clark n.d.).

On a walking trip to Poloko to try to identify some sites of Timbu performances photographed by Harland Kerr in the early 1960s, I heard for the first time a pidgin gloss of *ulo* sorcery, namely 'stone poison', a gloss that did not exist on my last trip to Pangia in 1985. Given the argument in Chapter 2 that *ulo* was connected to government patrols and the extension of European influence, in other words to the power of the periphery, I imagined it was a fitting irony that 'stone' now evokes the meanings of both money and sorcery—and the rapid spread of *ulo* suggests that this power is now embodied through encounters with the postcolonial state. The cyclical chronology of the Wiru experience of colonialism had come full circle, a movement from steel to stone in which stone (money) came to bear some of the amoral and dangerous attributes of the power of *kapona* (steel). The alienating promise of capitalism had borne its fruit in what Taussig would no doubt refer to as the evil inherent in commodity fetishism, in seeing in money the magical power of increase associated with whites and denied to Wiru. *Ulo* beliefs have become the most feared form of sorcery, mirroring the Wiru experience of the necessary evil of money as they moved from being subjects under colonialism to citizens of the independent state—history as sorcery (Taussig 1987). Recall too that *ulo* perpetrators are believed to be imported from the outside—particularly from the south, the traditional realm of deviance and power, where the state is now instantiated as Port Moresby—and recognizable by their white faces.[1] Having reached a suitable state of closure, steel to stone to steel, this would be an appropriate point upon which to conclude the monograph, but there are a few more points I wish to make about Wiru notions of history.

This history is more a particular attitude to the past than a linear, cause-and-effect model of change over time. In the West, history is invoked to explain the past in the present, but the point of this monograph is to establish that Wiru rhetorically claim to have abandoned the past, so that it has no influence on the present. 'Time before' is rendered sinful, and Wiru hold that they formerly inhabited a Satanic geography in which they behaved like wild pigs in a time of darkness. Yet even in the 1980s there was a certain nostalgia, evoked more by men than women, about a past in which men were warriors and more in control of their destinies.[2] Wiru always needed the outside world but it was only under colonialism that they became dependent upon it, and idioms of male shrinking refer to a perception of increasing powerlessness. Spirit cults, in the performance of which men were largely independent of external constraints, were often said to have worked better than Christianity—money and European power proving themselves difficult to access—and men have to work harder today, like women, to make the same sort of living as before.

Colonialism has created a particular form of local historical consciousness, and I doubt that Wiru had previously thought about the past in terms of abandonment and evil. Nostalgia is a peculiarly modern disposition, as is a view of the past as something that has to be denied or forgotten to enable 'progress'. The difference from the West is that Wiru use the present to explain the past: they acted like wild pigs and heathens because they were not yet Christians; they were 'kanakas' because they had no experience of wage labour or education. Stories of madness and shrinking have a short public life, recalled for the anthropologist but not, as far as I could determine, part of an oral historical 'archive' recounted over fires in the evening. Wiru—at least those in Takuru—live in the present and rarely resort to the past. Modernity has its local inflections in Pangia although, as I suggested in the introduction, the reference should perhaps be to postmodernity in so far as it allows for conflict rather than transition between the past and the present. Narratives of madness and shrinking are embodied histories of this conflict.

[1] Daribi identify the coast as a 'sacred space', and incorporated it into their 'cargo cult' narratives of power and wealth (Wagner 1979: 145).
[2] Many Huli women, while in favour of Christianity, are very nostalgic about a past in which men had been educated to behave as 'real' men through the bachelor cult, believing that men treated women better before than they do today (Clark and Hughes 1995).

I had wanted to limit this monograph to a discussion of the colonial divide, concluding with independence in 1975, but brief mention needs to be made of a spectacular event that took place in early 1992. I was making a visit to Pangia, taking time off from fieldwork in Tari, for a holiday and to catch up with old friends. My timing was fortuitous, as many of the inhabitants of the Catholic settlement of Apenda had been working for many months on a cultural 'revival' under the inspiration of a young unmarried man, Louis Warimi, educated in a Fine Arts degree at the University of Papua New Guinea. My experience of Christianity in Pangia, admittedly in a fundamentalist settlement, left me totally unprepared for any attempt at reconstructing the sinful past. The Catholic mission was very supportive of the revival, reflecting a provincial policy to acknowledge, celebrate, and incorporate local cultures.

The revival was not a product of a desire to return to the values and behaviours of the past, although to some extent it was a celebration of 'culture', this being the first time I had ever heard the concept reified in a positive sense in Pangia. Still, the revival was part of a larger project, namely the 'Wiru Culture and Tourism Development Project'. The revival was envisaged as a business, something to attract tourists to Pangia to view the richness of its cultural heritage, which they would support and perpetuate through paying admission fees, renting guest houses, and so on. This was development on Wiru terms, in which a particular claim was made on the past as a resource for the present. The cultural 'revival' was a quest to regain the lost autonomy denied by colonialism, and to withdraw to some extent from the control of the state. The irony is that the viability of Wiru 'culture' is vitally dependent on support from the outside—tourists and government funding—and when the former predictably failed to turn up in the months and years after the excitement and optimism of the opening, the 'Development Project' lost much of its momentum and rapidly became moribund. 'Culture' as Wiru understand it can perhaps only survive as a 'bisnis', and I do not mean this in a derogatory sense as another example of the pragmatic Highlander. The 'Development Project' is a continuation of the logic of the Kongono cult, an attempted colonial mimesis that failed to achieve the desired experience of alterity (Taussig 1993). The inhabitants of Pangia perhaps realize that they cannot be European and will settle for being independently Wiru, a force to be reckoned with against other Highlanders who may have reserves of gold, oil, and gas.

The interesting aspect of the revival is the form in which it was presented. A special enclosure was constructed and within it all of the Wiru spirit cult houses were once more constructed—Tapa, Timbu, and *Aroa Ipono*. The form in which 'culture' was resurrected was precisely that which the missions had condemned as the most 'heathen' and evil of Wiru practices. Tribal fighting, a diacritical marker of primitiveness, was also re-enacted. During the week of festivities and 'singsing' competitions preceding the official opening day, the dances associated with cults were performed in the enclosure, away from the majority of local spectators. If the central premises of this monograph are accepted, then the revival could have taken no other form. Wiru engagement with the cosmos of power had always been through the praxis of ritual and exchange. The iconic architecture of Wiru culture was firmly grounded in cults, and self-presentation to the 'other', be it tourists or important guests such as the Governor-General, had to take place through cults. The enclosure was in some sense a sacred space in which constructions of ethnicity in the context of state power took place; the cult houses and their dances were visible only to the few tourists who turned up and paid admission, and to the official guests and Catholic missionaries. Wiru visitors from other districts stayed outside the enclosure, where re-enactments of tribal fighting, 'singsings' for prizes, and the selling of foodstuffs took place.

Wiru, for the first time since the early 1960s, were looking at their past as a source of identity and a means of attaining recognition in the postcolonial state; this attitude to the recording and display of the past was very much in a museological rather than a literary mode.[3] The invention of culture, which for Wagner (1979: 141) only takes place between system and event, has to be interpreted as part of a *development* project, not as a return to the idealized values of the past (custom). The potential for a recasting of local historical consciousness exists, and the dynamism and open-ended potential of cultural innovation is once more demonstrated (cf. Merlan and Rumsey 1991). It may be that Wiru will invent a continuity with the past, and use it to help explain a postcolonial present. As the Comaroffs (1991: 18) cogently remind us,

history everywhere is actively made in a dialectic of order and disorder, consensus and conflict. At any particular moment, in any marked event, *a* meaning or *a* social arrangement may appear freefloating, underdetermined, ambiguous. But it is often the very attempt to harness that indeterminacy, the seemingly unfixed signifier, that animates both the exercise of power and the resistance to which it may give rise.

The colonial divide for Wiru was the experience of order and disorder, and such things as the Kongono cult and the cultural 'revival', along with a host of other more mundane practices, were attempts to 'harness the indeterminacy' of a colonial project that saw itself as rational, enlightened, and progressive. Wiru did not want to sell their souls to the state, but they were willing to exchange them to live in a stone-age world.

---

[3] According to Anderson (1991: 163), the colonial state in parts of Asia imagined its power and extent through the three institutions of census, map, and museum. In Papua New Guinea, the state did not use the museum as a technology of power to any great extent, although what is interesting in the Highlands is the indigenous construction of local museums or 'cultural centres' that postdate independence, and are used in the imagining of ethnic communities, perhaps in opposition to the state.

BIBLIOGRAPHY

Patrol Reports

Held at the National Archives of Papua New Guinea, Waigani, Port Moresby (referenced in the text as, for example, Erave PR3/55–56).

Erave Patrol Report 3, 1955–56.
Ialibu Patrol Report 2, 1954–55.
Ialibu Patrol Report 2, 1955–56.
Ialibu Patrol Report 3, 1955–56.
Ialibu Patrol Report 1, 1956–57.
Ialibu Patrol Report 2, 1958–59.
Ialibu Patrol Report 4, 1958–59.
Ialibu Patrol Report 1, 1959–60.
Ialibu Patrol Report 5, 1959–60.
Ialibu Patrol Report 10, 1959–60.
Ialibu Patrol Report 3, 1960–61.
Ialibu Patrol Report 6, 1960–61.
Kikori Patrol Report 13, 1921–22.
Kikori Patrol Report 19, 1928–29.
Kikori Patrol Report 2, 1937–38.
Mendi Patrol Report 5, 1952–53.
Mendi Patrol Report 5, 1953–54.
Mendi Patrol Report 3, 1955–56.
Mendi Patrol Report 7, 1955–56.
Pangia Patrol Report 1, 1961–62.
Pangia Patrol Report 3, 1961–62.
Pangia Patrol Report 1, 1962–63.
Pangia Patrol Report 3, 1962–63.
Pangia Patrol Report 7, 1962–63.
Pangia Patrol Report 4, 1963–64.

Pangia Patrol Report 6, 1963–64.
Pangia Patrol Report 8, 1965–66.
Pangia Patrol Report 1, 1966–67.
Pangia Patrol Report 4, 1966–67.
Pangia Patrol Report 7, 1966–67.
Pangia Patrol Report 9, 1966–67.
Pangia Patrol Report 5, 1969–70.
Pangia Patrol Report 8, 1969–70.
Pangia Patrol Report 1, 1970–71.
Pangia Patrol Report 2, 1970–71.
Pangia Patrol Report 3, 1970–71.
Pangia Patrol Report 4, 1970–71.
Pangia Patrol Report 8, 1970–71.
Pangia Patrol Report 3, 1971–72.
Pangia Patrol Report 10, 1971–72.
Pangia Patrol Report 16, 1971–72.
Pangia Patrol Report 2, 1972–73.
Pangia Patrol Report 9, 1972–73.
Pangia Patrol Report 10, 1972–73.
Pangia Patrol Report 13, 1972–73.
Pangia Patrol Report 4, 1973–74.
Pangia Patrol Report 5, 1973–74.
Pangia Patrol Report 2, 1976–77.
Pangia Patrol Report 1, 1980.

Other References

ALLEN, B. and FRANKEL, S. (1991). Across the Tari Furoro. In E. Schieffelin and R. Crittenden, *Like People You See in a Dream: First Contact in Six Papuan Societies*, Stanford: Stanford University Press, 88–124.

ANDERSON, B. (1991) *Imagined Communities: Reflections on the Origin and Spread of Nationalism*. London: Verso.

APEA, S. (1985). Footprints of God in Ialibu. In J. D. May (ed.), *Living Theology in Melanesia: A Reader*. Goroka: Melanesian Institute for Pastoral and Socio-Economic Service, 218–55.

APPADURAI, A. (1986). Introduction: Commodities and the Politics of Value. In A. Appadurai (ed.), *The Social Life of Things: Commodities in Cultural Perspective*, Cambridge: Cambridge University Press, 3–63.

BARHAM, H. (1984). First Contact and Social Change in the Wiru Area of Papua New Guinea. Undergraduate thesis, St Catharine's College, Cambridge University.

BARKER, J. (1992). Christianity in Western Melanesian Ethnography. In J. G. Carrier (ed.), *History and Tradition in Melanesian Anthropology*, Berkeley: University of California Press, 144–73.

BERNDT, R. (1962). *Excess and Restraint: Social Control Among a New Guinea Mountain People*. Chicago: Chicago University Press.

—— (1965). The Kamano, Usurufa, Jate and Fore of the Eastern Highlands. In P. Lawrence and M. J. Meggitt (eds.), *Gods, Ghosts and Men in Melanesia: Some Religions of Australian New Guinea and the New Hebrides*, Melbourne: Oxford University Press, 78–104.

BIERSACK, A. (1990). Histories in the making: Paiela and Historical Anthropology. *History and Anthropology* 5(1), 63–85.

—— (1991). Prisoners of Time: Millenarian Praxis in a Melanesian Valley. In A. Biersack (ed.), *Clio in Oceania: Toward a Historical Anthropology*, Washington, D. C.: Smithsonian Institution Press, 231–95.

—— (1995). Introduction: The Huli, Duna, and Ipili Peoples Yesterday and Today. In A. Biersack (ed.), *Papuan Borderlands: Huli, Duna, and Ipili Perspectives on the Papua New Guinea Highlands*, Ann Arbor: University of Michigan Press, 1–54.

Black Harvest. (1992). R. Connolly and R. Anderson (dir). Arundel Productions (Australia), 90 mins.

BREWSTER, H. C. (1934). *Pearls of Papua*. Sydney: Endeavour Press.

BROWN, P. (1970). Mingge-money: Economic Change in the New Guinea Highlands. *Southwestern Journal of Anthropology* 26(3), 242–60.

—— (1973). *The Chimbu: A Study of Change in the New Guinea Highlands*. London: Routledge & Kegan Paul.

—— (1992). Chimbu and Stranger: Many Histories in Intercultural Relations. *Ethnology* 31(1): 27–43.

BRUMBAUGH, R. (1987). The Rainbow Serpent on the Upper Sepik. *Anthropos* 82(1–3), 25–33.

BULMER, R. (1967). Why is the Cassowary not a Bird? A Problem of Zoological Taxonomy among the Karam of the New Guinea Highlands. *Man* 2(1), 5–23.

BURRIDGE, K. (1960). *Mambu: A Melanesian Millennium*. Oxford: Basil Blackwell.

—— (1965). Tangu, Northern Madang District. In P. Lawrence and M. J. Meggitt (eds.), *Gods, Ghosts and Men in Melanesia: Some Religions of Australian New Guinea and the New Hebrides*, Melbourne: Oxford University Press, 224–49.

—— (1969), *Tangu Traditions: A Study of the Way of Life, Mythology, and Developing Experience of a New Guinea People*, Oxford: Oxford University Press.

BUSTIN, G. T. (n.d.). *Four Years with My Savage Brothers*. Shoals: Evangelical Bible Mission.

CARRIER, J. G. (1992). Introduction. In J. G. Carrier (ed.), *History and Tradition in Melanesian Anthropology*, Berkeley: University of California Press, 1–37.

Catholic Diary (n.d.) Pangia Mission Station, Pangia, Southern Highlands Province, Papua New Guinea.

CHAMPION, I. F. (1936). Bamu–Purari Patrol Report. Australian Archives, Canberra.

—— (1940). The Bamu–Purari Patrol, 1936. *Geographical Journal* 96(3), 190–206; 96(4), 243–57.

CLARK, J. (1985). From Cults to Christianity: Continuity and Change in Takuru. Ph.D. thesis, University of Adelaide.

—— (1988). *Kaun* and *Kongono*: Cargo Cults and Development in Karavar and Pangia. *Oceania* 59(1), 40–57.

—— (1989). Gods, Ghosts and People: Christianity and Social Organisation among Takuru Wiru. In M. Jolly and M. Macintyre (eds.), *Family and Gender in the Pacific: Domestic Contradictions and the Colonial Impact*, Cambridge: Cambridge University Press, 170–92.

—— (1991). Pearlshell Symbolism in the New Guinea Highlands, with Particular Reference to the Wiru People of Southern Highlands Province. *Oceania* 61(4), 309–39.

—— (1992). Madness and Colonisation: The Embodiment of Power in Pangia. In A. Lattas (ed.), *Alienating Mirrors: Christianity, Cargo Cults and Colonialism in Melanesia, Oceania* [Special Issue] 63(1), 15–26.

—— (1993). Gold, Sex and Pollution: Male Illness and Mythology at Mt Kare. *American Ethnologist* 20(4), 742–57.

—— (1995). Shit Beautiful: Tambu and Kina Revisited. *Oceania* 65(3), 195–211.

—— (n.d.). *Mana* from Heaven: Ethnicity and Knowledge in Tari. Unpublished MS.

—— and HUGHES, J. (1995). A History of Gender in Tari. In A. Biersack (ed.), *Papuan Borderlands: Huli, Duna, and Ipili Perspectives on the Papua New Guinea Highlands*, Ann Arbor: University of Michigan Press.

CLARKE, W. C. (1973). Temporary Madness as Theatre: Wild-man Behaviour in New Guinea. *Oceania* 43(3), 198–214.

Close Encounters of the Third Kind. (1977). Steven Spielberg (dir.). Columbia, 135 mins..

COMAROFF, J. and COMAROFF, J. (1991). *Of Revelation and Revolution: Christianity, Colonialism and Consciousness in South Africa*, Vol. 1. Chicago: University of Chicago Press.

CONNOLLY, R. and ANDERSON, R. (1987). *First Contact: New Guinea's Highlanders Encounter the Outside World*, New York: Viking Penguin.

CRITTENDEN, R. (1991). Across the Nembi Plateau. In E. Schieffelin and R. Crittenden (eds.), *Like People You See in a Dream: First Contact in Six Papuan Societies*, Stanford: Stanford University Press, 168–97.

DAMON, F. H. (1982). Alienating the Inalienable. *Man* 17(2–3), 342–3.

EPSTEIN, A. L. (1979). *Tambu*: The Shell-money of the Tolai. In R. H. Hook (ed.), *Fantasy and Symbol: Studies in Anthropological Interpretation*, London: Academic Press, 149–205.

ERRINGTON, F. (1974). Indigenous Ideas of Order, Time, and Transition in a New Guinea Cargo Movement. *American Ethnologist* 1(2), 255–67.

FABIAN, J. (1983). *Time and the Other: How Anthropology Makes its Object*. New York: Columbia University Press.

FEIL, D. K. (1982). Alienating the Inalienable. *Man* 17(2–3), 340–2.

—— (1983). A World without Exchange: Millennia and the *Tee* Ceremonial System in Tombema-Enga Society (New Guinea). *Anthropos* 78(1), 89–106.

FINNEY, B. R. (1973). *Big-Men and Business: Entrepreneurship and Economic Growth in the New Guinea Highlands*. Honolulu: University Press of Hawai'i.

First Contact (1982). B. Connolly and R. Anderson (dir.). Arundel Publications (Australia), 54 mins.

FOUCAULT, M. (1979). *Discipline and Punish: The Birth of the Prison*, tr. A. Sheridan. New York: Vintage Books.

—— (1980). *The History of Sexuality I*, tr. R. Hurley. New York: Vintage Books.

FRANKEL, S. (1986). *The Huli Response to Illness*. Cambridge: Cambridge University Press.

FRANKLIN, K. J. (1972). Review article. *Practical Anthropology* 19(3), 133–6.

—— (1975). Comments on Proto-Engan. In S. A. Wurm (ed.), *Papuan Languages and the New Guinea Linguistic Scene*, Pacific Linguistics Series C, no. 38, Canberra: Department of Linguistics, Research School of Pacific Studies, Australian National University, 263–75.

—— and FRANKLIN, J. (1978). *A Kewa Dictionary: With Supplementary Grammatical and Anthropological Materials*. Pacific Linguistics Series C, no. 53. Canberra: Department of Linguistics, Research School of Pacific Studies, Australian National University.

GARDNER, D. (1984). A Note on the Androgynous Qualities of the Cassowary: Or Why the Mianmin Say it is Not a Bird. *Oceania* 55(2), 137–45.

GEERTZ, C. (1973). *The Interpretation of Cultures: Selected Essays*. New York: Basic Books.

GIBBS, P. (1977). The Cult from Lyeimi and the Ipili. *Oceania* 48(1), 1–25.

GLASSE, R. M. (1965). The Huli of the Southern Highlands. In P. Lawrence and M. J. Meggitt (eds.), *Gods, Ghosts and Men in Melanesia: Some Religions of Australian New Guinea and the New Hebrides*, Melbourne: Oxford University Press, 27–49.

—— (1968). *Huli of Papua: A Cognatic Descent System*, Paris: Mouton.

—— (n.d.), Report on the Huli. Southern Highlands Archives, Mendi, Papua New Guinea.

GODELIER, M. (1977). *Perspectives in Marxist Anthropology*, tr. R. Swyer. Cambridge: Cambridge University Press.

—— (1986). *The Making of Great Men: Male Domination and Power among the New Guinea Baruya*. Cambridge: Cambridge University Press; Paris: Editions de la Maison des Sciences de l'Homme.

GOULD, S. J. (1987). *Time's Arrow, Time's Cycle: Myth and Metaphor in the Discovery of Geological Time*. Cambridge, Mass.: Harvard University Press.

GRAY, J. N. (1987). *Bayu utarnu*: Ghost Exorcism and Sacrifice in Nepal. *Ethnology* 26(3), 191–99.

GREGORY, C. A. (1980). Gifts to Men and Gifts to Gods: Gift Exchange and Capital Accumulation in Contemporary Papua. *Man* 15(4), 626–52.

—— (1982a). Alienating the Inalienable. *Man* 17(2–3), 343–5.

—— (1982b). *Gifts and Commodities*. London: Academic Press.

GROSZ, E. (1990). Inscriptions and Body-maps: Representations and the Corporeal. In T. Threadgold and A. Cranny-Francis (eds.), *Feminine/Masculine and Representation*, Sydney: Allen & Unwin, 62–74.

HARKIN, M. (1988). History, Narrative and Temporality: Examples from the Northwest Coast, *Ethnohistory* 35(2), 99–130.

HARVEY, L. B. (1973). *Out of the Shadows in New Guinea*. Bicknell, Ind.: Fellowship Promoter Press.

HASTINGS, P. (1969). *New Guinea: Problems and Prospects*. Melbourne: Cheshire.

HAYANO, D. (1978). Cognitive Footprints from the Past: Clues to the Settlement of a New Guinea Village. *Mankind* 11(4), 461–7.

—— (1990). *Road Through the Rain Forest: Living Anthropology in Highland Papua New Guinea*. Prospect Heights: Waveland Press.

HEALEY, C. J. (1985a). Pigs, Cassowaries and the Gift of the Flesh: A Symbolic Triad in Maring Cosmology. *Ethnology* 24(3), 153–65.

—— (1985b). New Guinea Inland Trade: Transformation and Resilience in the Context of Capitalist Penetration. In D. Gardner and N. Modjeska (eds.), *Recent Studies in the Political Economy of Papua New Guinea Societies, Mankind* [Special Issue] 15(2), 127–44.

—— (1988). Culture as Transformed Disorder: Cosmological Evocations among the Maring. *Oceania* 59(2), 106–22.

HEIDER, K. G. (1988). The Rashomon Effect: When Ethnographers Disagree. *American Anthropologist* 90(1), 73–81.

HERDT, G. (1986). 'Madness and Sexuality in the New Guinea Highlands. *Social Research* 53(2), 349–67.

HIDES, J. G. (1936). *Papuan Wonderland*. London: Blackie.

HOPE, P. (1979). *Long Ago is Far Away: Accounts of the Early Exploration and Settlement of the Papuan Gulf Area*. Canberra: Australian National University Press.

HUGHES, I. (1977). *New Guinea Stone Age Trade: The Geography and Ecology of Traffic in the Interior*. Terra Australis 3. Canberra: Department of Prehistory, Research School of Pacific Studies, Australian National University.

—— (1978). Good Money and Bad: Inflation and Devaluation in the Colonial Process. In J. Specht and J. P. White (eds.), *Trade and Exchange in Oceania and Australia, Mankind* [Special Issue] 11(3), 308–18.

HURLEY, F. (1924). *Pearls and Savages: Adventures in the Air, on Land and Sea in New Guinea*. New York: G. P. Putnam's Sons.

JOLLY, M. (1992a). Specters of Inauthenticity. *The Contemporary Pacific* 4(1), 49–72.

—— (1992b). Custom and the Way of the Land: Past and Present in Vanuatu and Fiji. In M. Jolly and N. Thomas (eds.), *The Politics of Tradition in the Pacific, Oceania* [Special Edition] 62(4), 330–54.

—— and THOMAS, N. (1992). Introduction. In M. Jolly and N. Thomas (eds.), *The Politics of Tradition in the Pacific, Oceania* [Special Edition] 62(4), 241–8.

JOSEPHIDES, L. (1985). *The Production of Inequality: Gender and Exchange among the Kewa*. London: Tavistock Publications.

—— and SCHILTZ, M. (1991). Kewa Aftermath. In E. Schieffelin and R. Crittenden (eds.), *Like People You See in a Dream: First Contact in Six Papuan Societies*, Stanford: Stanford University Press, 278–81.

JUILLERAT, B. (1975). Transe et langage en Nouvelle-Guinée. *Journal de la Société des Océanistes* 31(47), 187–212; 31(49), 379–97.

KAPFERER, B. (1991). *Legends of People, Myths of State: Violence, Intolerance, and Political Culture in Sri Lanka and Australia*, Washington, D.C.: Smithsonian Institution Press.

KEESING, R. M. and JOLLY, M. (1992). Epilogue. In J. G. Carrier (ed.), *History and Tradition in Melanesian Anthropology*, Berkeley: University of California Press, 224–47.

KERR, H. B. (1975). The Relationship of Wiru in the Southern Highlands District to Languages of the East New Guinea Highlands Stock. In S. A. Wurm (ed.), *Papuan Languages and the New Guinea Linguistic Scene*, Pacific Linguistics Series C no. 38, Canberra: Department of Linguistics, Research School of Pacific Studies, Australian National University, 277–96.

—— (1984). Wiru Essentials for Translation: Anthropology Section. Drafted October 1967. Paper presented at the Research Workshop at Takuru, Pangia, 30 September to 4 October 1985. Waigani: Educational Research Unit, University of Papua New Guinea.

—— (1987). A Theory of Language Organisation based on Hjelmslev's Function Oriented Theory of Language. In E. W. Conrad and E. G. Newing (eds.), *Perspectives on Language and Text: Essays and Poems in Honour of Francis I. Andersen's Sixtieth Birthday, July 28, 1985*. Winona Lake, Ind.: Eisenbrauns, 101–21.

Bibliography

KNAUFT, B. M. (1993). *South Coast New Guinea Cultures: History, Comparison, Dialectic.* Cambridge: Cambridge University Press.

KRAUTH, N. (ed.) (1982). *New Guinea Images in Australian Literature.* St Lucia: Queensland University Press.

LACEY, R. (1982). History. In B. Carrad, D. A. M. Lea and K. K. Talyaga (eds.), *Enga: Foundations for Development.* Armidale: University of New England, 8–22.

LATTAS, A. (1992). Skin, Personhood, and Redemption: The Doubled Self in West New Britain Cargo Cults. In A. Lattas (ed.), *Alienating Mirrors: Christianity, Cargo Cults and Colonialism in Melanesia, Oceania* [Special Issue] 63(1), 27–54.

—— (ed.) (1992). *Alienating Mirrors: Christianity, Cargo Cults and Colonialism in Melanesia, Oceania* [Special Issue] 63(1).

LAWRENCE, P. (1964). *Road Belong Cargo: A Study of the Cargo Movement in the Southern Madang District, New Guinea.* Manchester: Manchester University Press.

—— and MEGGITT, M. J. (1965). Introduction. In P. Lawrence and M. J. Meggitt (eds.), *Gods, Ghosts and Men in Melanesia: Some Religions of Australian New Guinea and the New Hebrides,* Melbourne: Oxford University Press, 1–26.

LEAHY, M. J. (1991). *Explorations into Highland New Guinea, 1930–1935,* (ed.) D. E. Jones. Tuscaloosa: University of Alabama Press.

—— (n.d.). Diaries, photographs and speeches, 1930–1934. National Library of Australia, Canberra, MS 384.

—— and CRAIN, M. (1937). *The Land that Time Forgot: Adventures and Discoveries in New Guinea.* New York: Funk & Wagnalls.

LEDERMAN, R. (1981). Sorcery and social change in Mendi. *Social Analysis* 8, 15–27.

—— (1986). *What Gifts Engender: Social Relations and Politics in Mendi, Highland Papua New Guinea,* Cambridge: Cambridge University Press.

LeROY, J. D. (1985). *Fabricated World: An Interpretation of Kewa Tales,* Vancouver: University of British Columbia Press.

LÉVI-STRAUSS, C. (1966). *The Savage Mind.* Chicago: University of Chicago Press.

LONGLEY, R. (n.d.). The Mendi: A People of the Southern Highlands of Papua New Guinea. Unpublished MS.

McCARTHY, J. K. (1963). *Patrol into Yesterday: My New Guinea Years.* Melbourne: Cheshire.

MEGGITT, M. (1974). The Sun and the Shakers: A Millenarian Cult and its Transformations in the New Guinea Highlands. In *Studies in Enga History,* Oceania Monograph 20, Sydney: University of Sydney Press, 1–56.

MEILLASSOUX, C. (1981). *Maidens, Meal and Money: Capitalism and the Domestic Community.* Cambridge: Cambridge University Press.

MERLAN, F. and RUMSEY, A. (1991). *Ku Waru: Language and Segmentary Politics in the Western Nebilyer Valley, Papua New Guinea.* Cambridge: Cambridge University Press.

MIMICA, J. (1988). *Intimations of Infinity: The Mythopoeia of the Iqwaye Counting System and Number.* Oxford: Berg.

MODJESKA, N. (1991). Post-Ipomoean Modernism: The Duna Example. In M. Godelier and M. Strathern (eds.), *Big Men and Great Men: Personifications of Power in Melanesia,* Cambridge: Cambridge University Press; Paris: Editions de la Maison des Sciences de l'Homme, 234–55.

MORREN, G. E. B. (1981). A Small Footnote to the 'Big Walk': Environment and Change among the Miyanmin of Papua New Guinea. *Oceania* 52(1), 39–65.

MURPHY, R. F. (1972). *The Dialectics of Social Life: Alarms and Excursions in Anthropological Theory*. London: Allen & Unwin.

NEUMANN, K. (1992). *Not the Way It Really Was: Constructing the Tolai Past*. Pacific Islands Series Monograph 10. Honolulu: University of Hawai'i Press.

NEWMAN, P. L. (1965). *Knowing the Gururumba*. New York: Holt, Rinehart & Winston.

NIHILL, M. (1989). The New Pearlshells: Aspects of Money and Meaning in Anganen Exchange. *Canberra Anthropology* 12(1–2), 144–60.

O'HANLON, M. (1993). *Paradise: Portraying the New Guinea Highlands*. Bathurst: Crawford House and the Trustees of the British Museum.

PAIA, R. M. (1977). The Coming of Red Foreigners to the Wiru Area of Pangia Sub-Province in S. H. P. *Oral History* 5(4), 49–55.

—— and STRATHERN, A. J. (1977). *Beneath the Andaiya Tree: Wiru Songs*. Port Moresby: Institute of Papua New Guinea Studies.

PANNELL, S. (1994). Mabo and Museums: The Indigenous (Re-)appropriation of Indigenous Things. *Oceania* 65(1), 18–39.

PATTON, P. (1987). Michel Foucault. In D. J. Austin-Broos (ed.), *Creating Culture: Profiles in the Study of Culture*, Sydney: Allen & Unwin, 226–42.

RADFORD, R. (1987). *Highlanders and Foreigners in the Upper Ramu: The Kainantu Area, 1919–1942*. Melbourne: Melbourne University Press.

RAPPAPORT, R. (1968). *Pigs for the Ancestors: Ritual in the Ecology of a New Guinea People*. New Haven: Yale University Press.

READ, K. (1952). Missionary Activities and Social Change in the Central Highlands of Papua and New Guinea. *South Pacific* 5(11), 229–38.

REAY, M. (1959), *The Kuma: Freedom and Conformity in the New Guinea Highlands*. Melbourne: Melbourne University Press, on behalf of the Australian National University.

RIDGWAY, K. (1976). *Feet Upon the Mountains: A History of the First Five Years of the Wesleyan Missionary Work in Papua New Guinea*. Indianapolis: Wesleyan Church Corporation.

ROBIN, R.W. (1980). The Presence, Influence, and Effects of Christian Missionaries on the People of the Southern Highlands Province, Papua New Guinea. Ph.D. thesis, University of Papua New Guinea, Port Moresby.

—— (1981). Revival Movement Hysteria in the Southern Highlands of Papua New Guinea. *Journal for the Scientific Study of Religion* 20(2), 150–63.

—— (1982). Revival Movements in the Southern Highlands Province of Papua New Guinea. *Oceania* 52(4), 320–43.

RODMAN, M. (1979). Introduction. In M. Rodman and M. Cooper (eds.), *The Pacification of Melanesia*, ASAO Monograph 7, Ann Arbor: University of Michigan Press, 1–23.

ROSALDO, R. (1980). *Ilongot Headhunting, 1883–1974: A Study in Society and History*. Stanford: Stanford University Press.

SAHLINS, M. (1981). *Historical Metaphors and Mythical Realities: Structure in the Early History of the Sandwich Islands Kingdom*. ASAO Special Publication No. 1. Ann Arbor: University of Michigan Press.

—— (1985). *Islands of History*. Chicago: University of Chicago Press.

SALISBURY, R. F. (1962). *From Stone to Steel: Economic Consequences of a Technological Change in New Guinea*. Melbourne: Melbourne University Press.

SALISBURY, R. F. (1966). Possession in the New Guinea Highlands: Review of Literature. *Transcultural Psychiatric Research* 3, 103–8.

SCHIEFFELIN, E. L. (1976). *The Sorrow of the Lonely and the Burning of the Dancers*. New York: St Martins Press.

—— (1991). The Great Papuan Plateau. In E. L. Schieffelin and R. Crittenden (eds.), *Like People You See in a Dream: First Contact in Six Papuan Societies*, Stanford: Stanford University Press, 58–87.

—— and CRITTENDEN, R. (1991). *Like People You See in a Dream: First Contact in Six Papuan Societies*. Stanford: Stanford University Press.

—— and GEWERTZ, D. B. (1985). Introduction. In E. L. Schieffelin and D. B. Gewertz (eds.), *History and Ethnohistory in Papua New Guinea*. Oceania Monograph 28, Sydney: University of Sydney Press, 1–6.

SILLITOE, P. (1979). *Give and Take: Exchange in Wola society*. Canberra: Australian National University Press.

—— (1991). From the Waga Furari to the Wen. In E. L. Schieffelin and R. Crittenden (eds.), *Like People You See in a Dream: First Contact in Six Papuan Societies*, Stanford: Stanford University Press, 147–67.

SIMPSON, C. (1954). *Adam in Plumes*. Sydney: Angus & Robertson.

SINCLAIR, J. P. (1969). *The Outside Man: Jack Hides of Papua*. London: Angus & Robertson.

—— (1981). *Kiap: Australia's Patrol Officers in Papua New Guinea*. Sydney: Pacific Publications.

—— (1988). *Last Frontiers: The Explorations of Ivan Champion of Papua*. Broadbeach Waters, Qld.: Pacific Press.

SMITH, R. M. (1980). The Time that Anthropology Forgot. *Canberra Anthropology* 3, 81–94.

SORENSON, E. (1972). Socio-economic Change among the Fore of New Guinea. *Current Anthropology* 13(3–4), 349–83.

STEPHEN, M. (1979). Dreams of Change: The Innovative Role of Altered States of Consciousness in Traditional Melanesian Religion', *Oceania* 50(1), 3–22.

STOW, R. (1981), *Visitants*, London: Picador.

STRATHERN, A. J. (1968). Sickness and Frustration: Variations in Two New Guinea Highlands Societies. *Mankind* 6(11), 545–51.

—— (1971a). Wiru and Daribi Matrilateral Payments. *Journal of the Polynesian Society* 80(4), 449–62.

—— (1971b), *The Rope of Moka: Big-men and Ceremonial Exchange in Mount Hagen*. Cambridge: Cambridge University Press.

—— (1977). Souvenirs de 'folie' chez les Wiru (Southern Highlands). *Journal de la Société des Océanistes* 33(56–7), 131–44.

—— (1978). 'Finance and Production' Revisited: In Pursuit of a Comparison, *Research in Economic Anthropology* 1, 73–104.

—— (1979). Gender, Ideology and Money in Mount Hagen. *Man* 14(3), 530–48.

—— (1979–80). The Red Box Money-cult in Mount Hagen, 1968–71. *Oceania* 50(2), 88–102; 50(3), 161–75.

—— (1982a). Alienating the Inalienable. *Man* 17(3), 548–51.

—— (1982b). Social Change in Mount Hagen and Pangia. *Bikmaus* 3(1), 90–9.

—— (1982c). Witchcraft, Greed, Cannibalism and Death: Some Related Themes from the New Guinea Highlands. In M. Bloch and J. Parry (eds.), *Death and the Regeneration of Life*, Cambridge: Cambridge University Press, 111–33.

—— (1984). *A Line of Power*. London: Tavistock Publications.

—— (1991). Struggle for Meaning. In A. Biersack (ed.), *Clio in Oceania: Towards a Historical Anthropology*, Washington, DC: Smithsonian Institute Press, 205–30.

STRATHERN, M. (1984). No Culture, No History. Paper presented at the German Historical Institute, London.

—— (1988). *The Gender of the Gift: Problems with Women and Problems with Society in Melanesia*. Berkeley: University of California Press.

—— (1990). Artefacts of History: Events and the Interpretation of Images. In J. Siikala (ed.), *Culture and History in the Pacific*, Helsinki: Finnish Anthropological Society, 25–44.

—— (1992). The Decomposition of an Event. *Cultural Anthropology* 7(2), 244–54.

STRAUSS, H. (1990). *The Mi-Culture of the Mount Hagen People, Papua New Guinea*, tr. B. Shields. Pittsburgh: University of Pittsburgh Press.

TAUSSIG, M. (1980). *The Devil and Commodity Fetishism in South America*. Chapel Hill: University of North Carolina Press.

—— (1984). Space of Death, Culture of Terror: Roger Casement and the Explanation of Torture. *Comparative Studies in Society and History* 26(3),464–97.

—— (1987). *Shamanism, Colonialism and the Wild Man: A Study in Terror and Healing*. Chicago: University of Chicago Press.

—— (1993). *Mimesis and Alterity: A Particular History of the Senses*. New York: Routledge.

THOMAS, N. (1991), *Entangled Objects: Exchange, Material Culture and Colonialism in the Pacific*. Cambridge, Mass.: Harvard University Press.

—— (1992). The Inversion of Tradition. *American Ethnologist* 19(2), 213–32.

—— (1994). *Colonialism's Culture: Anthropology, Travel and Government*. Oxford: Polity Press.

TORGOVNICK, M. (1990). *Gone Primitive: Savage Intellects, Modern Lives*. Chicago: University of Chicago Press.

TURNER, T. (1991). Representing, Resisting, Rethinking: Historical Transformations of Kayapo Culture and Anthropological Consciousness. In G. W. Stocking, Jr. (ed.), *Colonial Situations: Essays on the Contextualization of Ethnographic Knowledge*, Madison: University of Wisconsin Press, 285–313.

TURNER, V. (1974). *Dramas, Fields and Metaphors: Symbolic Action in Human Society*. Ithaca, NY: Cornell University Press.

WAGNER, R. (1967). *The Curse of Souw: Principles of Daribi Clan Definition and Alliance*. Chicago: University of Chicago Press.

—— (1972). *Habu: The Innovation of Meaning in Daribi Religion*, Chicago: University of Chicago Press.

—— (1975). *The Invention of Culture*. Chicago: University of Chicago Press.

—— (1978). *Lethal Speech: Daribi Myth and Symbolic Obviation*. Ithaca, NY: Cornell University Press.

—— (1979). The Talk of Koriki: A Daribi Contact Cult. *Social Research* 46(1), 140–65.

—— (1986). *Symbols that Stand for Themselves*. Chicago: University of Chicago Press.

WALTER, M. A. H. B. (1981). Cult Movements and Community Development Associations: Revolution and Evolution in the Papua New Guinea Countryside. In R. Gerritsen, R. J. May and M. A. H. B. Walter (eds.), *Road Belong Development: Cargo Cults, Community Groups and Self-Help Movements in Papua New Guinea*, Canberra: Department of Political and Social Change, Research School of Pacific Studies, Australian National University, 81–105.

WEINER, A. B. (1987). Dominant Kings and Forgotten Queens. *Oceania* 58(2), 157–60.

—— (1992). *Inalienable Possessions: The Paradox of Keeping-While-Giving.* Berkeley: University of California Press.

WEINER, J. F. (1988). Introduction: Looking at the New Guinea Highlands from its Edge. In J. F. Weiner (ed.), *Mountain Papuans: Historical and Comparative Perspectives from New Guinea Fringe Highlands Societies*, Ann Arbor: University of Michigan Press, 1–38.

—— (1991). *The Empty Place: Poetry, Space and Being among the Foi of Papua New Guinea.* Bloomington and Indianapolis: Indiana University Press.

WILLIAMS, F. E. (1944). Mission Influence amongst the Keveri of South-East Papua. *Oceania* 15(2), 89–141.

—— (1976), *The Vailala Madness and Other Essays*, (ed.) E. Schwimmer., St Lucia: University of Queensland Press.

WURM, S. A. (1975). Eastern Central Trans-New Guinea Phylum Languages. In S. A. Wurm (ed.), *Papuan Languages and the New Guinea Linguistic Scene*, Pacific Linguistics Series C no. 38, Canberra: Australian National University Press, 461–526.

YOUNG, F. S. H. (1926). *Pearls from the Pacific.* London: Marshall Books.

INDEX

Printed in the United States
135106LV00002B/9/A